Rights of Way
Restoring the Record

By Sarah Bucks and Phil Wadey

Bucks & Wadey
PUBLISHING

Rights of Way: Restoring the Record

Published by:
Bucks & Wadey Publishing
Bryants Farm
Dowlish Wake
Ilminster TA19 0NX

hq@restoringtherecord.org.uk

First edition by Sarah Bucks and Phil Wadey, published 2012

British Library Cataloguing in Publishing Data.
A catalogue record for this book is available from the British Library.

ISBN 978-0-9574036-0-4

Cover Photo: 'Oakridge Lane', currently not on the definitive map. Application made to Hertfordshire County Council in December 2006 (reference HTM/172). At going to press this route is in the process of being recorded by the Hertfordshire County Council (Aldenham 83 and 9) Modification Order 2009. Photo taken by Phil Wadey.

Designed and typeset by Free Range Book Design & Production Limited

Printed and bound in the United Kingdom by Latimer Trend & Company Ltd, Plymouth.

CONTENTS

LIST OF ILLUSTRATIONS

ACKNOWLEDGEMENTS

The authors are indebted to Dr Janice Bridger, Catriona Cook, Geri Coop, Peter Kidner, Sue Rogers and Stephanie Wheeler for their comments on an early draft; to the Hertfordshire County Council Rights of Way department for permission to reproduce their flow charts in Chapter 5; and to The National Archives, the British Library, Hertfordshire Archives and Local Studies and to Somerset Heritage Centre for permission to reproduce extracts of documents in their custody.

PREFACE

The beauty of England and Wales can often be seen best from paths, tracks and meandering lanes that cross the countryside. Many of these routes are of ancient origin, and many fell into disuse in the last century after the rise in the use of the motor car and the metalling of principal routes. Sometimes it was just the case of metalling one road rather than another.

In 2000, Parliament decided that old unrecorded ways should be extinguished to provide certainty to landowners, but 25 more years would be allowed for the legal record to be brought up to date. This is an incredibly important point as, although those routes that are already formally recorded will retain their public rights, unrecorded ways will cease to exist in 2026. In this book, we use the term 'unrecorded' for routes where there is no public right recorded and for routes where a highway is recorded with some public rights (for example as a footpath) but where additional rights (for example as a bridleway or carriageway) exist.

Often, people in a village may feel that they know the landowner, he knows a path is used by the public and has never done anything to prevent use, so why is there a need for action? While of initial appeal, this line of thought is often found to be wanting only when there is a change in landowner, or the land acquires development potential, and it becomes necessary to deal with unhelpful owners or people who have a large financial interest in denying rights. It follows that it is always best to record the rights that exist sooner rather than later, and, of course, this must be before 2026.

When a path is obstructed by a fallen tree or overgrown by brambles, it is only its public right of way status that *enables* the local authority to take action. Indeed, it is the duty of the highway authority (county or unitary council) to assert and protect the rights of the public to use highways, including footpaths and bridleways. Once a route is recorded, it makes it easier to *persuade* a local authority to take appropriate enforcement action, such as preventing motor vehicular use of routes that are truly bridleways, or clearing fly-tipping on the route.

Experience suggests that there are more unrecorded routes waiting to be re-established than permanent routes waiting to be created by benevolent landowners. Short-term, permissive, routes are perhaps more easy to come by, but they carry no permanent public rights and so can be withdrawn at any time. It is vitally important that in the time remaining until 2026, those who value their rights of way become more active in researching those routes that are missing from the definitive map, and making applications for them to be recorded.

This book sets out to help those new to rights of way research to get started. It is equally of use to those who wish to show a route exists as to those that wish to show one doesn't.

This book is primarily to aid the researcher. It includes references to Acts, Regulations and case law to help explain how research materials are used, but the reader should be aware that the law is constantly changing, and so other sources may be needed to give the latest interpretation to the evidence found.

Sarah Bucks
Phil Wadey

1. INTRODUCTION

1.1 What is a Public Right of Way?

The term 'public right of way' is a common expression for what is usually called a 'highway' in the legislation. A highway exists if there is a public right to pass and re-pass along a defined particular route. At common law, a highway may be for people on foot only (a public footpath), on foot, leading a horse or riding a horse (a public bridleway) or for all traffic (a carriageway). A highway is available for use by all of the Queen's subjects (i.e. everyone), not just residents of a particular parish or locality. Statute law has added the right to use bicycles to the common law rights on a public bridleway.[1] These public rights can exist over publicly held or privately owned land.

We use the term 'minor highways' to mean highways other than clearly identifiable public roads. In broad terms, this expression encompasses all public footpaths and bridleways, and any carriageways that are either more used as footpaths and bridleways, or have had their motor vehicular rights stopped up, or are in danger of being forgotten about because they are not made up for motor vehicles.

1.2 Once a Highway, Always a Highway

Once a public right of way, or highway, has come into existence, it needs a specific legal act to stop it up. Lack of use, for however long, does not stop the route from carrying highway rights.[2] Stopping up can take many forms, including court orders, extinguishment and diversion orders, and Acts of Parliament. If such a stopping up mechanism is found to have been used, it negates all prior evidence.

It is the use of the 'Once a highway always a highway' rule that enables evidence of highway status from long ago to be used to record minor highways today.

1 s.30 Countryside Act 1968.

2 *Harvey v Truro Rural District Council* (1903).

1.3 How are Public Rights of Way Recorded?

Every surveying authority (county or unitary authority) in England and Wales, except for inner London, is required to have and keep up to date the 'definitive map and statement of public rights of way' for its area. The definitive map is an official record of those minor highways that have been recorded. The presence of a route on the definitive map is conclusive proof in law that the public had the rights shown on a particular date, without prejudice as to whether any additional rights exist.[3] The definitive statement is a textual record of the route that may contain information about the width and position of the highway, and whether there are any limitations or conditions on the way's use by the public (for example, a limitation that the landowner has the right to erect a stile on the route of the path).

Anyone can apply for a change to the definitive map. All that is needed is (1) a completed application form, (2) a map showing the route to be added, reclassified (from one sort of highway to another), or deleted from the map, and (3) evidence to show why the change should be made. If the council agrees with the application, it will make a 'definitive map modification order' which is then advertised to see if anyone disagrees. If there are objections, the order will be determined by an Inspector acting for the Secretary of State. Depending on the nature and number of objections, he may deal with the process by an exchange of written representations, a hearing or a public inquiry. The process does not relate to what anyone would like, it relates only to establishing the historical truth of the status of a way. Full details of the process are given in Chapter 5.

While talk of legal orders and public inquiries can put off all but the most determined, the aim of this book is to guide readers through the process, from collecting evidence of highway status to making the application. This book has been written to guide the beginner but should be equally valuable as a reference guide for the serious researcher. The subject is particularly rewarding for those interested in local history, re-establishing unrecorded ways, or defending their property against highway applications.

Fortunately, if a good case is put forward explaining how the historical rights can be proven to exist, landowners may agree to having the path recorded by the surveying authority without opposition, enabling the whole process to be concluded much more quickly.

3 s.56 Wildlife and Countryside Act 1981.

1.4 Getting Started

People often wonder how to get started. For some, the identification of a route of interest is forced on them by someone else applying to change the rights that are recorded over it, while some may realise that the route they've ridden for years is only recorded as a footpath, and yet others are simply seeking unrecorded[4] rights to record. In the latter case, there are several options, of which the following are suitable, depending on your purpose.

One starting point is a current Ordnance Survey Explorer or Landranger map. These show rights of way recorded on definitive maps, and routes described in the map keys as 'Other Routes with Public Access' (ORPAs). In some areas, the ORPAs are worth investigating to establish exactly what public rights exist. Depiction on an OS map indicates the physical presence but provides no protection to the legal rights over the land. However, if these are evaluated and added to the definitive map then the rights are safeguarded. Other routes worth investigating are those which appear to change status for example from footpath to bridleway, stop in the middle of nowhere for no apparent reason, or appear to be the continuation of a road which now turns a corner. While for some abrupt changes of status there will be a good reason, for many it is simply the result of each parish making its own record in isolation during the original surveys for the definitive map in the 1950s.

The reprints of the old Ordnance Survey maps by companies such as Cassini Publishing Ltd[5] or old county maps often reprinted by local history associations or county record offices can be a great source of inspiration. While the growth of towns and cities will have altered the highway network in places, the fact that an old route is shown in the same way as other routes which are roads today means there is something worthy of investigation. At worst there will be a simple explanation, like a stopping up order (see section 3.20), but at best there could be a highway that needs to be recorded, all depending on the evidence available.

When driving, you may see tracks, hedged grassy lanes or tree-lined avenues that immediately raise suspicions. Some will, of course, be private accesses but a quick check against the old OS maps, or with the

4 'unrecorded' includes the case where footpath rights are shown on the definitive map but bridleway or carriageway rights are not.

5 Cassini Publishing Ltd: http://www.cassinimaps.com.

Inland Revenue valuation maps (section 3.17), will enable the researcher to form a view.

Discussions with people who have lived in an area for many years can be highly beneficial. It is common to hear how the postman or delivery man used to go this way or that before the roads were metalled.

Those more interested in ensuring a whole area is thoroughly researched rather than looking at one or two specific paths might find a trip to The National Archives helpful or, if they hold the documents, their County Record Office, to look at the Inland Revenue valuations maps. The showing of a route as a 'white road' (so called because they are omitted from the coloured-in land holdings) is a primary indicator of carriageway rights at that time, and hence that there is an investigation to be carried out.

Once a possible route has been identified for detailed investigation, it is worth checking whether anyone else has already applied for it to be added, changed or deleted from the definitive map as this may enable time to be saved by not duplicating research that has already been done.

Suggested approaches to performing research are given in Chapter 2.

1.5 Historical Evidence

The criterion for recording rights on the definitive map is not that the route conclusively exists or even that it exists beyond reasonable doubt. The test used is the normal civil law test of the 'balance of probabilities' rather than the criminal test of 'beyond reasonable doubt'.[6] That is, does the evidence show that it is more likely than not that the right exists?

The basis of the application to change or record the status of a route is the discovery of evidence which suggests that the definitive map is in error. Section 32 Highways Act 1980 sets out the basis for using historical evidence to determine highway status:

6 *Todd and another v Secretary of State for the Environment, Food and Rural Affairs* [2004] 4 All ER 497.

> 32. Evidence of dedication of way as highway
>
> A court or other tribunal, before determining whether a way has or has not been dedicated as a highway, or the date on which such dedication, if any, took place, shall take into consideration any map, plan or history of the locality or other relevant document which is tendered in evidence, and shall give such weight thereto as the court or tribunal considers justified by the circumstances, including the antiquity of the tendered document, the status of the person by whom and the purpose for which it was made or compiled, and the custody in which it has been kept and from which it is produced.

This means that it is very important to record, whenever a document is examined, the provenance of a document, who made it and why, and where it has been kept since then. This information should be included when applications are made to record highway rights.

In examining the evidence, it is important to consider the evidence *as a whole*: over the range of documents and a span of time. Each individual map or document may not be conclusive and only suggestive of rights. When this pattern is repeated across many different types of evidence produced by different people for different purposes at different times, though, it suggests that the common theme was that public rights existed.

1.6 Layout of Contents

Chapter 2 provides a suggested order for the research, giving separate methods depending on whether single routes or area-based research is being performed.

Chapter 3 sets out the most important frequently-consulted types of evidence, lists where they may be inspected and copies obtained, and considers their value in terms of proving or disproving highway status. A system is adopted where the value of each piece of evidence is indicated by a star rating. In the authors' view, once a route has accrued seven stars, it is worth making a modification order application, unless of course there is later evidence of a stopping up order.

Chapter 4 briefly describes evidence of use of a path as a concurrent or alternative to historical documentary evidence, and notes that full consideration of this possibility is beyond the scope of this book.

Chapter 5 provides the mechanics of making the application to record or remove rights from the definitive map, and provides examples of the statutory forms that are to be used.

Chapter 6 contains helpful hints and suggestions for record office visitors, including thoughts on how to make the best of the time spent there.

Chapters 7 and 8 provide a guide to archive and record offices in England and Wales. Each office is slightly different but all are very knowledgeable and helpful. Many do now have much of their collection indexed on an electronic catalogue and where this information is available, we have given the internet addresses. It is necessary to visit the record office to obtain the most information. The authors hope that the information given will enable researchers to plan their visits to record offices so as to make the most of the time available and minimise the chances of wasting time or inconvenience. Opening hours may be subject to change, and an internet search will usually reveal any recent changes.

Chapter 9 provides the glossary and explanation of abbreviations used.

Chapter 10 provides a list of further reading.

Chapter 11 lists reference material that may be of value to the researcher.

1.7 Information on Other Public Rights

A researcher may come across information that indicates the existence of other types of public rights (or at least suggests that an investigation is needed). Such rights could be related to common land, manorial waste, or deeds made under the Law of Property Act 1925, for example. These are all outside the scope of this book, but are worth noting, if found, and following up when time permits.

2. ORGANISING YOUR RESEARCH

The suggested order for looking at documents depends on the purpose for which the research is being undertaken and the convenience of the location of the various documents.

Landowners and tenants are likely to be interested in particular routes, often after someone has applied for the route to be recorded. Solicitors and licenced conveyancers might be suspicious about the status of a route and wish to investigate it before a land purchase is completed. Walkers, riders and vehicle users might find a route they have been using blocked one day. In each case, the rights relating to the specific route will need to be investigated and modified if it looks as though they are different from those on the current definitive map. An approach for researching a single route is in section 2.1.

For the rights of way researcher, local history group or very large estate, a more efficient method of checking for highways is to consider parishes or groups of parishes at a time. The objective is to find which routes in the parish or estate need to be investigated and to collect the required evidence. A method of doing this is given in section 2.2.

Some people prefer to work on discrete research projects rather than go through the full process of restoring the record. For these and for friends of archives or local history groups, we suggest some projects that will index useful highway information from various document sources, and which will then save time for anyone seeking to collate evidence prior to applying for a route to be recorded or modified. This information is in section 2.3.

While each of the projects will help in assembling the historical evidence in a form to assess whether highway rights exist, the researcher should always have an eye to what has happened more recently, to avoid doing work on a route that has relatively recently been stopped up. If the modern map shows evidence of major infrastructure works (such as railways, motorways and bypasses) since definitive maps were produced in the 1950s, the authorities at the time will have either extinguished all crossings and dedicated new routes in lieu, in which case all historical evidence prior to that date will be void, or they will have stopped up or diverted each crossing individually. In the latter case, under-recorded rights on the definitive map at that time will not usually have been extinguished, and will therefore still exist. A modification order application can be made based on historical evidence and could result in the old line of the route being recorded. It would be prudent for a highway authority to divert this to the nearest suitable crossing. It is therefore always worth looking for works that have happened in the last 60 or so years before deciding which routes should have time spent on them.

2.1 Confirming the Status of an Individual Track

Whether a researcher is for or against the recording of a particular highway status of a route, similar work needs to take place. In essence, it is worth looking at as many of the documents described in Chapter 3 as can be reasonably examined or obtained. The authors have found that drawing up a summary sheet for an investigation, listing each document type and what has been found when it was examined, helps form a view on the merits of a case, before spending too much time writing a statement of case. Do not forget, the name of the route, if it has one, may have changed over the years.

For those seeking to record additional rights on the definitive map, the summary sheet shows eventually whether there is enough evidence to show that rights exist or can be reasonably alleged to exist. For those seeking to disprove rights, for example in a modification order that has just been made, it highlights inconsistencies and deficiencies that, if left unexplained, cast doubt on the changes that the order seeks to make. Figure 1 gives an example of a summary sheet. The sheet shows the typical document set used in that county, and in italics, the researcher's notes on the documents examined, and his notes on additional work to be performed. Blanks indicate where the researcher has not yet checked the document. If any of the terms are unknown, do not worry, they will be clear by the end of Chapter 3. The numbers on the white background to the left of the sheet are the section numbers where that sort of document is discussed. The National Grid references for the ends of the paths are given to help locate them on modern maps. A description of how to work out a grid reference is given in section 11.4.

2.2 Completing the Record for a Parish or Locality

A simple way of getting started is to buy an extra Ordnance Survey Explorer map of the area to use as a research index map. The authors have found it helpful to mark additional information onto the research index map to speed up identifying individual documents when at the archive. First mark on the boundaries of the maps forming the Ordnance Survey county series as these will help with, for example, finding the sheet numbers for the Inland Revenue valuation survey. Secondly, mark on the parish boundaries, as these will help with documents such as tithe maps.

Then, individual routes that are excluded from the Inland Revenue valuation can be marked. Similarly, routes shown as roads on old maps can be marked. Any changes in highway status that do not have an immediate explanation, for example cul-de-sac paths or a footpath changing to a bridleway at a parish boundary, should be marked, perhaps in a different colour, for investigation. Once several sources have been examined, the research index map provides a good indication of routes that may need to be recorded.

If employing this method, especially for the researcher who lives some distance from the archive office, it is helpful to identify the documents that will be of interest, pre-order them if possible, and then spend a visit simply photographing (at sufficient resolution) the documents. This means that the document does not need to be retrieved more frequently than absolutely necessary and so aids its preservation. In those archive offices where photography is not permitted, it will be necessary to work from the source document and mark up the research index map in pencil. Regrettably, this may mean that the document is handled much more than would otherwise be necessary.

Generally, it is helpful to start with documents such as old maps sold to the travelling public (see section 3.3), inclosure records (section 3.5), tithe records (section 3.6), and Inland Revenue valuation maps (section 3.17), but the actual list used will vary from place to place.

When any document suggests that highway rights exist on a route, mark the route on the research index map and number it. Start a summary sheet for the route (as in Figure 1). If the route is already marked on the map, add the notes to the summary sheet for that path.

Figure 1: Example summary sheet for a single route investigation[1]

	Route description	*Route from Hitchin Road, over the railway, to Fishers Green Road (currently recorded as Stevenage 57 FP)*	
	Name (if any)	*Fishers Green Lane*	
	Parish	*Stevenage*	
	OS County Grid	*Hertfordshire 12 – 11*	
	Grid References	*TL 22512591 to TL 22512591*	★**Stars**[2]
3.3	Dury and Andrews (1766)	*Shows the route in the manner of 'Roads enclosed by Hedges'.*	*2/2*
3.3	Bryant (1822)	*This shows the route in the style of 'Lanes and Bridle Ways'.*	*2/2*
3.4	Turnpikes	*None found*	*0/5*
3.5	Inclosure	*[Record office reference QS/E/63B] The Inclosure map shows the application route as separate from the land to either side. It is not numbered. Other vehicular highways are shown in the same way. Need to examine the accompanying Award.*	*/10*
3.6	Tithe	*None found*	*0/5*
3.7	Parish, Estate Maps		*/2*
3.8	River/Drainage	*None found*	*0/5*
3.9	Railway Plans	*The railway plan for the London and York Railway shows the route as plot numbers 1, 175, 175A, 165 and 181.*	*5/5*
	Railway Book of Reference	***Book of Reference of the London and York Railway*** *(built) (CRO reference R337)* *Shows plot 1 as 'Public Highway', owner 'John Howard, Surveyor of Highways of the Parish of Stevenage'.* *Shows 175 as 'Arable Field and Footpath', owner 'Benjamin Hornet'.* *Shows 175a as 'Public Highway', owner 'Surveyor of the Highways of the Parish of Stevenage as aforesaid'.*	

1 This route was subsequently recorded as a restricted byway by The Hertfordshire County Council (Stevenage 57) Modification Order 2008. (Confirmed 5 March 2009.)

2. The star rating system is explained in section 3.2.

	Railway Book of Reference	*Shows 177 as 'Arable Field and Footpath', owner 'Benjamin Hornet'.* *Shows 165 (currently Fishers Green Road) as 'Public Highway', owner 'Surveyor of the Highways of the Parish of Stevenage as aforesaid', that is in exactly the same way as the investigation route.* *Shows 181 as 'Pasture Field', owner 'Mary Jane Weldon Bishop', occupier 'Thomas Cass'.* *Summary: The investigation route is shown in the same way as other routes which are (vehicular) roads today (e.g. 165). Footpaths appear to have been included with the land they crossed (e.g. 175, 177). This route was not included in other land. It is listed as being owned by the Surveyor of Highways, in the same way as other routes which are today roads.* *Conclusion: good evidence of vehicular status.*	
3.10	OS Area Books		*/3*
3.11	Highway Board		*/4*
3.12	HCC Main Roads		*/5*
3.13	Quarter Sessions	*None found*	*0/10*
3.14	OS Boundary Records	*None found*	*0/5*
3.15	OS Object Name Book	*Route is named 'Fishersgreen Lane' so need to check the object name book.*	*/4*
3.16	Other OS		*/2*
3.17	Inland Revenue		*/5*
3.18	Sales Documents		*/3*
3.19	Handover Maps		*/5*
3.20	Stopping Up Orders		*/0*
3.21	MAF		*/2*
3.22	CC information		
3.23	Other Landowner-supplied information		*/2*

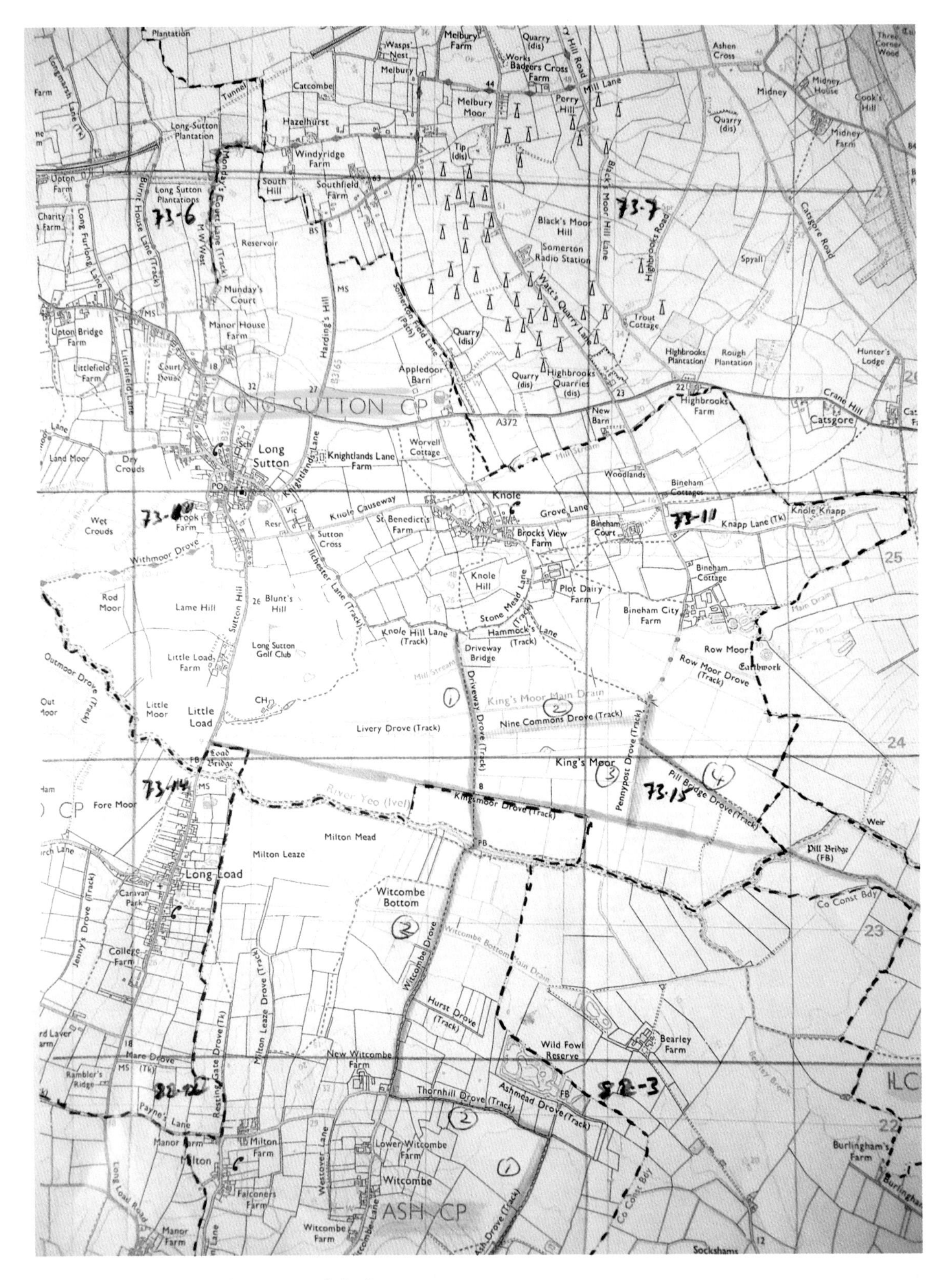

Figure 2: Example of a research index map

Figure 2 shows an extract from a research index map, based on the Ordnance Survey Explorer map of the area. The researcher has marked the parish boundaries with dashed black lines and highlighted the parish names in yellow. The Ordnance Survey county grid map boundaries have been drawn on in pencil and the map number marked in each top left-hand corner. Bridleways already recorded on the definitive map have been marked in green.

Pink lines are routes for which some evidence has been found, and so have been numbered and will be under investigation. Each researcher will come to a personal view on the priority to be placed on making an application for any particular path – for example, one which provides a through route might well have a higher priority than a route that would end up as a cul-de-sac.

The authors have found it helpful, when visiting an archive office, to make a note of the reference numbers of all the commonly used documents, whether they have been examined or not. This is particularly important for those offices that do not have an online document catalogue, and means that documents will be able to be pre-ordered to save time at the next visit.

Local knowledge is valuable. Finding a place on a map is so much quicker when familiar with the area. Knowing that a track depicted as a bridleway in an old record is still a bridleway on the definitive map saves time. Knowing the dates of infrastructure projects such as airfields and construction of reservoirs helps to make more sense of some of the records. It can speed the research if such information is determined from local people before spending time in the record office.

There are a few practices which make keeping and using research easier. It is most important to compile the record in a form that is going to be easy to reference, easy to sort, and is comprehensive, for future use. Before computers, the researcher's notes were often kept in card indexes. However, now with computers, it is sensible to record the information where it can be stored, sorted and shared. The authors recommend that information from source documents is retained in folders relating to those source documents on the computer. The folder may then contain either just the researcher-compiled index of where exactly in a large document relevant entries can be found, or the photographs of those extracts, if they have been taken. This means that original records that are sorted by parish will be indexed on the researcher's computer by parish, and originals that follow a grid system will be indexed by grid. When applications start to be compiled, always 'copy and paste' (rather than 'cut and paste') the extracts needed from the source document collection rather than store photographs only by route or application. This will keep the original research intact and usable for researching a nearby path.

2.3 Discrete Research Projects

While some will be interested in researching particular routes or all the potential routes in an area, others will find their skills lie better in examining particular historical documents to ensure that all relevant highway information has been extracted in good time. This essentially allows a catalogue to be produced for a record source, which will be of value to the wider community, as well as helping to identify routes for more detailed consideration.

Although such records should be checked from start to finish, it is most unlikely that the job of reading, researching and cataloguing these records can be carried out in a short time or single visit. However, they can usually be divided into discrete sections and examined in stages, for example by parish, grid square, linear distance, or a time period depending on the type of record being examined.

Where the status of a specific route is being researched, most of the evidence will be saved as photographs of source documents or print outs of microfiche copies, together with a note of the document location and reference. In the research projects in this section, the output is often an index to findings which may be of value to future specific-route studies, and where in the source document they can be found, to facilitate later copying. Note that when making an application for a modification order, it is essential to provide copies of evidence and not simply the references.

2.3.1 Example of a Linear Project: The Railway Project

Railways and canals are examples of linear features that would have been crossed by minor highways. Their records are described in section 3.9. For this project, the researcher should start at the beginning of the railway line (or relevant section, often 20 miles of railway is a manageable length), with the deposited plan and book of reference. Each land parcel that is described as belonging to the surveyor of highways or is described as a footpath, bridleway, carriageway or road should be noted, and marked on the research index map. Take a note of the plot number and parish on the plan and the wording in the book of reference (by photograph if permitted). Any other information that will help find this exact spot in the records would also be useful, whether the page number in the book of reference, or the distance from the railway terminus, as appropriate. This will enable unrecorded minor highway crossings of the railway or canal prior to construction to be identified. By comparing the list with the rights of way information shown underlying the research index map, and subsequently checked against the definitive map, this provides a list of crossings that appear to warrant further investigation.

This project can also be performed on railway lines that received their Act of Parliament but were never built, as the statutory process of checking all the landowners, including for the proposed crossings, will still have been carried out.

Other linear projects could relate to navigation or drainage records (see section 3.7) or Ordnance Survey boundary records (section 3.14) or, where available, route cards formerly produced by organisations like the Ancient Order of Packriders.

2.3.2 Example of an Area or Grid Project: Inland Revenue Valuation

The Inland Revenue valuation maps show most vehicular highways as excluded from the valuation, as described in section 3.17. For this project, the researcher should make a list of the numbers of the Ordnance Survey county grid maps in which he is interested, and systematically work through the list, examining each document and marking these excluded routes ('white roads') on his research index map. Keep a note of the document reference, and if permitted take a photograph of those white roads that are not shown as modern roads on the current Ordnance Survey map, or are shown but also with a footpath or bridleway symbol.

This will provide quick reference information for the parish or area research described in section 2.2, and ensure that none of the roads identified in 1910 are lost through lack of research.

While doing this project, it is also worth noting any routes marked on the base Ordnance Survey map as 'B.R.', whether on defined tracks or cross-field, as these will also need to be investigated if they do not have the same level of rights recorded today.

This methodology is equally applicable to other area-based records such as inclosure maps and awards (section 3.5), tithe maps and awards (section 3.6), and highway board maps (section 3.11).

2.3.3 Example of a Time-based Project: Highway Board Minutes

Highway board minutes were produced every month or quarter (depending on locality). Where there is not yet an index, it is worthwhile for a researcher to start reading from the earliest records, recording in a notebook or on a computer each reference to a highway take over, diversion, maintenance expenditure or dispute. The route should be marked on the research index map once it has been identified, and each time the route is mentioned photographs of the records or detailed notes should be retained, so that copies of the minutes can be retrieved later if necessary.

This sort of project enables time to be saved by researchers working on a single route or area-based research project.

Other documents suitable for a time-based research project are travel diaries, court records from Quarter Sessions and council committee minutes.

2.3.4 The Digital Archive Research Project

Rights of way research is something everyone can help with. While some are best suited to taking information from documents and synthesising proofs of highway status, others could be spending time at the record office (where permitted) simply photographing documents at the right resolution in a systematic way. When this is done, it is essential that the file names of the photographs are changed to something meaningful, by including the document reference number or name. For example, photographs of the Inland Revenue valuation plan IR 126/8/178 might be named simply as ir126-8-178-NW.jpg where NW is varied to NE, SW, SE to indicate which portion of the map is in which image.

A set of minutes might have the page number appended to the minute book reference.

The benefit of this sort of research is that it can provide data to those who are perhaps unable to visit the archive offices during normal opening hours or can form an electronic library for a team of researchers to call on when researching specific routes or areas.

2.3.5 The Cataloguing Project

Some rights of way sources are not indexed well enough for rights of way purposes, meaning that researchers need to visit the sources simply to rule out their applicability to a particular case.

An example is the MT 78 series of stopping up orders at The National Archives. Online sources allow the researcher to find out which orders relate to a county, and the parishes that each order affects, but there is seldom enough information to identify which route is altered by the order without looking at the order itself.

A second example might be a series of minute books for a highway board, where references to potential under-recorded highways could be noted with the date or page number in the minute book for future reference.

A good cataloguing project is for someone to spend time at The National Archives simply noting which route each order relates to in a specified parish or group of parishes and which highways are created in lieu, so that other researchers can make use of this information.

Similar projects can be performed on other records held by county record offices.

3. STANDARD DOCUMENTARY EVIDENCE SOURCES

3.1 Introduction

In this chapter we examine over 20 documents that are often used as evidence when applying for an unrecorded or under-recorded highway to be correctly recorded or an over-recorded highway to be lowered in status or removed.

The significance of early evidence is brought home by the general presumption in law in favour of the regularity and validity of ancient documents. This presumption applies in both civil and criminal proceedings and applies to documents that are over 20 years old.[1]

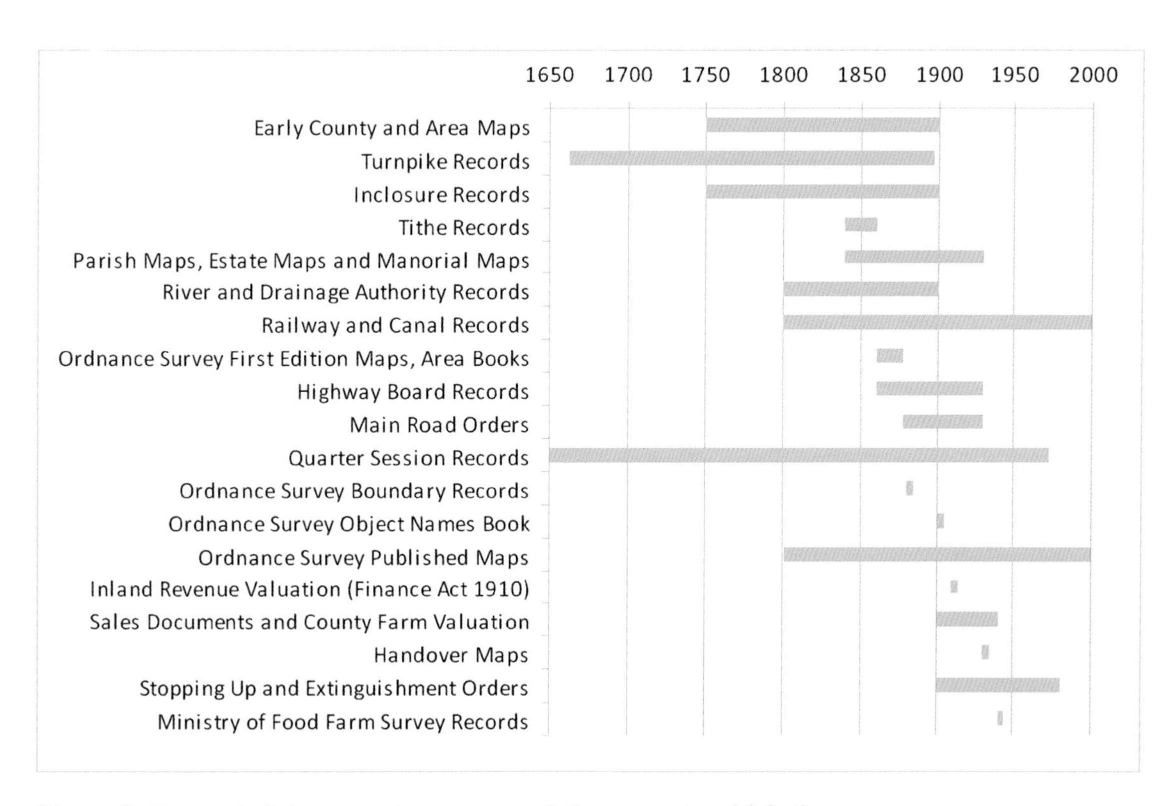

Figure 3: Suggested document sources and the years to which they typically apply

1 Section 4, Evidence Act 1938. See also Halsbury's Laws, Vol 18 Evidence, 4th edn reissue.

For any particular path, only a subset of the documents will be available. For example, railway and canal records only assist when the path crosses or runs adjacent to a railway or canal.

For each document class, a guide is given to where it might be found, how valuable it can be for rights of way research and how it can be used. An example of how the evidence might appear in a definitive map modification order application is given. Further reading suggestions are given: it is emphasised that these do not need to be read for the majority of applications but can sometimes provide assistance in confirming the existence of documents, or interpreting them when they are not quite as the preceding text suggests.

The standard documentary evidence sources are given in approximate chronological order, with the oldest documents first. The researcher should be aware that early evidence could be invalidated by a subsequent stopping up or diversion order. For example, Inclosure Awards often extinguished existing routes and set out new ones. Accordingly, any earlier evidence is invalid, and any 'stars' under the rating system described in the next blue box are wiped out.

The research will involve a visit to the relevant county record office, The National Archives and, perhaps, the council's rights of way office. There are various researchers who will visit a record office for a fee, and some organisations, like The British Horse Society, have volunteers who will examine documents at places like The National Archives or the British Library for their members.

The list of standard sources cannot cover all possible records that may add weight one way or another in determining the question of highway status. Record offices often hold uncatalogued papers, which, when they are eventually indexed, could be of use and researchers may sometimes find additional evidence in other places.

The more information that can be given about a particular document submitted in evidence, the stronger its effect when determining an application, so for all sources consulted, record as much information about the document as possible. Section 6.3 contains helpful hints in this regard.

For each of the standard sources considered, we provide the information described below in a blue panel. The researcher should not be daunted by the long list: for many areas only some of the documentation was prepared or survives and for some paths the documentation may not be relevant.

Star Rating	For each document type, we provide a star rating. In short, the more stars, the more valuable a document will be for highways researchers. The authors generally make applications when a route has seven or more stars in total. A discussion of the star rating system is given in section 3.2. The value stated here is the most the document can be worth.
Held at	This describes where the document can usually be inspected. Where reference is made to a county record office, it is worth checking if the office has the particular document type before travelling, as the records held vary greatly across the country. Because of local government reorganisation over the years, some records may in fact be in an adjacent area's office.
Coverage	This relates to geographical extent. For example, some records will only relate to matters within London or in England rather than in Wales. Others will only exist for a particular county.
Appearance	A note on what the document looks like or how it is laid out.
Shape	Parish – if documents are likely to cover a whole parish (or group of parishes) Grid – if documents are based on rectangular maps Linear – if documents provide information along a linear route Ad hoc – other
Date	This will indicate the date or dates that the relevant record was produced.
Use with	Some documents were made in two parts, or naturally work well with others. Where this is the case it is identified here.
Locating	How to go about finding the relevant document reference.
Interpretation	This entry explains how the document may be used in the context of highway status investigation. Terminology may have changed since the records were created. If this is the case, explanation will be provided.
Caveats	Sometimes a document may not be as useful as the earlier text may have suggested. An entry here will alert the reader to known situations. Others may apply.

In the yellow section, we provide an example of how the document could be used in a definitive map modification order application. This is set out in a standard order. For each paragraph in a proof of evidence, we give a brief title saying what the document is, and a description of where it can be found, and what it shows.

Most applications will only have evidence available from some of the document sources listed. Each example is taken from an application that one of the authors has actually made, so more than one application had to be used to ensure every document source had a relevant example.

Further Reading

Here we provide a list of references for those who wish to delve further into the subject. They are not required for the majority of our readers, but could help explain documents that appear slightly out of the ordinary in what they show.

3.2 The Star Rating System for Evidence

Those new to highways research might well wonder how much evidence is needed before an application is made to modify the definitive map and statement. There is no statutory requirement for a particular number of documents, and each case is, formally, taken on its merits. However, in order to give some sort of value to what is shown on documents, the authors have devised a star rating system which can be used as a guide. The authors emphasise that this is just a guide to sufficient evidence for the making of an application. The evidence has to be considered as a whole, not as a series of individual documents each of which may be inconclusive. The allocation of stars allows one method of assessing whether the application satisfies some basic evidential test.

Each document is rated as follows:

10 star – Legally conclusive e.g. Acts of Parliament, court orders affecting the subject path, administrative orders

5 star – Evidence of reputation in a legally conclusive document, but where the legally conclusive document is not written specifically about the subject path, for example court orders that show the route as an adjoining highway but do not make changes to it

4 star – Evidence of expenditure that would be unlawful unless the route was a public highway e.g. highway board records.

3 star – Evidence of reputation coupled with public scrutiny, or evidence of highway status in a landowner produced document

2 star – Evidence of reputation but without formal public scrutiny for example old maps sold to the travelling public

1 star – Physical evidence only

In the examples that follow throughout this chapter, an explanation of the number of stars allocated is given, as this is not always the same as the maximum value given in the blue box. The authors usually require at least seven stars for a route before making an application. This does not set a minimum: some paths have fewer stars but have compelling cases when the documents are looked at in the context of local circumstances. Equally, seven stars does not guarantee success in recording highway status. This means that even though enough documents have been found to justify an application, other documents should still be sought, if they exist, to make an application as robust as possible. The production of a later stopping-up order will negate all the stars earned from earlier documents.

An example researcher's summary sheet, showing documents examined and stars allocated, is given in section 2.1.

3.3 Early County and Area Maps

Although the Ordnance Survey had been preparing maps for government use for many years, it only started to publish maps for the public in 1801. Many map makers and cartographers had produced maps for sale to the public before this date. The maps that are most useful to rights of way researchers are not the ornamental maps often framed for display (although these can occasionally provide evidence of a former major route), but the more detailed and extensive maps sold to the travelling public.

The depiction of a route on such a map suggests that it could be used by the map purchaser; word would soon get round that a map was useless for navigation if it contained many apparent roads that were not open for public use.

Star Rating	2 (While all old maps can count in evidence, do not count more than two old maps' worth when totalling the stars.)
Held at	County Record Offices
Coverage	Widespread
Appearance	Various
Shape	Ad hoc
Date	Various
Use with	Modern mapping to identify potentially unrecorded highways If a key to the map is available, always include this with your map extract, to aid interpretation.
Locating	Many county record offices will hold originals, and some sell reprints, of useful old maps. For example, Somerset holds maps by Day and Masters (1782) and Greenwood (1822). Hertfordshire sells reprints of the county maps by Dury and Andrews (1766) and Bryant (1822), and Norfolk sells those of Fayden (1795) and Bryant (1826). Many record offices hold copies of maps by John Bartholemew, which were based on the Ordnance Survey maps and produced for the cycling public.

Interpretation	These maps have two main uses. Firstly, they can be used as an aid to research to compare routes shown on the old maps with the modern Ordnance Survey Explorer map, and to identify routes shown on the old map that are not shown on the modern map with at least restricted byway status (or bridleway status if shown as a lesser status route on the old map). The research index map then provides a record of paths to be researched in more detail with other sources. Secondly, for any route that has sufficient evidence, include the extract from the old map to illustrate that it existed physically at the time of the old map, and argue (unless there is contrary evidence) that the route shown must have had some public significance because it was sold to the travelling public. This means that such maps are more likely to show roads for public use than those of a purely private nature. They may also be more likely to show roads than bridleways, but each map must be considered separately on this point, after taking into account its scale and key. Include any notes that add weight to the value of a map – for example, Fayden was the 'Cartographer to the King' which might give his surveys additional weight. The key to many of Cary's maps includes the term 'Parochial Roads' indicating that the specified routes were the responsibility of the parish. Many inspectors find it helpful to compare several routes on the old map with their status today: if all the other local routes shown in the same way on the old map are today shown as (for example) bridleway, then it adds weight to the unrecorded route also having that status.
Caveats	Some early cartographers may not have been so accurate with the exact alignment of routes, but would still have been accurate with showing road junctions and destinations. Such maps may not provide quite so much evidence for modification order purposes, but remain useful for identifying routes needing investigation. Some early maps may have been produced from the plates of even earlier maps, and so the date of publication and date of survey may differ. Be careful to specify which date is being used.

Example for use in an application[2]

1. Dury and Andrews' Map of Hertfordshire (1766)

a. An original is held by the Hertfordshire Archives and Local Studies (HALS) under reference CM26.

b. This was made for sale to the public, and so is unlikely to show routes that the public could not use. It has a key in which different types of route are distinguished.

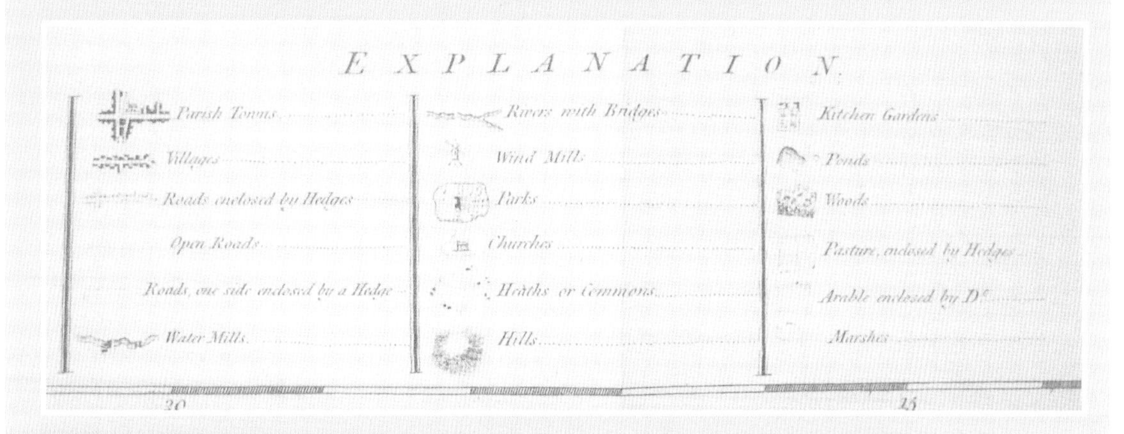

Figure 4: Extract from Dury and Andrews' Map (1766) showing the Key

c. The application route is shown in the manner of a 'Road enclosed by Hedges'. It is indistinguishable in depiction from the adjoining road that leads to Nape End (now 'Nup End'), suggesting similar status to that route, which is today a public road. Accordingly, this suggests that the route was considered to have vehicular rights in 1766.

2 Application made to Hertfordshire County Council on 18 Jan 2010. Their reference NH/209.

Figure 5: Extract from Dury and Andrews' Map (1766) showing the application route

Example for use in an application[3]

2. Bryant's Map of Hertfordshire (1822)

a. An original is held by the Hertfordshire Archives and Local Studies (HALS) under reference CM88.

b. This was made for sale to the public, and so is unlikely to show routes that the public could not use. It has a key in which different types of route are distinguished.

c. The route is shown in the manner of a 'Good cross or driving road'. This suggests that the route was considered to have vehicular rights in 1822. Other routes in the vicinity that are shown in the same way are today public (vehicular) roads, so adding to the conclusion about vehicular rights.

Figure 6: Extract from Bryant (1822) showing the application route as good cross or driving road

3 Application made to Hertfordshire County Council on 18 Jan 2010. Their reference NH/209.

The Turnpike & Mail Roads
Good Crofs or Driving Roads
Lanes & Bridle Ways

Figure 7: Extract from Bryant (1822) showing the Key

The maps in the above examples each show the route in question. In both cases, the key is suggestive of vehicular rights and a comparison of other routes shown in the same way on the map with the status today shows that, for consistency, the application route would also need to have vehicular rights. Each map scores 2 stars, giving a total of 4. If a third old commercial map gave similar results, it would give no more stars as the total that can be counted from the old commercial map source is four.

Further Reading

Cobbett, William, *Rural Rides* (1830) reprinted as Cobbett, William and Dyck, Ian (2001) *Rural Rides*, Penguin, ISBN 978-1-150-09035-6.

Taylor, Susan and Hogg, Sue (1997) *What is a Cross Road?* South Pennine Packhorse Trails Trust, ISBN 978-0-9530573-0-6.

3.4 Turnpike Records

Originally, when roads were predominantly used by local traffic, they were maintained by the local people. This was firstly under the manorial system; then under the Highway Act 1555, the parishes took control of supplying labour and materials. As the number of longer journeys increased, and the traffic changed from just horses to wagons and carriages, so the wear and tear on the road system was increased, to the point where the local people were both unable and unwilling to maintain the roads in their parish to the standard required for long distance coaches and wagons. It was thought more equitable if every user contributed to the repair of the roads in the proportion to the use they made of them. The idea of a turnpike system came into being with the cost and responsibility for maintaining the roads being taken into a trust which charged the passing public. The trustees would put up the funds to bring the roads up to a good state of repair and then receive interest from the tolls.

Turnpike Acts were usually for a period of 21 years in which time the roads would be made up to an acceptable standard, although many turnpike acts were renewed. Renewal acts could also allow for new lengths of road and sometimes dis-turnpiking of others. Between 1750 and 1770 the number of Turnpike Trusts trebled. They were unconnected with any of the county, parish, manor or borough authorities. In 1773 a General Turnpike Act was passed which facilitated the process so that by 1820 some 20,000 miles (32,000km) of roads in England and Wales had been improved.

Up until around 1815, most Turnpike Acts were to improve existing roads. Later, with the improved methods of construction and the use of large and heavy vehicles, more new roads were built.

Eventually Turnpike Trusts were responsible for over 23,000 miles of roads. Some Turnpike Acts state how much, if any, statute labour could be used. It was thought that once a road had been brought up to a good state of repair, and all the debts paid off, then the toll gates would be removed.

All Turnpike Acts are available at the Parliamentary Archives. Some are in manuscript form which can be hard to read for the untrained eye. Useful sources are lists of new Turnpike Acts as given by Albert (1972) (England only) and Pawson (1977) which ends in 1800 so will not list all. Neither is complete.

Not all roads were turnpiked as many did not need repair and maintenance; there will be sections of public road between turnpikes.

Drovers and the masters of packhorse trains, amongst others, avoided the turnpikes wherever possible. Circumventing a tollgate was comparatively easy in open countryside, but as routes converged on towns many turnpike trusts negotiated with landowners to prevent the use of side roads and back lanes by erecting obstacles which may still be evident in local names such as Chain Bar Lane and the Chainway.

The presence of milestones is usually regarded as evidence of turnpike roads, although many important roads had milestones and guide posts predating turnpikes. The General Turnpike Act of 1822 required trusts to mark points at which their roads crossed parish boundaries.

The dawn of the canal and then the railway age changed methods of long distance travel and transportation of goods, and the age of the turnpike slowly came to an end.

The Highways and Locomotives (Amendment) Act 1878 provided that all turnpike roads that were dis-turnpiked after 31 December 1870 became main roads, with the county authority responsible for providing half of the maintenance costs.[4] This means that if a route can be shown to have been a turnpike road, and no stopping up order exists, it will still carry carriageway rights.

4 s.13, Highways and Locomotives (Amendment) Act 1878.

Star Rating	5 (for former turnpike routes), 3 (for routes linking to former turnpike routes) Some maps are not very detailed so may only offer supporting evidence. These can score at most 2 stars.
Held at	Parliamentary Archives Some county record offices
Coverage	Wherever there was a turnpike road.
Appearance	Either roll maps or bound books with maps that extend out.
Shape	Linear, with little or no regard for north.
Date	Turnpike trusts created in 1663, then 1696 to 1836. Between 1700 and 1750, four hundred road acts were passed, Between 1751 and 1790, one thousand six hundred acts were passed. Turnpike trusts ended around 1895.
Use with	Any indication that there were milestones on a route is good evidence that it was either a main or a turnpike road.
Locating	Ask for help at the record office.
Interpretation	For a route which used to be a turnpike, use the 1878 Act to conclude it became a main road (and hence a carriageway). If there has been no subsequent stopping up order, and the route is not an ordinary road today, apply for byway status. Turnpikes also provide supporting evidence for linking routes. Follow the line of the turnpike, many of which are still major roads now. The spurs off the turnpike, which may say 'to xxx', are most useful. These maps were for the general travelling public and 'to xxx' would most likely indicate a public route to that place.

Example for use in an application[5]

3. Langport, Somerton and Castle Cary Turnpike Trust (1830)

a. The Langport, Somerton and Castle Cary Turnpike Trust was set up by Act of Parliament in 1753 and extended several times. The Act providing the Trust with powers covering the date of this map was 5 Geo 4 c98 in 1824. The Trust's main responsibilities were the east-west road above the Somerset levels, and a network of minor roads into the three market towns of mid-Somerset.

b. This map is held by the Somerset Heritage Centre under reference D/T/lsc H10.

c. This map was produced by the Turnpike Trust. It sets out the roads that were under the Trust's control. Near to Shepherds Cross turnpike gate there is a cross road. The right hand branch is labelled 'From Hadspan Road'. This information would only have been of value if the route could have been used by the public. The conclusion is that this is evidence in favour of public highway rights along the route 'from Hadspan Road'.

[Note: a copy of the Act would be enclosed with the modification order application. This part of a proof of evidence would need to be read in conjunction with other evidence setting out the full route that had been applied for, as this only covers one end of the route.]

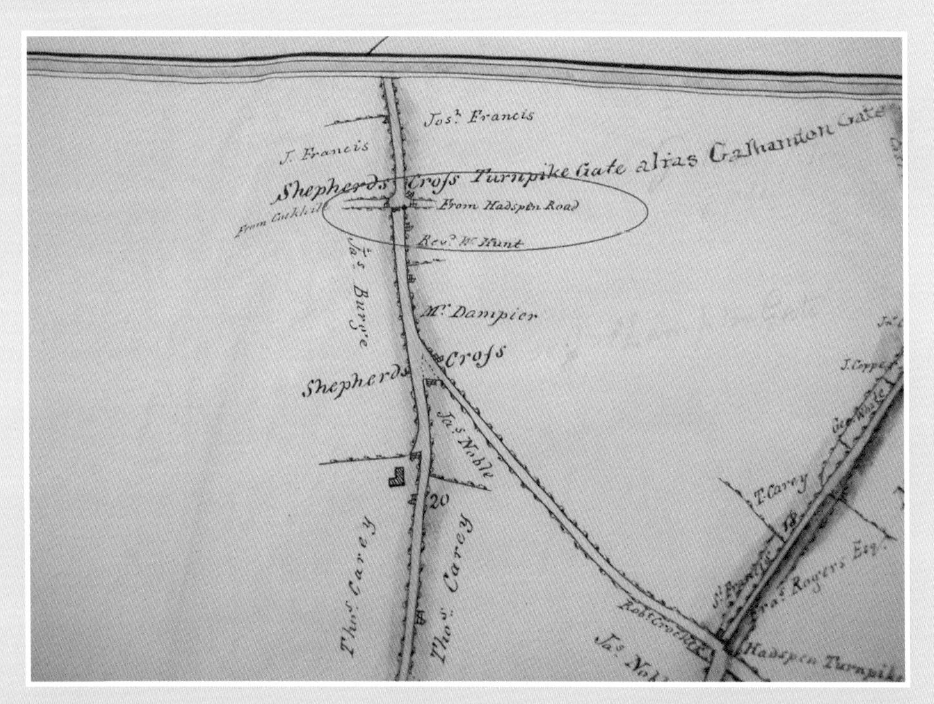

Figure 8: Extract of map produced by the Langport, Somerton and Castle Cary Turnpike Trust

5 Application made to Somerset County Council on 12 Mar 2009. Their reference 638M.

The application route is not the former turnpike route itself, so does not get the full five stars possible for turnpike evidence. However, it is shown in a way indicating likely highway status on the turnpike plan, and so scores three stars.

Further Reading

Friar, Stephen (2001) *The Sutton Companion to Local History*, Sutton Publishing Ltd, ISBN 978-0-7509-2723-9.

Hindle, Paul (2001) *Roads and Tracks for Historians*, Phillimore & Co Ltd, ISBN 978-1-86077-182-8.

The Planning Inspectorate (2011) *Definitive Map Orders: Consistency Guidelines.*

Webb, S & B (1913) *English Local Government: The Story of the King's Highway*, Volume V, Longmans, Green & Co.

http://www.turnpike.org.uk – a general resource giving information about various turnpike trusts.

3.5 Inclosure Records

These records were compiled when a few landowners grouped together to combine and reallocate lands in order to improve methods of agriculture. This process ring fenced lands and reduced the common grazing areas. The landowners would apply to Parliament for an Inclosure Act to be passed, after which Commissioners were appointed to carry out their survey, prepare the map(s), set out the new road network, and make the distribution/award and land ownership allocations. The award could be made several years after the enabling Act. In some cases all existing roads, with the exception of turnpike roads, were extinguished and a completely new road network was set out.

Because the process was authorised by Act of Parliament, and followed a statutory process including rights of complaint by the public, any road or other highway set out at inclosure is highly conclusive evidence of highway status. For any area that was subject to Parliamentary inclosure, there will be an Act setting out the powers to inclose and the procedure to be followed. In 1801, Parliament passed the Inclosure (Consolidation) Act 1801 which contained clauses that were generally applicable (and so did not need to be cited in each area's local Act), so adding more uniformity to the powers of the Inclosure Commissioners and the procedure used. The General Inclosure Acts 1836 and 1845 also provided standard rules.

Whenever Inclosure Act evidence is used, it is necessary to determine the powers of the Commissioners, which means working out precisely which Acts govern the process in that instance. It is worth getting a copy of the Act authorising the local inclosure, and a copy of any general Act to which it refers.

The various Inclosure Acts all make provision for publicity of the proposed changes, and mechanisms for appeal. These processes mean that documents from the inclosure are weighted more highly in today's definitive map work than, say, a private communication of the era.

By way of example, consider the Inclosure Act 1836. This set out the process to be followed in order to redistribute lands in a parish. It provided scope for local agreements to be endorsed, independent people to assess where local agreements could not be reached, and an appeals and hearing process. It follows that any evidence relating to the inclosure process will have substantial weight.

> If two-thirds (both in number and value) of the owners and occupiers of land could agree then the lands and commons in an area could be inclosed (s.1). This process required notice on the door of the local church, and also advertised in a newspaper circulating in the county in which the affected lands were located. Consent in writing of the two-thirds was required after the meeting to make the agreement binding. Commissioners to work out the detail of the local inclosure process and who were not to have any interest in any of the affected lands were appointed by the majority of the landowners (s.3). All notices given by the Commissioners had to be on the church door and in a newspaper (s.8). Four-fifths (by number and value) of the landowners could agree rules to guide the Commissioners' work (s.12) and any other landowner who disagreed could appeal to the Quarter Sessions (s.13). Commissioners were required to set out who had the right to herbage growing on 'private roads' (s.29).
>
> If seven-eighths of the landowners agreed the terms of an inclosure, they could proceed without the use of commissioners (s.40) but in this case, the proposals had to be deposited with the Clerk of the Parish, the Clerk of the Peace of the county, placed on the door of the church for three weeks, and advertised in a newspaper that circulated in the county (s.41). Any person interested in the inclosure could object in writing to the Clerk of the Peace (s.43), who would collect all the objections and place them before Quarter Sessions for determination (s.44).
>
> When the process was completed, the Commissioners had to deposit the Inclosure Award and any maps with the local Parish church and with the Clerk of the Peace (s.51). Anyone aggrieved by anything done under the Act could appeal to the Quarter Sessions (s.53).

Typically the following were set out: public carriage roads, private carriage roads, halter paths, bridleways, and footpaths. The Act will provide the powers to be exercised by the Commissioners, and sometimes these will vary from Act to Act. Compare, for example the highways provision in the Inclosure (Consolidation) Act 1801 and the Inclosure Act 1845:

> The Inclosure (Consolidation) Act 1801 provided that public carriage roads had to be set out before allocating lands, and that they had to be at least 30 foot wide (s.8). Private roads, bridleways and footways were also to be set out (s.10).

> The Inclosure Act 1845 provided that public roads and ways were to be set out and made, and existing public roads and ways could be widened, before allocating lands (s.62). No statement of width was given in this Act, but any public road or way set out was to have the width required (s.65) by the Highways Act 1835, which set minimum widths. Private or occupation roads and ways could be set out (s.68).

Commissioners will normally record where maintenance responsibility fell.

Each inclosure award comes with a map or set of maps. Each track awarded will have a description and will often be numbered. If a number is given, it will be indexed in the Award where a description will be found.

Star Rating	10 for routes set out in the Award
	5 for others
Held at	County Record Offices
	The National Archives, class/series MAF 1 (post 1845 onwards) and a few earlier ones in other classes.
Coverage	England and Wales, but only in areas that were inclosed. Figures range from a few in one county to nearly 200 in another county. They can cover part of one parish or a combination of parts of several parishes; the area covered may be from a few acres up to a few thousand acres
Appearance	They may be in volume, roll or folio format. All will have the map(s) and the award which is many pages of handwritten script. Some will have the Act included with the document, other record offices will keep the Acts separately.
Shape	Parish system
Date	Could be anywhere between the mid-1700s to the very early 1900s.
Locating	At county record offices: ask the archivist how to find the document reference; there will probably be a list of their holdings. Sometimes the Acts are included with the document and sometimes they will have separate document references.

The TNA holds the awards for post 1845 inclosure acts in MAF 1. (Section 146 of the General Inclosure Act 1845 required two copies to be made). Pre 1845 awards will only be found at TNA if a second copy of the award was made and enrolled. This might have happened when one or more of the parties decided to pay for an extra copy to be made enrolled where it would be held safe for future reference; these would have been deposited with the Kings Bench, the court of Common Pleas or other courts, and hence they will be held in a variety of classes at TNA.

Some parishes are covered by more than one inclosure award. A listing of most inclosure awards is available for England at WE Tate's *Domesday of English Enclosure Acts and Awards* (1978), and for Wales at J Chapman's *Guide to Parliamentary Enclosures in Wales* (1992).

A comprehensive guide to inclosure maps is contained in Roger JP Kain, John Chapman and Richard Oliver's book, *The Enclosure Maps of England and Wales, 1595-1918*. There is an associated database which gives current location and document references available at http://hds.essex.ac.uk/em/index.html

Note the variation in spelling from 'Inclosure' to 'Enclosure' and be prepared to look under both versions.

Interpretation

Because it is a legal document with a good description of each track, it is necessary to read through the Act and the award, which is typically verbose, and pay attention to any subsequent paragraphs which may detail additional information such as maintenance responsibilities and other rights.

Although a track may have been set out as a private carriage road, the commissioners may also have awarded public bridleway rights over it, so do not be misled by an early entry in the award not giving the full picture.

The *PINS Consistency Guidelines* note that the facts in an inclosure award carry significant evidential weight,[6] but that interpretation can be difficult. The *Guidelines* draw attention to a Court of Appeal judgment[7] in which it was held, 'Even if the Commissioners in this case have acted *ultra vires*, it would be impossible to hold that the award at this distance of time could be impeached'.

Caveats

Private carriage road could be taken in modern parlance to mean a private route able to take carriages. Historically, other interpretations are possible. Cook (2011) gives examples that show the only possible interpretation of some documents is that a private carriage road was a carriage road for the use of the public, but which was privately maintained, for example maintained by a specific person. Other commentators have found documents where the interpretation is that of a road

6 *Roberts v Webster* [1967] QBD 298.
7 *Micklethwaite v Vincent* [1893] 69 LT 57.

for private carriages, so meaning, perhaps, that it was a less significant route than that intended to be used by mail coaches or stage coaches, for example.[8]

In respect of Charlton Musgrove (Somerset Heritage Centre reference Q/RDe 127), the Act is dated 1814, the Award is dated 1821, and the General Inclosure Act of 1801 is relevant. Only one 'Public Carriage Road' was awarded. This goes diagonally across the parish and does not pass through the main village. The only way of reaching the village is on one of the nine 'Private Carriage roads' that were also set out. It seems reasonable to argue that either there was some way in which these routes could be used by the public, or that some quickly became highways by usage after the award had come into effect. However, corroborating evidence will be needed to back up such a statement.

It is important to read the local and any general Act in order to understand how the language was used, and what its effect would have been. In *Buckland, Buckland and Capel v Secretary of State for Environment, Transport and the Regions* [2000] CO/1682/1998 it was held in connection with a local Act of 1797 that it was not open to the Commissioners to circumvent strict requirements as to width for public carriage routes by awarding them as private carriage routes that the public could use. It was also confirmed that there was nothing that stopped subsequent use from turning the privately awarded route into a public highway.

For the latest information given to Inspectors, the *PINS Consistency Guidelines* are essential reading.

The following examples relate firstly to a route shown as a bridleway, and secondly to a route shown as a private road.

Example for use in an application[9] (route shown as bridleway)

4. Inclosure Act and Award for Chilthorne Domer, Somerset

a. An Act of Parliament passed in the seventh year of the reign of King George IV entitled 'An Act for dividing allotting and inclosing the open and common lands within the parish of Chilthorne Domer in the county of Somerset' provided authority for the inclosure of the land in this parish subject to the terms of the Act.

b. The inclosure of this area was implemented by William Keen of Godalming in the County of Surrey and recorded in the Award for Chilthorne Domer, and the award, including the map, is now held at the Somerset Heritage Centre under reference Q/RDe 9.

8 This meaning has since been discounted by *Dunlop v SSE and Cambridgeshire County Council* [1995] 70 P & CR 307, *The Times*, 5 May 1995.

9 Application made to Somerset County Council on 5 May 2011. Their reference 713M.

c. The award sets out, amongst other routes, a public bridleway. The transcript of the section from the Chilthorne Domer Inclosure Award contains the entry,

> BRIDLEWAY ALSO one bridleway of the breadth of ten feet marked C on the said map hereto annexed extending from the public highway leading from Yeovil aforesaid to Tintinhull in the said county of Somerset through a certain common field called Girdle Field unto and into the present public bridleway from Girdle Field aforesaid to Montacute in the said County of Somerset.

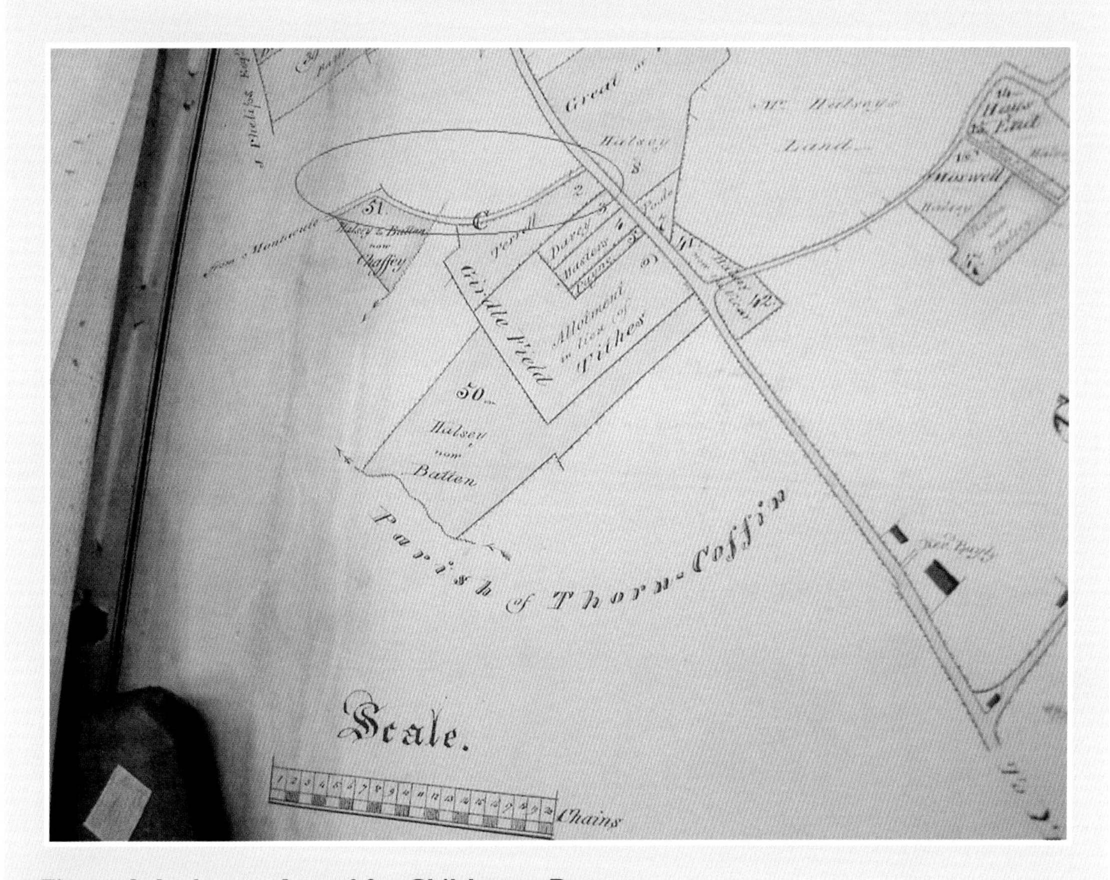

Figure 9: Inclosure Award for Chilthorne Domer

d. The route is set out in the award and the map shows it going into the next parish, Montacute, to join up with a public bridleway. This record has the advantage of validating that the continuation was regarded as a public bridleway.

e. The inclosure process was authorised by an Act of Parliament. The award recitals show that the process was correctly implemented. Accordingly the Act and award are strong evidence that this route carried public bridleway status.

The document in the above example is worth ten stars because the award recitals show the correct process was followed, the route was set out in the award and it is clearly identifiable from the plan.

Example for use in an application[10] (route shown as private road)

5. Inclosure Act (1833) and Award (1838) for West Moor, Somerset

a. An Act of Parliament passed in the third year of King William IV entitled 'An act for inclosing certain moors or commons called West Moor East Moor and Middle Moor in the County of Somerset' provided authority for the inclosure of the land in named parishes subject to the terms of the Act. This Act gives the Inclosure Commissioner the powers set out in the Act of 41 Geo III c.109 (i.e. the Inclosure (Consolidation) Act 1801). Section 8 of the 1801 Act provides that Public Carriage Roads shall be set out at 30 feet width and section 9 provides for money to be raised to pay for the setting out and maintenance of these public carriage roads. In section 10 the Commissioner is given the power to set out (with no particular width) private roads, bridleways, footways, watering places, bridges, and other things that are public in nature, and then provides for the maintenance of them to be the responsibility for ever of the owners and proprietors for the time being.

b. The inclosure of this area was implemented by Thomas Best of Haselbury Plunknett in the County of Somerset, and the Award, including the map, are now held at the Somerset Heritage Centre under reference Q/RDe 101.

c. The key to the Inclosure Map sets out the colours used for land in each of the parishes covered by the award. Roads are coloured sienna or ochre, regardless of parish.

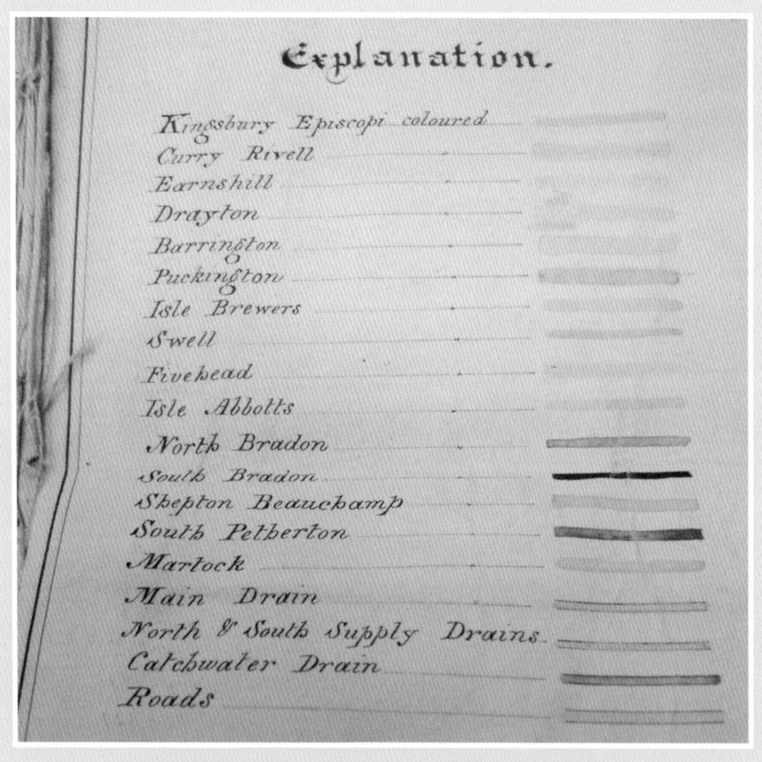

Figure 10: Inclosure Award for West Moor Extract 1 (Key)

10 Application made to Somerset County Council on 13 Oct 2009. Their reference 550M.

d. The award sets out, amongst other routes, a private road, number 16: The West Moor Inclosure Award provides:

> 16. One other private road of the width of twenty feet numbered 16 on the said map branching out of the said last mentioned private road numbered 15 at the north east corner of an allotment numbered 248 and proceeding in a southerly direction by the same allotment and allotments numbered 305, 331, 332, 333, 334, 379, and 403 to a bridge marked G made and erected by me under the said act across the said catchwater drain at a place called Palmers Lane End **And** I have adjudged and determined and do hereby declare that this road (numbered 16) as lies between the said Private Road numbered 15 and a bridge marked F and erected by me across the said Main Drain at the south west corner of an allotment numbered 334 together and one half part of the said bridge and as far as the keystone thereof on the north side thereof shall be and shall be deemed to be situate and lying in the said parish of Curry Rivell[.] And that the remainder of the same bridge and road together with the said bridge marked G made and erected by me over the said catchwater drain marked G made and erected by me over the said catchwater drain at Palmers Lane End shall be and shall be deemed to be situate and lying in the said parish of Kingsbury Episcopi.

e. The route is long, and requires two photographs to be seen in context.

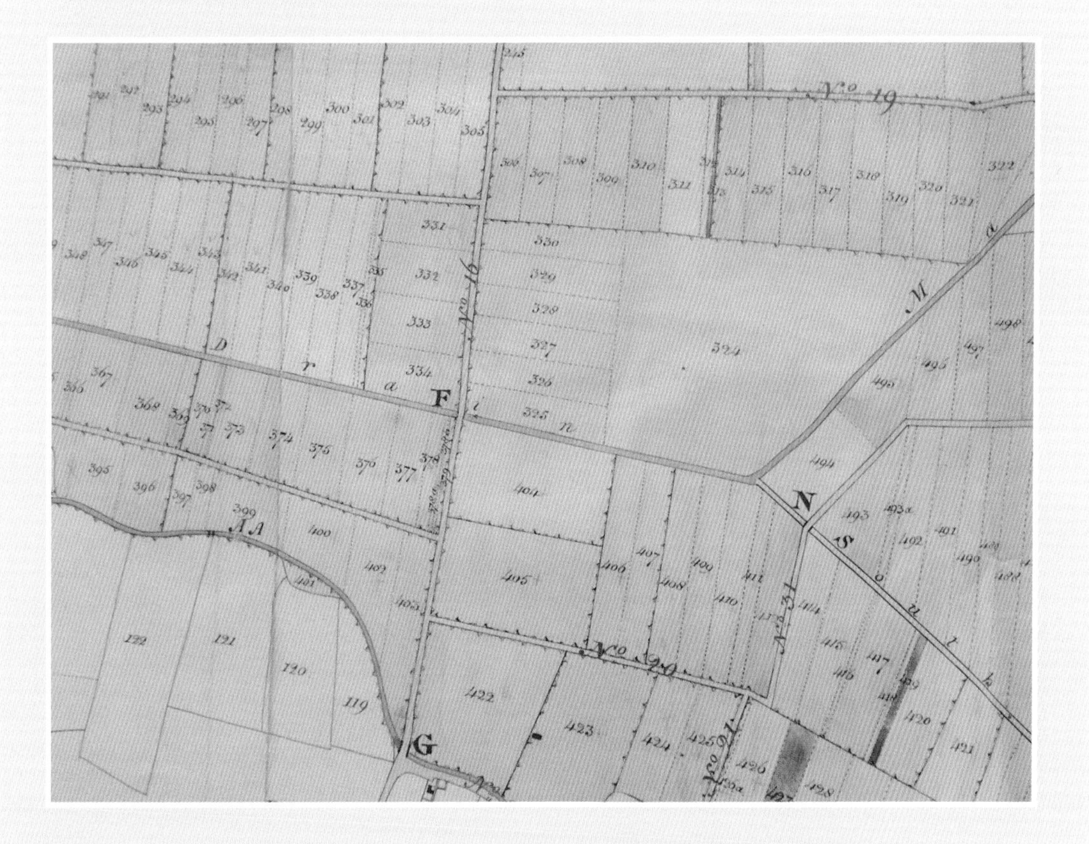

Figure 11: West Moor Inclosure Award Extract 2 (Southern section)

Figure 12: West Moor Inclosure Award Extract 3 (Northern section)

f. The application route (road number 16) is set out as a private road in the award. The 1801 Act's description of private road as part of a list of things which are public in nature, and the allocation of perpetual maintenance responsibility to the owners and proprietors for the time being suggests that it was only the maintenance responsibility that was private, and that in all other respects the road was a public highway. In other words, the term 'private road' is simply being used to mean 'public highway without public responsibility for maintenance'.

g. The inclosure process was authorised by an Act of Parliament. The award recitals show that the process was correctly implemented. Accordingly the Act and award are strong evidence that this route carried public vehicular rights and hence should be recorded as a byway. Unless any of the exemptions set out in the Natural Environment and Rural Communities Act 2006 apply, this route will today carry restricted byway rights.

The document in the above example is worth five stars because the award recitals show the correct process was followed, the route was set out in the award and it is clearly identifiable from the plan. Although there may be a discussion about the meaning of 'private road', the context of that expression has been explained as meaning 'privately-maintained public highway'. However, because this is not crystal clear from the award, we give it 5 stars so ensuring that there is some corroboration before 7 stars are attained.

3.5.1 Inclosure Awards – Exchanges

These records were compiled as and when landowners exchanged lands, typically after inclosure.

Star Rating	Up to 2
Held at	The National Archives, class/series MAF 11 and occasionally at county record offices
Coverage	England and Wales, where exchanges took place and the records were deposited. The authors have found them in TNA, and a few in the county record office. They will only be found when they have been deposited with an archive office.
Appearance	The document comprises a written record of the legal exchange of land, sometimes with a schedule if there are many land parcels. The date and title are on the back of the document, the front has the map and the legal exchange. There is often a wax seal attached. The sheets are large, around 80cm by 80cm and the map is usually in colour. At TNA, the exchange documents are contained in brown envelopes.
Shape	Area, generally only the immediate area of the parcels of land being exchanged.
Date	Generally around 1857 to 1880.
Use with	Can be used independently.
Locating	The MAF 11 series are referenced by county, and by parish within that county. There is often more than one exchange in a parish, and each exchange has its own document in a separately marked envelope. MAF 11 are produced in boxes containing around 30 envelopes each containing an exchange document which has an individual reference number. Finding them: put the parish name in the top line of the search engine, and MAF 11 in the third line. If there are any, and there may not be, the reference will be MAF 11/xxx/yyyy. Order the MAF 11/xxx and the document will be in a box with the last reference number on the outside of a brown envelope. Very occasionally they are stored as rolls.

Interpretation	These exchanges were usually between two large landowners and, although were not compiled for rights of way work, show the road system as it was then, and this frequently shows the surfaced roads which are tarmacked today in the same way as those which have not been tarmacked. The example below also shows the piece of land being exchanged and there is no mention of any easement, so it may be concluded that the drove it is accessed from (Lakehouse Drove) was for use by the public.
Caveats	Limited coverage so there may not be any in the area of interest.

Example for use in an application[11]

6. Exchange of lands in Drayton and Curry Rivel (1867)

a. When land was exchanged to give effect to an Inclosure Award, documents evidencing the land transfer were often drawn up by the respective landowners, and some survive.

b. This exchange document is held at The National Archives under reference MAF 11/137/3230, dated November 1867.

c. The map forming part of this exchange document shows Lakehouse Drove (circled by the applicant and running from left to right) in the same manner as other routes which are part of the public road network today.

d. The exchange document shows that the process of advertising the proposed transfer for three consecutive weeks was followed, and the required wait of three months was completed with no objections raised.

e. The exchange plan shows that the land to be exchanged is accessed off the spur to Lakehouse Drove. No right of easement is given in the Award, and the adjoining fields had different owners. The land would be inaccessible if there were no public highway to reach it.

f. Lakehouse Drove is coloured sienna. Surrounding routes also coloured sienna are today recorded as public roads, or are the subject of separate applications for addition to the definitive map at restricted byway status.

g. The showing of the Lakehouse Drove route on the map in the same way as other public vehicular highways, and the lack of recording, in the exchange document text, of any means of access (such as an easement) are good evidence that the landowners of the day considered Lakehouse Drove to be a public vehicular highway.

11 Application made to Somerset County Council on 26 Jun 2010. Their reference 687M.

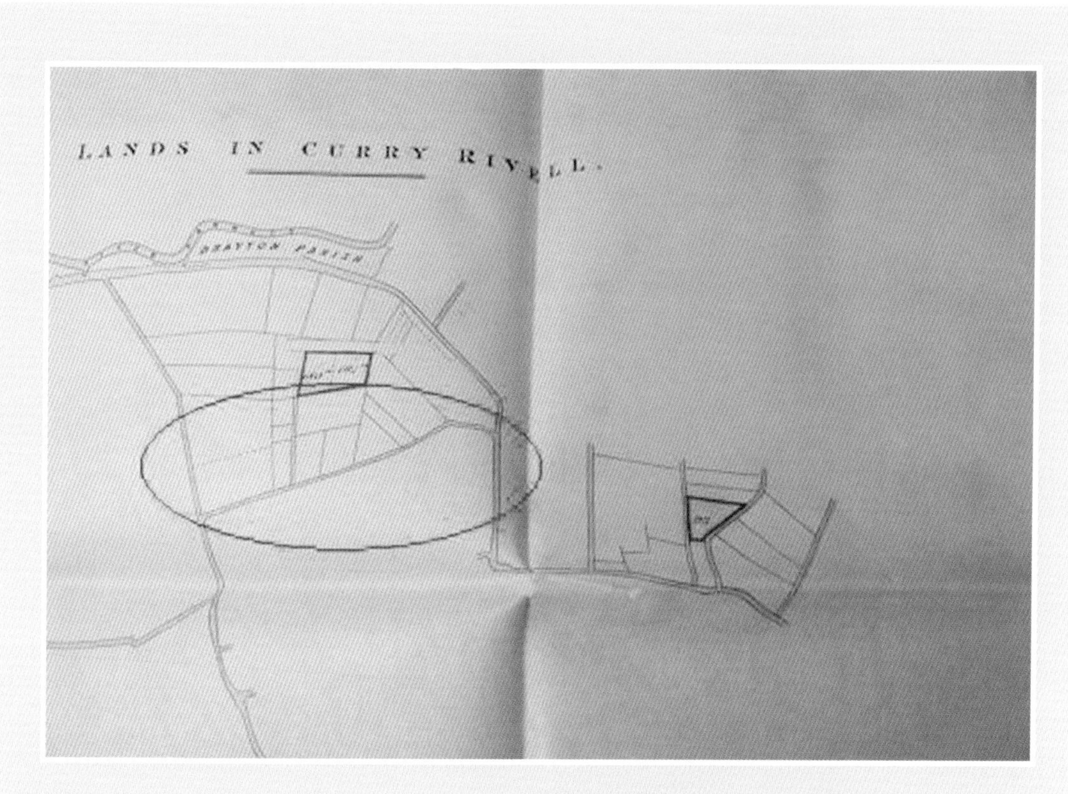

Figure 13: Exchange of lands in Drayton and Curry Rivel

[Note: photographs of the exchange document text, and a transcript, would be attached to the modification order application but are not reproduced here for space reasons.]

The document in the above example is worth two stars because the exchange document recitals show the correct process was followed, the route was set out in the award and it is clearly identifiable from the plan, and the information was supplied by the landowner or his agent.

Further Reading

Braham, D (October 2001) 'Inclosure Awards: law and practice', Rights of Way Law Review 9.3 pp 139–145.

Chapman, J (1992) *Guide to Parliamentary Enclosures in Wales*, University of Wales Press, ISBN 978-0-7083-1111-0.

Cook, C (2011) 'A journey through private roads', in *Byway and Bridleway*, 2/2011, Byways and Bridleways Trust, ISSN 1357-9737.

Hammond, JL & B (1924) *The Village Labourer 1760-1832*, Longmans Green & Co (reprinted 1987 by Alan Sutton Publishing Ltd).

Hart, T (January 1994) 'Inclosure Awards', Rights of Way Law Review 9.3 pp 57–66.

Hodson, Y (September 2011) 'Footpaths and bridleways in Inclosure Acts 1801-1845', Rights of Way Law Review 9.3 pp 179–97.

Hollowell, S (2000) *Enclosure Records for Historians*, Phillimore Press, ISBN 978-1-86077-128-6.

Kain, R J P, Chapman, J and Oliver, R (2004) *The Enclosure Maps of England and Wales, 1595–1918*, Cambridge University Press. ISBN 978-0-521-82771-3.

The Planning Inspectorate (2011) *Definitive Map Orders: Consistency Guidelines.*

Sugden, J (May 1992) 'Inclosure Commissioners at Work', Rights of Way Law Review 9.3 pp 39–48.

Tate, WE (1967) *The English Village Community and the Enclosure Movements*, London: Gollancz.

Tate, WE (1978) *Domesday of English Enclosure Acts and Awards*, University of Reading. ISBN 978-0-7049-0486-6.

Willmore, C (July 1990) 'Inclosure Awards: public rights of way', Rights of Way Law Review 9.3 pp 1–15.

3.6 Tithe Records

From the ninth century tithes were paid in kind by parishioners and landowners to support the church and the parish priest. The tithe was 10 per cent of the produce of the land (for example, crops, animals, and wool) and these were collected in the tithe barn. Much of the tithe was perishable produce. The priest or vicar would have used some of it to distribute to the poor and needy. Tithes were not due on manufactured goods. Non-conformists had to pay tithes as well as any contribution to their own church. Some tithes had been commuted before the Tithe Act 1836. At the dissolution of the monasteries some church land and rectorial tithes passed into private ownership (although the vicar would still receive the vicarial tithes). There were difficulties in the collection of tithes. The Inclosure Acts and awards were made to improve the productivity of the land and this would have increased the tithe income and in some inclosure awards, parcels of land were awarded to the church/vicar in lieu of tithes. It was generally felt that the tithe system was inefficient and unfair, and there was a desire to change delivery of actual produce into a money payment. In 1835 around two thirds of the country was still paying tithes in kind.

The Tithe Act 1836 extinguished all remaining tithe charges once its procedures had been followed. Although contentious at the time, it provided scope for local agreements to be endorsed, independent people to assess where local agreements could not be reached, its own appeals and hearing process, and penalties for withholding or giving false evidence. It follows that any evidence relating to the tithe process will have substantial weight.

> The Tithe Act 1836 set out the process to be followed in order to commute the tithes payable in a parish, overseen by Tithe Commissioners appointed under s.1 of the Act. Sufficient land owners or tithe owners in a parish could call a meeting and two-thirds of the owners by value could agree a commutation scheme which would then be binding on all of the owners (s.17). Forms for agreements and notices were specified by Tithe Commissioners (s.22). Any disputes about the right to tithes were to be referred to arbitration (s.24). Agreements pending at the passing of the Act (13 August 1836) which were completed within six months were to remain valid (s.25). All signed

> agreements were to be sent to the Commissioners, who would make inquiries to ensure that the agreement had not been made fraudulently before confirming the agreement. After confirmation, the agreement would be binding on all persons interested in tithes in the parish (s.27). In parishes where no agreement had been made by 1 October 1838, the Commissioners were empowered to investigate and make an Award in place of an agreement (s.36). Objectors had a right to be heard before an Award was confirmed (s.51). Some payments were linked to the price of crops, and s.56 provided for average prices to be calculated centrally and published in the *London Gazette*. Two copies of every confirmed Award were to be sealed by the Commissioners; one for the Diocese and one for the local church incumbent. The giving of false evidence to the Commissioners was deemed to be perjury, and withholding evidence was an offence (s.93). Proceedings under the Act were not to be quashed or removed by any court (s.95).

Commissioners were appointed to agree the level of payment where they were disputed, and these records are catalogued in the tithe files (TNA IR 18 series). The files vary in content, and although they can be interesting, they are not as useful as the tithe maps and apportionments.

All expenses incurred in the making of an award (except the salary of the Commissioners, and expenses that could be specifically assigned) were attributable to the landowner and tithe owners interested in that award (s.74). To reduce the cost of providing a map, many tithe records were compiled on any suitable map that was available at the time. In some cases, maps were made specifically and in most of those cases they would have conformed to the criteria set out by Lieutenant Robert Kearsly Dawson, in which roads were to be coloured sienna. Lt Dawson was at that time superintendent of the tithe survey. His background was as a military surveyor and his career was with the Ordnance Survey. He had wanted the tithe survey to become a national survey with all maps done to the same standard and using the same key, but this did not happen. Landowners also had to pay for the apportionments to be written. Maps are either first or second class maps. The first class maps will be sealed and signed and are a legal and accurate record of all matters shown; only 16 per cent of maps are first class. All other maps are called

'Second class maps'. Three sets of tithe records would have been compiled for each tithe district; one for the tithe commissioners, now held by The National Archives; a copy for the diocese, and a copy for the parish/tithe district. In a few cases the copy for the tithe commissioners is a first class map, and the other two may not be signed and sealed and are second class maps. Therefore whenever possible it is advisable to check the record held at The National Archives.

Star Rating	5
Held at	The National Archives, class/series IR 29 and IR 30 County Record Offices
Coverage	England and Wales. All parishes except for those where the tithes were commuted before 1836. One award each for a parish or tithe district (group of parishes). In some areas tithes were commuted early and so tithe records may not be found.
Appearance	The records compose a map and an apportionment. The maps can be relatively small (2 ft by 3 ft) or enormous (10 ft by 12 ft), and occasionally for very big parishes, in several parts. They are usually a roll map. The scale of maps varies, but a common scale is three chains to 1 inch (26.67 inches to a mile). If the parish already had a suitable map, it would probably be used, if not, a new map would be prepared. The apportionments are often in large flat folders, but this can vary. The apportionment gives an acreage, ownership and land use.
Shape	By parish or tithe district
Date	Mainly around the mid-1800s

Locating

At The National Archives they are in the IR class of documents, and the series is IR 29 for the apportionments and IR 30 for the tithe maps. The document reference number is IR 29 (or 30) followed by a county number, and then a piece number. Using The National Archives' online catalogue (http://www.nationalarchives.gov.uk/catalogue/), type the parish name in the top line and IR 30 in the third line.

Search the catalogue

Search | Places, prominent people & subjects

Word or phrase (Mandatory)	Hardington Mandeville
Year range (optional)	to
Department or Series code (optional)	IR 30

Clear | Search >

Figure 14: TNA search for IR30 records

The result is one reference (unless there are parishes with the same name in more than one county). Some years ago The National Archives started a project to microfiche all tithe maps but this project was abandoned half way through the alphabet. So, maps for counties beginning with a letter from the first half of the alphabet are on microfiche. For counties in the second half of the alphabet the original maps are produced. If the original map is required (so the colouring can be checked), ask at the help desk for the appropriate form which then should be filled out and taken to the document production counter. All the apportionments are on microfiche and stored in the white cabinets by the windows of the Map Room.

Alternatively, Kain and Oliver's *The Tithe Maps of England and Wales – A Cartographic Analysis and County by County Catalogue* is on the open shelves at The National Archives. It lists the tithe maps alphabetically by parish within a county and gives The National Archives' document reference number.

County record offices will generally produce the original apportionments, and some produce the maps on microfiche. Some parishes have a copy of the tithe map in the village hall or held by the Clerk. If possible, it is worth going to where the original, rather than microfiche, can be produced.

Interpretation

These records were compiled in order to agree the commutation of the tithes and, rather than the church receiving one tenth of the produce from the land, they were to have land instead from which to raise a living, thus ending the system of collecting tithes annually.

Land that was not subject to tithes was generally accepted to either be public, or owned by the church or the crown estates etc. Such land would not have an apportionment number on it. In many cases, public roads were coloured a sienna (light brown) colour; this was prescribed by Lieutenant Dawson to the Tithe Commissioners[12] and although widely used, was not mandatory. Occasionally there will be an indication of where the road went as it left the Parish and words such as 'to xxx' or 'from yyy' are unlikely to have been written on roads that were only for a landowner's private use.

The majority of tithe maps were dated 1836 to 1845. They vary greatly in size and quality. First class maps were signed and sealed by the commissioners; second class maps, which might not be so accurate, were signed but not sealed. There was a proposal to be consistent with the colouring but this was not compulsory. However, it is worth consulting Lieutenant Dawson's paper and map key which indicated that land surveyors use sienna colouring for public roads and bridleways.

Note that very occasionally wide droves would be subject to tithes if a crop (for example of hay) could be taken from them. The presence of a tithe does not negate public rights.

Caveats

Although a tithe map may have been prepared for a whole parish, those areas that were exempt from tithes (such as glebe land and Crown land) may be left blank. If a candidate highway crosses such an area, part of it may be omitted. Such omission does not count as evidence that the route was not a highway.

In some tithe apportionments all the roads are grouped together at the end of the document instead of being in numerical order.

Note that in some areas, tithes were commuted prior to the Tithe Act 1836 under a different process.

12 The National Archives Map Room cabinet reference HC-1/1160 in 'Chest A' within the Map Room.

Example for use in an application[13]

7. Tithe maps for Hardington Mandeville (1841) and West Coker (1838)

a. The Tithe Commutation Act 1836 enabled tithes (literally a tenth of the produce of the land) to be converted to a monetary payment system. Maps were drawn up to show the titheable land in order to assess the amount of money to be paid. The Act was amended in 1837 to allow maps produced to be either first class or second class.

b. First class maps are legal evidence of all matters which they portray and were signed and sealed by the commissioners (Tithes Act 1847). They had to be at a scale of at least 3 chains to the inch. Second class maps, signed but not sealed, were evidence only of those facts of direct relevance to tithe commutation, and are often at 6 chains to the inch. There was a proposed convention of signs and symbols to be used, which included Bridle Roads and Footpaths, but this was not strictly adhered to.

c. The tithe process received a high level of publicity as landowners would be particularly keen not to be assessed for more tithe payment than necessary. Non-titheable land deemed to be unproductive was usually excluded from the process. It is common therefore for no tithe to be payable on roads, although wide grass drovers' routes could carry a tithe as they were used as pasture. It was in the interest of the landowners for untithed roads to be shown correctly to minimise their payments. Footpaths and bridleways were more likely to be at least partially productive (for example as pasture). Therefore, although the process was not directly concerned with rights of way, inferences can be drawn from tithe documents regarding the existence of public rights, and in particular, public vehicular rights. In some cases highways are coloured yellow or sienna to indicate public status.

d. The maps are held at The National Archives under reference IR 30/30/208 (Hardington Mandeville) and IR 30/30/132 (West Coker). They are both second class maps and so are only conclusive of matters of relevance to the tithe commissioners.

e. Both these maps show the route, Coker Hill Lane, Hardington Mandeville where it passes from one parish into the next. There is no apportionment number on any section of the route. This indicates that no tithe was assessable. The route is depicted in the same way as the public metalled roads it connects to.

f. This depiction is consistent with the route being a public vehicular highway at the time of the assessments.

13 Application made to Somerset County Council on 22 Oct 2008. Their reference 588M.

Figure 15: Tithe map for Hardington Mandeville (1841)

Figure 16: Tithe map for West Coker (1838)

The documents in the above example are worth five stars in total because the process was authorised by Act of Parliament and received a high level of publicity, the route is clearly identifiable, is depicted in the same way as neighbouring routes which are today roads, and was set out on the map with no tithe payable. Although there is good evidence from two tithe maps, we do not allocate ten stars since five is the most allowed from this source.

Further Reading

Beech, G and Mitchell, R (2004) *Maps for Family and Local History*, The National Archives, ISBN 978-1-903365-50-2 (although now out of print, there is at least one copy on the shelves in the Map Room).

Kain, RJP (June 1998) 'Interpreting Tithe Map Evidence', Rights of Way Law Review 9.3 pp 97–106.

Kain RJP & Oliver, RR (1995) *The Tithe Maps of England and Wales – A Cartographic Analysis and County-by-County Catalogue*, Cambridge University Press, ISBN 978-0-521-44191-9.

Kain, RJP and Prince, HC (2000) *Tithe Surveys for Historians*, Phillimore & Co Ltd. ISBN 978-1-86077-125-5.

The National Archives, *Tithe Records: A Detailed Examination*, Domestic Information Leaflet 41 (available from The National Archives).

The Planning Inspectorate (2011) *Definitive Map Orders: Consistency Guidelines.*

3.7 Parish Maps, Estate Maps and Manorial Maps

Although these maps may have been prepared for different reasons, when taken in conjunction with other maps of the same area made at different times, they can provide useful supporting evidence. They are of varying degrees of scale and accuracy. Some were to sell to travellers, sometimes a parish wished to have a map made for its own records, and sometimes maps were made when owners of large landholdings exchanged lands. Some will be old manorial or estate maps which were compiled for owners of large estates who lived away from the landholding. Smaller landholdings where the owner lived nearby often did not have the need for maps.

Star Rating	2 (While all parish, estate and manorial maps can count in evidence, do not count more than two maps' worth when totalling the stars.)
Held at	County Record Offices Manorial records are held in various locations, including public and private archives. The National Archives is the official repository for the Manorial Records Register.
Coverage	Patchy. They are only available if compiled, and if subsequently deposited with the record office. The very early maps may be pictorial or schematic rather than accurate, but they remain of some value particularly if indicating part of a through route. Some, typically those compiled for major landowners, will cover large areas, others may be relatively small. Some will show areas of land owned and be blank where not owned, so appearing patch-like.
Appearance	Generally roll maps, or sometimes folded maps, or very occasionally in books if they cover more than one parish.
Shape	Parish, area or manor system. North may not be at the top of the map, the map may not be accurate, especially in scale.
Date	Vary widely, predominantly in the 1800s and early 1900s, although a few are much earlier (1600s).
Use with	If available, it is useful to show maps of the adjacent parish where the continuation of the route is marked.
Locating	Probably by parish name in the county record office catalogue/map file.

Interpretation	Roads and routes which appear to be through routes and have 'to xxx' or 'from yyy' would add to the likelihood that the route was for use by the public. Estate maps made for a landowner would be unlikely to show the status of a route that the landowner did not agree with, so these can be good evidence of highway status.
Caveats	Sometimes the vanity of the owner made the scale of the map a little suspect. Some county record offices have not catalogued the private collections deposited with them, and so some estate maps, although held by the county archive office, may not be catalogued and therefore may not be found. Specific permission maybe required to use a map from a private collection.

Example for use in an application[14]

8. Parish Maps

a. Parish maps of South Petherton are held by the Somerset Heritage Centre dated 1828 (under reference DD/SAS c/212) and 1849 (under reference DD/SCL 36).

b. They are of use because they show how the parish viewed routes within the parish at the time the maps were compiled. Here, two maps of the same parish, surveyed 21 years apart, show the same route marked as a through route, and depicted in the same way as other routes which are today public roads. These maps both indicate that the route, Frogmary Lane in South Petherton, was considered in the same way as roads that are public on today's definitive map.

c. We conclude that the route carried the same rights as modern public roads immediately prior to the Natural Environment and Rural Communities Act 2006, namely that of byway. The precise depiction on the definitive map will therefore be restricted byway unless one of the exemptions in the 2006 Act applies.

14 Application made to Somerset County Council on 22 Sep 2008. Their reference 573M.

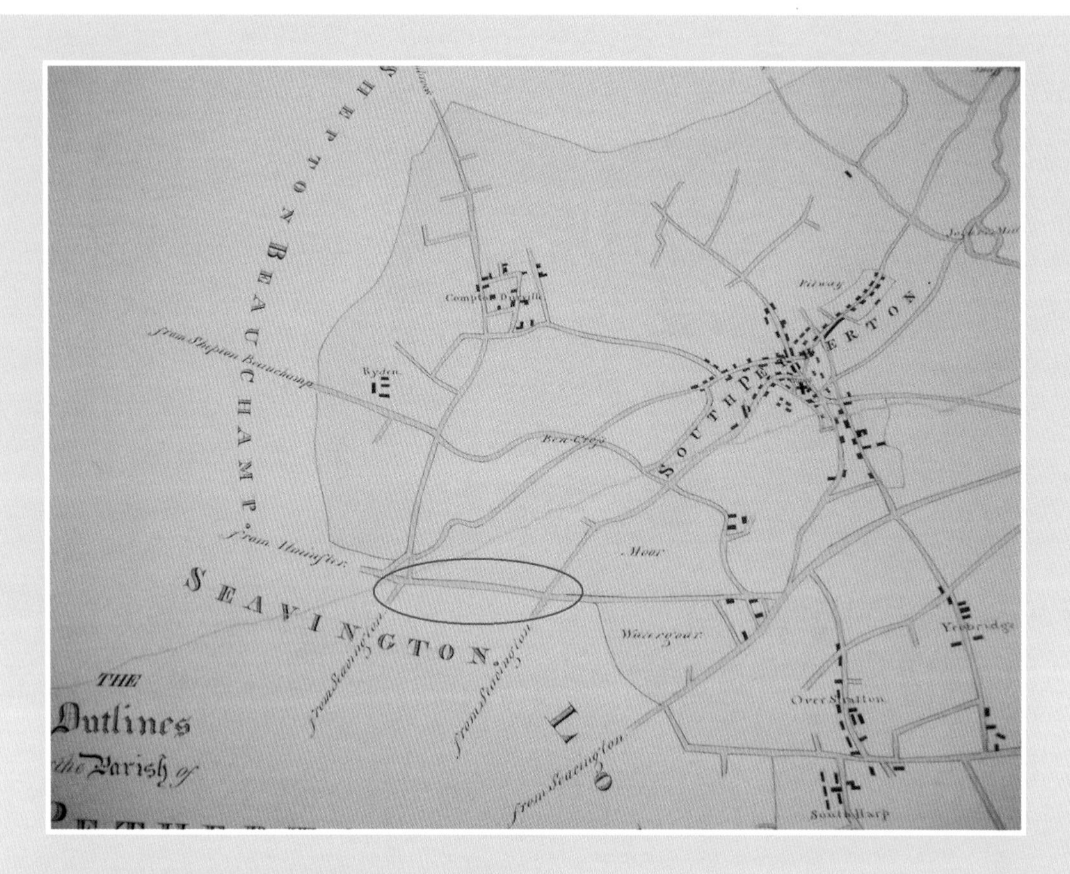

Figure 17: Map of South Petherton (1828)

Figure 18: Map of South Petherton (1849)

The document in the above example collects two stars from the 1828 map. The route is clearly identifiable and is depicted in the same way as neighbouring routes which are today roads. The route in the 1849 map also attracts two stars for the same reasons. If a third parish map gave similar results, it would give no more stars as the total that can be counted from this source is four.

3.8 River and Drainage Authority Records

River and Drainage boards were set up as local authorities and charged with maintaining the rivers. Each one would have its own enabling Act.

Star Rating	5
Held at	County Record Offices
Coverage	Where there were drainage boards or river authorities.
Appearance	Variable, usually a large map in either flat or roll form and a book of reference.
Shape	Linear
Date	Most records were compiled in the 1800s.
Locating	Will differ from record office to record office, usually found via the name(s) of the parishes it passes through or the river system it drained.
Interpretation	The river crossings will be shown and probably annotated, in some cases the crossing and/or the routes leading up to it will be numbered and the book of reference entry will say 'public drove' or some such. Fords may also be shown. Often a footbridge is shown alongside a ford. Many of these records were deposited with the Clerk of the Peace.

Example for use in an application[15]

9. Parrett and Yeo Navigation Plan (1836)

a. The Parrett and Yeo Navigation Plan was commissioned by the Company of the Proprietors of the Parrett Navigation (a company formed by the Parrett Navigation Act 1836) and deposited with the Clerk of the Peace to show where the river was navigable. This was important, as part of the navigation was only available in winter as the river was too shallow for navigation in summer. This map shows the section from Langport to Ilchester.

b. The document was deposited with the Clerk of the Peace in 1836. It is currently held by the Somerset Heritage Centre under reference Q/RUP/132. The 1836 Act itself is in a bound volume on the open shelves.

15 Application made to Somerset County Council on 27 Aug 2008. Their reference 557M & 558M.

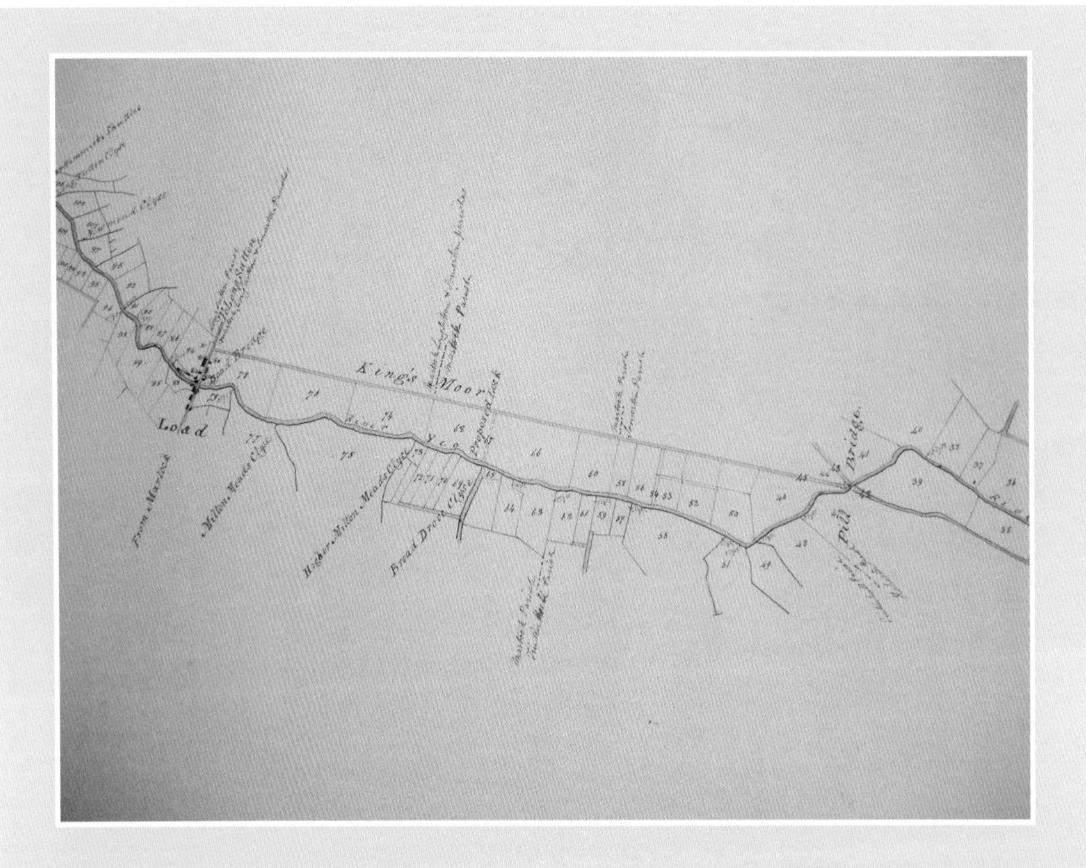

Figure 19: Extract from the Parrett and Yeo Navigation Plan (1836)

c. The record shows a highway (coloured sienna) leading to the river crossing at the end of Witcombe Drove to the south of the river, and a parallel set of dotted lines going north from the other side of the river numbered 67. It is not named on the plan. The book of reference entry for number 67 is 'public drove' and it is signed for by the Waywarden of the parish.

d. This item provides evidence of reputation of the route (as public drove) at the time the records were compiled. The fact that the route is shown as owned by the 'Waywardens of the parish', and the document was placed on deposit with the Clerk of the Peace, means that this is good evidence of highway status.

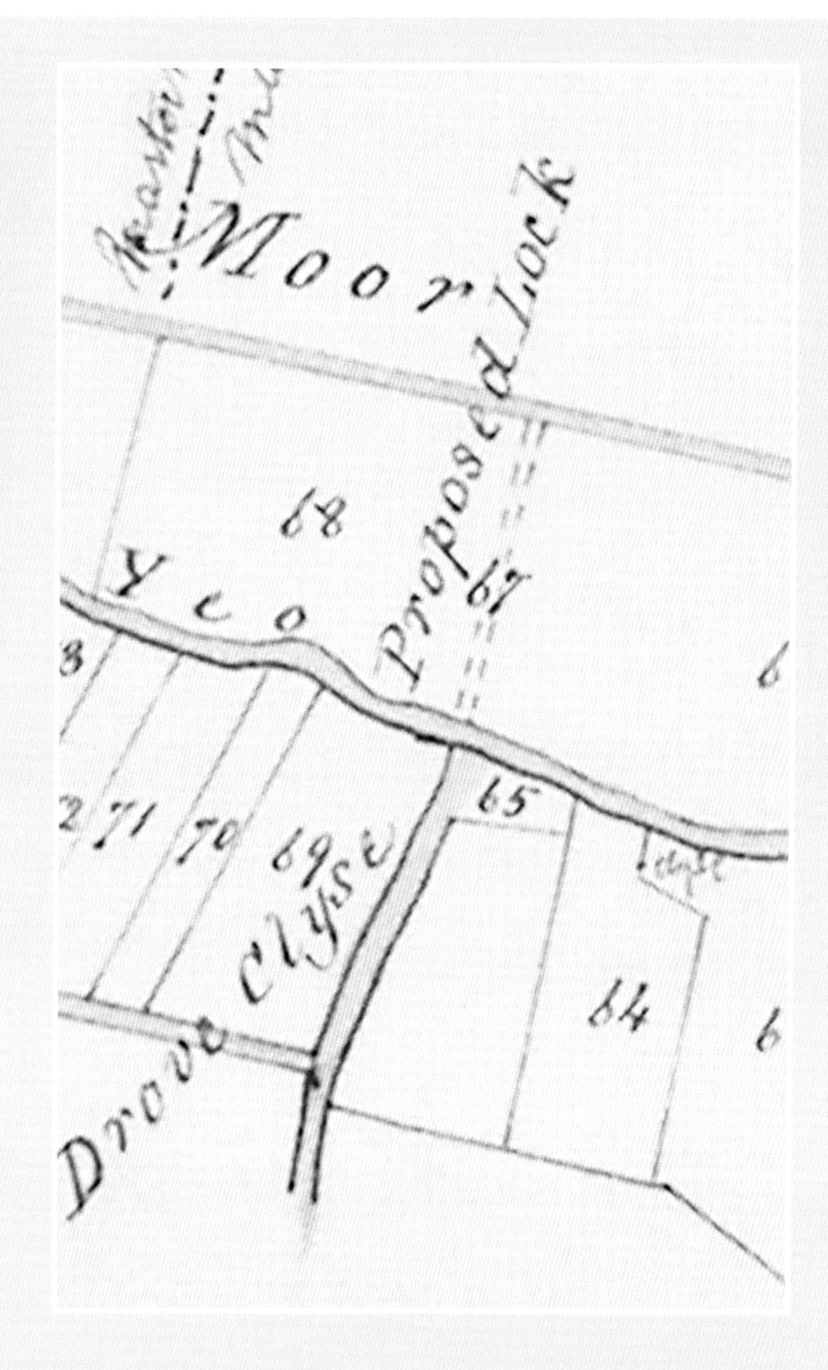

Figure 20: Enlargement from the Parrett and Yeo Navigation Plan (1836)

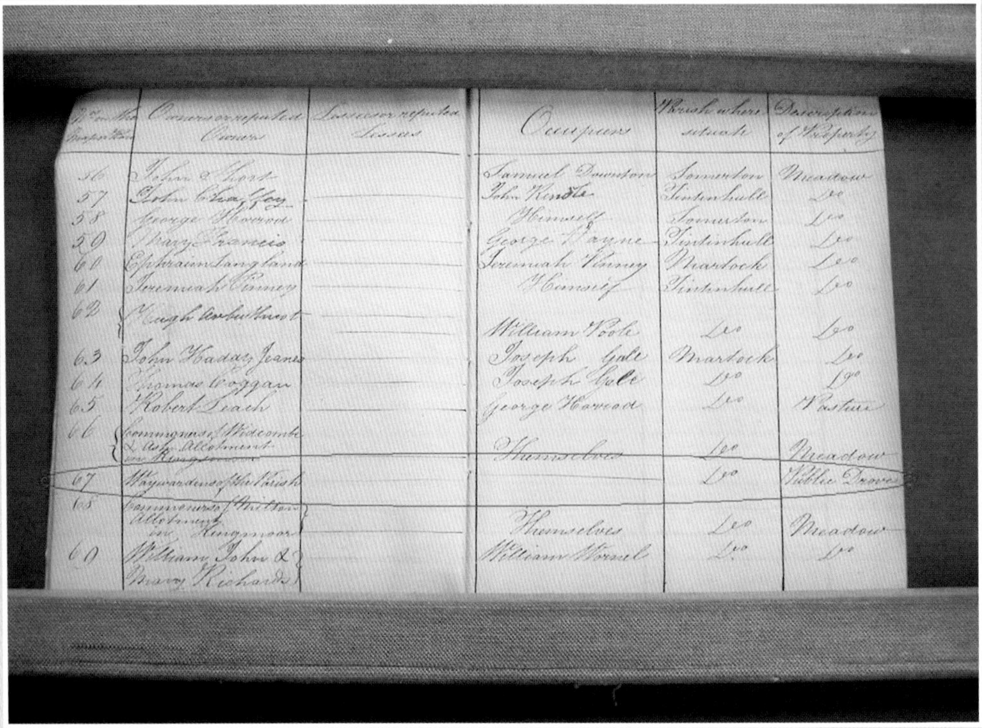

Figure 21: Extract from the Parrett and Yeo Navigation Book of Reference

The document in the above example is worth five stars (for an application at bridleway status) because the process followed was pursuant to an Act of Parliament, the plan was deposited with the Clerk of the Peace, the route is clearly identifiable on the plan and recorded as owned by the Waywardens in the book of reference accompanying the award.

3.9 Railway and Canal Records

These records were compiled when the suggestion of a new railway or canal was first mooted. The new company had to work up a prospectus and attract financial backers. The route would be worked out first in rough and then in detail. Each railway company had its own Act of Parliament which conferred on it the right to acquire land by compulsory purchase. The detailed plans would be placed on deposit open to public inspection and these plans showed, inter alia, what had been suggested for each crossing of the route by a public right of way. Some of the rights of way would have been diverted, or crossings, either at grade or by a bridge or underpass, specified. Canals would have had reservoirs planned to keep the water levels sufficiently high, and rights of way over the land to be covered by the reservoir would have to be diverted or stopped up.

Some canals were superseded by railways which bought the canal companies and used the same ribbon of land.

Many of the original railway companies were very small. Over time there was a move to consolidate these small companies (sometimes referred to as 'merger mania'). George Hudson, a Yorkshireman, sometimes known as 'the Railway King', was behind a move to consolidate a lot of railways into what became the London Midland and Scottish, and also the Great Central Railway. By the 1860s there was a clear pattern of several large companies who controlled all the major routes. This continued with further consolidation, either by lease or by selling out to the big operating companies. There were also a lot of infill branch lines built like the Chard to Taunton branch line to make connecting routes.

In the First World War, the government commandeered the railways and made the railway companies operate to government instructions for which they were paid. Afterwards, in the 1920s, the government never really gave back complete control and authority to the railway companies and instead placed them into four groups until nationalisation in 1947. The groups were the London North-Eastern Railway (LNER), the Great Western Railway (GWR), the London Midland and Scottish Railway (LMSR) and the Southern Railway.

Star Rating	5
Held at	Parliamentary Archives (all) National Archives (some) County Record Offices (some)
Coverage	Where there are or were railways or canals. Note: plans were deposited for all proposed railways and canals, whether built or not.
Appearance	In large bound volumes. Often with bound sets of maps which unfold. The plan of the route will be shown from left to right, possibly two strips per page, with mileages from one end. The books of reference which accompany the deposited plans are often in a lined 'exercise' type book and often found with the deposited plans. If they have been filed separately, ask the archivist for the separate reference number. Not all books of reference have survived, and the only remaining copy might be available at a different archive (for example, at the CRO if the copy intended for TNA had perished). There are also files of correspondence which are less useful for rights of way purposes.
Shape	Linear. They are shown from left to right on the pages, with the mileage from one of the termini shown along with the parish boundaries.
Date	circa 1830 to 1960s
Use with	Measurements taken from a site visit. If the railway was constructed and an archway was provided for access from one side to the other, measure the width of the arch at ground level. Section 49 of the Railway Clauses Consolidation Act 1845 provided that 'The Width of the Arch shall be such as to leave thereunder a clear Space of not less than Thirty-five Feet if the Arch be over a Turnpike Road, and of Twenty-five Feet if over a public Carriage Road, and of Twelve Feet if over a private Road'. It would have been in the interests of the railway company to provide the narrowest underbridge it could get away with, to minimise costs, so a width of the legal minimum for a public carriageway is highly persuasive that such rights existed.

Locating	It is probably easiest to locate the documents in the county record office which will have the section for the county, rather than the whole line which may be over a hundred miles long. Identifying the name of the line is not always obvious. The name, especially for branch lines, is usually written on the County series Ordnance Survey map. The lines can also be known by the termini, with the location nearest to London possibly the first of the two names. Some CROs keep deposited plans filed under 'public undertakings'. The Parliamentary Archives This archive should have all the deposited plans, including those for railways planned but not built. The National Archives This is not an official repository for railway records and may not have the deposited plans of the railway in question. Records were delivered to The National Archives in different batches from different sources and have been catalogued in various ways. Many were catalogued by the operating company (GWR, LMSR, LNER and the Southern Railway), and also by their termini. Further information can be found in Railway Records by C Edwards. The records are most likely to be found in the RAIL or MT class of documents. Look for the maps or plans, although some of the plans are for station buildings and no use for rights of way purposes. Correspondence or publicity material is unlikely to be of use. County Record Offices Ask at the individual county record office.
Interpretation	Identify where the track crosses the railway or canal, and check what the book of reference shows at the time. It may say 'public road', or 'farm road', and will show if the route was diverted to accommodate the line of the proposed railway/canal, and whether the crossing was going to be at grade (level crossing), or with a bridge or underpass. It will show who the owner of the land was, and the description 'Surveyor of Highways', 'Waywardens' or 'Overseer' indicates highway status. Accommodation works (bridges and level crossings over railways) will not appear in the book of reference as they were not in existence before the railway was planned.
Caveats	When photographing these, make sure that you follow along the mileages shown, starting at one end, rather than photograph sections which can then be awkward to join up when moving from one photograph or page to the next.

Example for use in an application[16]

10. Railway Plan

a. This record is of part of the Castle Cary to Langport section of the Great Western Railway.

b. Companies wishing to build railways were required to show the owners of all the land within a certain distance of the proposed railway, and to place this information on deposit so that it could be inspected by the public and objections made, before Parliament would give the powers needed for the railway's construction. Railway records were well researched as mistakes would have been costly, with the possibility of the private bill being thrown out and a rival railway company being given permission.

c. This plan is held by the Somerset Heritage Centre, under reference number Q/RUP 500 and dated November 1897.

d. The railway plan shows the route of the proposed railway line from left to right as a solid line marked with distances in furlongs. It shows where the application route, Withybed Lane, which runs along the parish boundary between Keinton Mandeville and Charlton Mackrell, crossed the route of the proposed railway line. The plan indicates that this route runs between Stickle Bridge and Coombe Lane. These directions would be unlikely to be printed on the map unless the route was used by the public.

e. The plan shows the route as plot number 79. The associated book of reference (under the same Somerset Heritage Centre document number) gives the description of the parcel as 'Road' and the owner as 'Langport Rural District Council'. No lessee or occupier is given. This entry is consistent with the route being a public road at the time of the survey.

16 Application made to Somerset County Council on 15 Feb 2009. Their reference 637M.

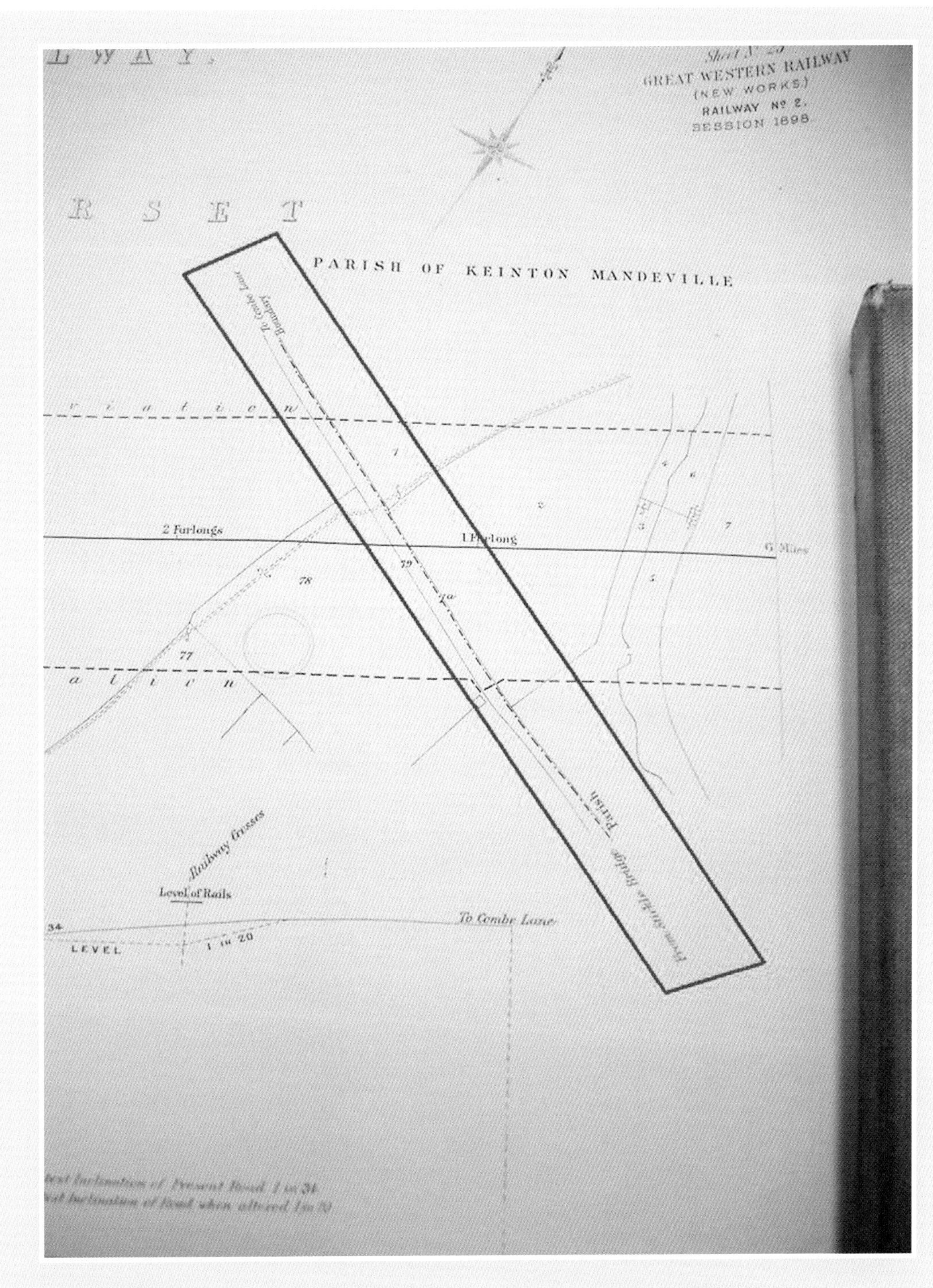

Figure 22: Extract from the Castle Cary to Langport Railway Plan

Parish of Charlton Mackrell, in the County of Somerset—*continued.*

No. on Plan.	Description of Property.	Owners or Reputed Owners.	Lessees or Reputed Lessees.	Occupiers.
77	Field and footpath	John Huntly Thring Charlton Mackrell Parish Council Langport Rural District Council	... ...	Thomas Hawkins
78	Field and footpath	John Huntly Thring Charlton Mackrell Parish Council Langport Rural District Council	... ...	Thomas Hawkins
79	Road	Langport Rural District Council		

Figure 23: Extract from the Castle Cary to Langport Railway Book of Reference

The document in the above example is worth five stars (for an application at byway status) because the process followed was to obtain an Act of Parliament, the plan was deposited with the Clerk of the Peace, the route is clearly identifiable on the plan and given the description 'road' and owned by a named council in the book of reference.

Further Reading

Edwards, C (2001) *Railway Records, a guide to sources*, The National Archives, ISBN 978-1-903365-10-6.

Garnett, AF (2005) *Steel Wheels*, Cannwood Press, ISBN 978-0-9550257-0-9.

Jackson, A (1992) *The Railway Dictionary*, Sutton Publishing, ISBN 978-0-7509-4218-8.

The Planning Inspectorate (2011) *Definitive Map Orders: Consistency Guidelines*.

Wolmar, Christian (2007) *Fire and Steam: How the railways transformed Britain*, Atlantic Books, ISBN 978-1-84354-630-6.

3.10 Ordnance Survey First Edition Maps and Area Books

While most Ordnance Survey maps carry a disclaimer that they do not show public rights of way, the first edition maps at 25 inch scale were accompanied by books of reference, often called 'Area Books' which can provide additional evidence of reputation, particularly for routes which ought to be recorded as restricted byways or byways open to all traffic.

Star Rating	3 (where area books provide land use information) 1 (otherwise)
Held at	British Library Some County Record Offices
Coverage	Area books (sometimes known as 'parish area books', or 'books of reference') are available for many of the maps and, if published before about 1879, contain land use information. Later area books only provide areas for the land parcels, and they were discontinued once acreages were printed on the maps themselves. The inquiry desk in the Map Room holds a book 'Ordnance Survey Books of Reference – A listing of the holdings of the British Library, Map Library' by RP McIntosh which lists the area books for those counties for which they were issued, and whether they provide land use information. The following counties had land use information; (P) denotes partial coverage: Berkshire (P), Breconshire (P), Buckinghamshire (P), Caernarvonshire, Cheshire, Cornwall (P), Cumberland, Denbighshire, Derbyshire, Devon (P), Dorset, Durham (P), Essex (all except Canvey Island), Flintshire, Glamorgan (P), Gloucestershire (P), Hampshire, Hertfordshire (P), Isle of Man, Kent, Merionethshire, Middlesex, Monmouthshire (P), Montgomeryshire (P), Northumberland, Nottinghamshire (P), Oxfordshire (P), Pembrokshire, Shropshire (P), Staffordshire (P), Suffolk (P), Surrey, Sussex, Westmorland, Wiltshire (P)
Appearance	Small books, approximately A5 size. For some counties the British Library has bound collections of parishes together.
Shape	Parish system. Occasionally more than one parish will appear in the same book. Detached parts of parishes may appear in the area book of the home parish or of the one where the detached part is situated.
Date	circa 1860 to 1878 (books after 1878 have no land use information)

Locating

If you have a British Library reader's pass, then you will be able to order the relevant area books so that they are available when you arrive. The document production time is about 70 minutes, so pre-ordering is beneficial.

Using the British Library's online catalogue (http://catalogue.bl.uk/), log in as a reader pass holder, select 'Reservation list' and then 'Maps (OS large scale pre-1950)'. In the resulting form, type the county and parish names and select 'area book'. This will add the document to the list, but does not order it. It is necessary to click on 'Reservation List' again and then 'Reserve' to order the document.

Some county record offices also hold Ordnance Survey Area Books, and this may be an easier way of inspecting them.

Figure 24: British Library search for OS area books

Interpretation

First identify the route on the first edition Ordnance Survey 25 inch map of the area. Microfiche copies are held in the Map Room at the British Library, and in many county record offices. If the prospective route has a land parcel number, order the relevant area book, and check the description given. If this is 'road', then it is likely that it carries highway rights by analogy with how other highways are shown.

Example for use in an application[17]

11. Ordnance Survey First Edition 25 inch

a. Copies of the first edition Ordnance Survey 25 inch maps are held by the British Library. As well as originals, they have created microfiche copies, which can be inspected by the public. The extracts here are taken from the microfiche copies.

b. The Ordnance Survey (OS) maps are not usually of use for rights of way purposes as they usually purport only to show physical features and not legal rights. However, the early maps in the first edition series contain valuable extra information when cross referenced to the books of reference, often called simply the 'area books', that were published to go with them. The British Library holds these books of reference. These are indexed by parish within each county.

c. This extract of OS sheet Hertfordshire 39 – 12 was obtained from the British Library. It shows the application route 'Malt Lane'. At the time of the mapping, the route was split by the parish boundary between Aldenham and St Stephen. The route is shown on the OS map as land parcel number 29 in the parish of Aldenham and land parcel 912 in St Stephen.

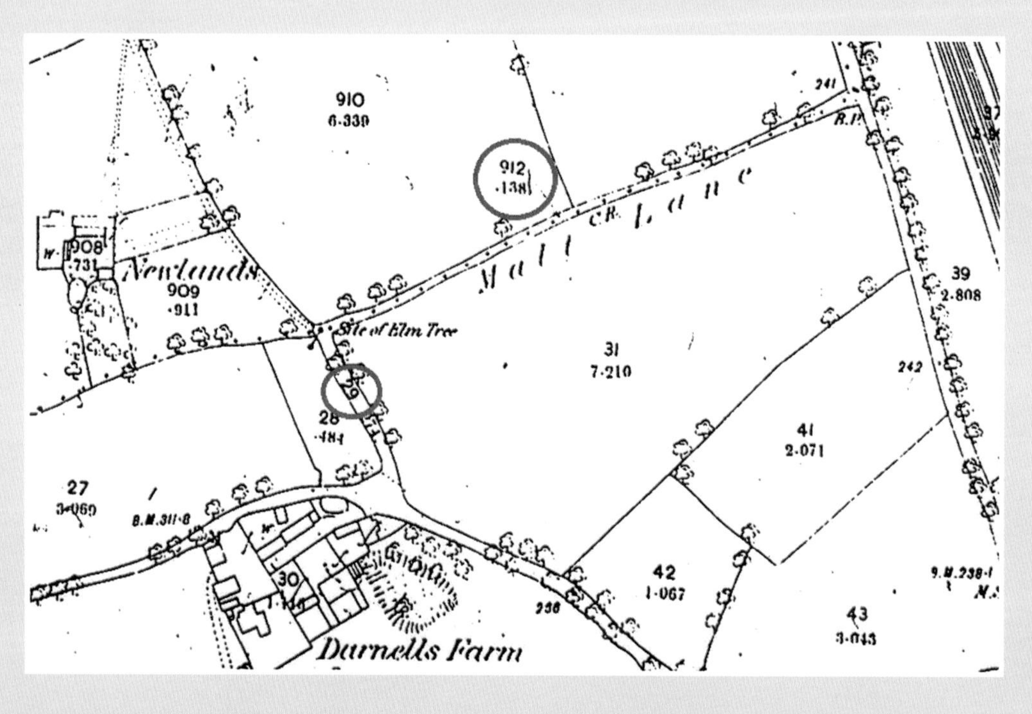

Figure 25: Extract from the Ordnance Survey first edition 25 inch map of the area, sheet Hertfordshire 39 – 12
Copyright © The British Library Board, All Rights Reserved, microfiche in Map Room

17 Application made to Hertfordshire County Council on 1 Jan 2010. Their reference HTM/184.

d. In the entry for the Area Book for Aldenham, there is a description for land parcel 29. The description reads, 'Road'.

27	3·969	Arable.	64	·528	Pasture.
28	·484	Stackyard.	65	·087	Wood.
29	·274	Road.	66	·106	Garden.
30	1·116	Farmsteading, &c.	67	·789	Road.
31	7·210	Arable.	68	·622	Water.
32	·137	Lodge, &c.	69	84·027	Wood.
33	1·144	Pasture.	70	3·289	Wood.

Figure 26: Extract from The Book of Reference to the Plan of the Parish of Aldenham, published by the Ordnance Survey of England in 1872

e. The entry for the Area Book for St Stephen has a description for land parcel 912. This reads 'road (part of)'.

891	7·812	Pasture, &c.	907	5·416	Pasture.
892	15·034	Arable.	908	·731	Houses, garden, &c.
893	13·936	Arable.	909	·911	Pasture, &c.
894	·914	Pasture.	910	6·339	Arable.
895	·803	Wood.	911	7·688	Arable.
896	8·753	Arable, &c.	912	·138	Road (part of).
897	·791	Pasture.	913	1·460	Arable.
898	7·774	Pasture, &c.			
899	1·630	Pasture, &c.		7387·475	
900	14·979	Arable.			

Figure 27: Extract from The Book of Reference to the Plan of the Parish of St Stephen, published by the Ordnance Survey of England in 1874

The document in the above example is worth three stars (for an application at byway status) because the route is clearly identifiable on the plan and given the description 'road' in both the books of reference. This happens in both of the parishes through which the route runs, but no additional stars are earned for this, as the maximum allowed in this category is three. If the area book did not contain land use information, the most the map could have provided on its own would have been one star for physical location. Although the route is shown in two area books, we do not allocate six stars since three is the most allowed from this source.

Further Reading

Harley, JB (1979) *Ordnance Survey and Land Use Mapping: Parish Books of Reference*, Historical Geographic Research Series, Geo Books, ISBN 978-0-86094-037-1.

McIntosh, RP (undated) *Ordnance Survey Books of Reference – A listing of the holdings of the British Library, Map Library*, unpublished, held at the British Library.

3.11 Highway Records (Highway Boards, District and County Councils)

The Highways Act 1862 allowed the court of Quarter Sessions to combine rural parishes into highway districts administered by an appointed board. These boards were then responsible for the upkeep of highways in their area. This power did not extend to urban areas.

The highway board had the power of improvement including the conversion of earth roads to stone. Not all previous earth roads were made into stone roads, but the improvement was such that most vehicular traffic diverted to those that were. The earth roads declined in importance to become the green lanes of the twentieth century. The improvement of roads led to the decrease in the use of packhorses and saddle horses as the primary means of transport.

The Local Government Act 1894 started the process of transferring the responsibilities of highway boards to the relevant rural district councils, or for more important roads, the county council. The transfers took place gradually over many years. Cambridgeshire County Council notes that in some instances the inheriting rural district council simply carried on using the same book as the outgoing highway board, so that the same volume contains the minutes of both the board and the succeeding highways committee, but this is not always the case.

Often the newly formed highway board would have compiled maps to show the routes for which they were responsible. Where they have survived, the minute books and supporting papers and maps are relevant for highway research.

Records for rural areas will cease around 1930 when the county councils became responsible. Details of this transfer process and the resulting records are in section 3.19, while information about the earlier takeover of specified routes by the county council are in section 3.12.

Highway board records can be used in a variety of ways. They may refer to the board spending money repairing a route. This would be outside the board's powers, and so unlawful, if the route had not been a highway, and so provides good evidence of highway status. They may refer to the taking over of former turnpike roads, or of the board seeking to have the county council take a route over as a main road. This can provide evidence of the status as perceived by the board and others at the time of the proposed transfer and so enable inferences about status and maintenance liability to be made. In some cases local people asked the highway board to take over a road, and whether they did or not might have depended on the state of the road. In many cases, the highway board would only take over a road after it had been brought up to a better state of repair. The records will often provide information about whether the processes were fully completed so enabling the route to be maintainable at the public expense.

The mere fact that a route is a highway that is maintainable at the public expense does not necessarily mean that it will always have had money spent on it. It has been judicially noted that many routes 'have never had a spadeful of gravel thrown upon them, or a shilling's worth of repairs done to them at any spot' yet the highway authority has a duty to maintain them should repairs be needed.[18]

Although many of the records survive and are available at county record offices, the authors believe that there may be further and more detailed records archived in County Highway departments which are not generally available to the public. A large number of records were submitted to the various historical government transport departments, in particular with the setting up of the Road Board, and these too may still be in existence but not available to the public. Classifications of roads produced many records, and maps were deposited at the Road Board, but these have never come into the public domain.

18 *Eyre v New Forest Highway Board* (1892) 56 JP 512 – Mr Justice Wills.

3.11.1 Highway Board Maps

These were compiled to show the roads and bridleways for which the highway boards were responsible

Star Rating	4
Held at	County Record Offices
Coverage	Variable, not all have survived.
Appearance	Some are large bound volumes, may have an index and a map for each parish. Others are large roll maps.
Shape	The records are of individual parishes within a district or of all the parishes on one large map.
Date	Around the mid-1860s.
Use with	Highway Board Minutes – if available.
Locating	Will vary between different counties. Probably located by parish, rural, or district name. Searching the electronic catalogue for 'highway board' or 'highway' AND 'map' may also help.
Interpretation	These show roads maintainable by the board, and their lengths. In some cases bridleways or halter paths are also shown, probably in a different colour. Some may show other roads and it is reasonable to assume that these roads existed, but may not have been maintainable by the highway board.
Caveats	Not all parishes combined into highway boards so records may not have been compiled.

Example for use in an application[19]

12. Yeovil Highway Board maps

a. Highway boards were created by Quarter Sessions following the Highway Act 1862 to discharge highway functions for groups of rural parishes. They were created under statutory authority to execute statutory powers, and so their documents have more evidential weight than completely private documents.

b. The Yeovil Highway Board maps are held by the Somerset Heritage Centre under reference D/R/Yeo 32/4/1. There is a separate map for each parish.

c. This record shows the roads and halter paths in each parish which was part of the Yeovil Highway Board. The key to the map shows that halter paths are shown in green.

19 Application made to Somerset County Council on 15 May 2009. Their reference 591M.

N.B THE HIGHWAYS *are colored* YELLOW.
HALTER-PATHS „ GREEN.
TURNPIKE ROADS „ RED.
The References contain the lengths of the Highways as scaled. and are as follows.— The Highways= 144„ 4„ 30 Halter Paths= 27 „5„ 28

Figure 28: Key to the Yeovil Highway Board maps

d. The extract of the Yeovil Highway Board map covering Pendomer parish shows two routes shaded in green. The longer one, crossing the railway, is currently shown on the definitive map as a bridleway while the circled one is currently recorded as a footpath. The combined length of the two routes is the same as the total of the halter paths listed in the record (424 perches). This excludes the possibility that the surveyor miscoloured the routes and that a different route was intended as a halterway.

e. This shows that the circled route was considered to be a halter path (which we would now call a bridleway) by the highway board at the time the map was produced.

f. In the absence of any stopping up order, the common law maxim 'once a highway always a highway' means that the route still carries halter path rights and so the definitive map should be updated to record the route as a bridleway.

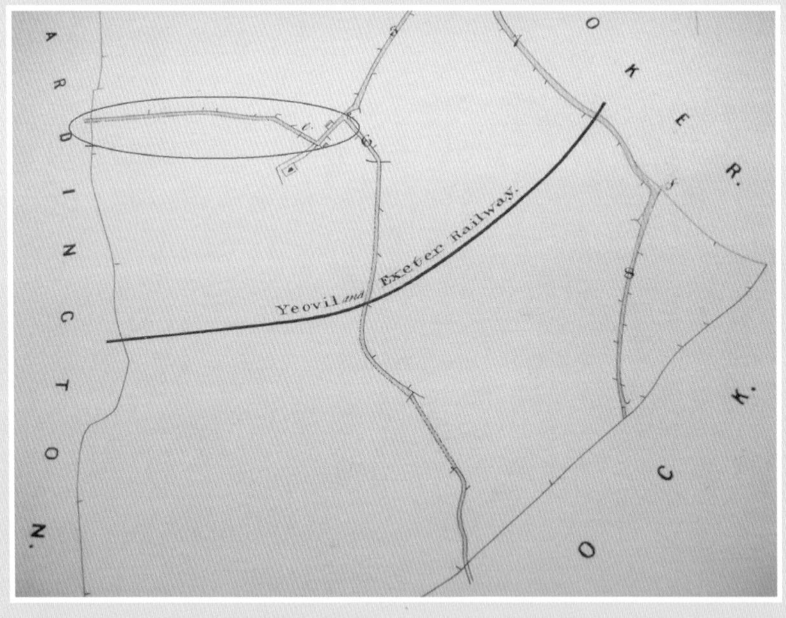

Figure 29: Extract from Yeovil Highway Board map of highways for Pendomer Parish showing the application route (circled)

S

L

REFERENCE.

Number	Description of Highway	Length by Scale in Perches.
1	From a. to b.	128
2	Short Lane	48
3	From b. to c.	184
4	Lane	74
5	From d. to e	212
6	Lane in Village	40
7	From d. to f	232
8	Lane	136

M. F. P
Total = 3 .. 2 .. 14

Halter Paths 424

Figure 30: Extract of Yeovil Highway Board map for Pendomer Parish showing lengths of highways. The numbers and letters also appear on the plan

The document in the above example is worth four stars (for an application at bridleway status) because the plan was produced by the highway authority for highways purposes. The route is clearly identifiable on the plan, the only way of making the lengths of halter paths add up to the total given is for the route to have that status, and the other routes shown in the same way are bridleways on today's definitive map.

3.11.2 Highway Board Minutes

These documents are minutes of meetings of various boards responsible for the maintenance of highways. Various Acts enabled the responsibility to pass to groups of parishes but this was not fully completed until 1929.

From 1835, elected surveyors, sometimes unpaid and often unqualified, were responsible for organising the maintenance to be carried out. Although highway boards could be formed in 1862, many parishes preferred not to do so. By as late as 1913 there were nearly 1,900 separate local authorities responsible for the roads (132 county or county borough authorities, 279 non-county and metropolitan borough councils, 812 Urban Districts Councils, and 661 Rural District Councils). It is quite usual for the highway maintenance records for any parish to start with parish minutes and progress through highway boards, urban/rural sanitary authorities, and urban/rural district councils, although not all areas used each stage of this progression. Finding references for these records is likely to be different in every county archive and it is probably easiest to seek the help of the staff. The researcher should first identify which authorities were responsible between which dates and then which references are needed for this trail of records. These minutes are well worth using as they show public money being spent on routes, which could not have been spent if the routes were for only private use.

Star Rating	4
Held at	County Record Offices
Coverage	Where Highway Boards and Rural District minutes were compiled and the records still exist and have been deposited at record offices.
Appearance	Leather bound volumes, typically approximately foolscap size. The early ones are handwritten. They usually each cover a period of a few years. These are notes of meetings and unlikely to contain any maps or plans.
Shape	Area
Date	Approximately mid-1860s to late 1920s, may vary around the country.
Use with	Can be used with Highway Board maps – where available

Locating	County record offices: ask the archivist. Unless these records have been read through and catalogued, they will be almost impossible to use, or at best a lengthy read. Highway boards may have changed over the years, so be prepared to look at the minutes of what may sound like adjacent areas in case responsibilities or boundaries altered.
Interpretation	These records can show a wide variety of entries which can be of importance to public rights of way. Subjects include, amongst others: • Roads and halter paths requiring maintenance. The original entry concerning a maintenance problem will be followed by a note at a subsequent meeting reporting whether the fault has been rectified. • Roads proposed for being 'taken over' by the highway board. The highway board would only be able to take over a road which was, or was to become, a highway. The entry in the minutes will reveal the situation. Note that a common reason for a route being turned down was that it was not in a good state of repair. Even if this is the case, the wording of the minutes will usually show whether the applying parish or board considered that it had highway status; if it did not then no discussion would be needed. • These records can also show that a road was not due to be repaired by the highway board, but nevertheless carried public rights of way. • Sometimes the entry will mention the road and that a bridle road or halter path continues on to a further destination. • Sometimes there is an entry listing 'roads little used by the public' which would indicate that they were able to be used by the public and so had highway status. There are a large number of entries stating how much money was available to maintain unclassified county or district roads, and funding for main roads.
Caveats	May not have survived for all areas. Records of minutes are only useful if the records have been catalogued. Unless the road is named or its location defined, it is not specific enough to be of use in modification order applications. The records in Somerset have no maps included with the minutes.

Example for use in an application[20]

13. Crewkerne Highway Board Minutes dated November 1864

a. Highway boards were created by Quarter Sessions following the Highway Act 1862 to discharge highway functions for groups of rural parishes. They were created under statutory authority to execute statutory powers, and so their documents have more evidential weight than completely private documents.

b. The Crewkerne Highway Board minutes are held by the Somerset Heritage Centre under the Chard Rural District Council records at D/R/Ch 32/1/1.

c. The minutes for a meeting dated November 1864 contain the following entry:

> A complaint having been made that the approaches to the Horse Bridge leading from Wayhill to Oathill are in a very imperfect state, and this board having recognised the liability of the parish of Wayford to repair the bridge and the approaches, on the grounds that the Bridge was placed in its present position at the expense of the Parish of Wayford and that it is a Public Halter Path. Resolved that the parish officers of Wayford be requested to convene a vestry at an early day for the purpose of deciding whether the Bridge shall remain in its present position or be removed to its former place and that our clerks to furnish the Parish officers of Wayford with a copy of this Resolution with a request that they will report to this board the result of their vestry, and that in the meantime the repair to the approaches to such Bridge be suspended.

d. This is strong evidence of the existence of bridleway rights over the Horse Bridge and its approaches. Taken in conjunction with other contemporary maps it is also evidence in favour of the whole route to and from the bridge carrying bridleway rights.

20 Application in preparation. Will be sent to Somerset County Council.

Resolved that the Overseers of the
Parishes of Middle Chinnock. West Chinnock
Crewkerne. Combe & Hewcombe. Oathill,
Misterton Seaborough and South Petherton
be applied to by the Clerks for the
immediate payment of the second
Instalment of the Calls.

Ordered that a Cheque be drawn
for One Hundred and Thirty Pounds for
Mr Harris on account of Current Expenses.

A Complaint having been made
that the Approaches to the Horse Bridge
leading from Wayford to Oathill are in
a very imperfect state, and this Board
having recognised the liability of the
Parish of Wayford to repair the Bridge
and the Approaches, on the ground that
the Bridge was placed in its present
position at the expense of the Parish of
Wayford and that it is a Public Horse
Path. Resolved that the Parish Officers
of Wayford be requested to convene a
Vestry at an early day for the purpose
of deciding whether the Bridge shall
remain in its present position or be
removed to its former place and that
our Clerks do furnish the Parish Officers

Figure 31: Photograph of Crewkerne Highway Board Minutes, page 53, November 1864

[Note: the application to record this route as a bridleway would also quote the entries from the several following meetings discussing the potential diversion, showing the involvement of the landowner, and the eventual conclusion that the bridge should stay where it is.]

The document in the above example is worth four stars (for an application at bridleway status) because there had been a complaint that the route was out of repair, the highway authority had investigated, and the route was acknowledged to be a public bridleway (halter path) in its minutes. The parish responsible for maintenance was notified. The discussions continued over several meetings, so the risk of error is low.

Example for use in an application[21]

14. Chard Rural Highway Board Minutes for period 1923 to 1928

a. [Introduction about highway boards as in Example 13 above]

b. The Chard Rural Highway Board minutes are held by the Somerset Heritage Centre under reference D/R/Ch 3/3/1.

c. These minutes show the results of a complaint in 1924 that Fout's Lane in Shepton Beauchamp had been closed. The three photographs show the entries from the meetings on 14 March 1924, 18 July 1924, and 15 August 1924.

d. The fact that the Rural Highway Board acted on the complaint and reopened the route is very good evidence of highway status. In addition, the minutes refer to the Fout's Cross crossroads, so adding weight to the theory that all four limbs of the crossroads had highway status.

[Note: a definitive map modification order application has been made in respect of Fout's Lane and Frogmary Lane, two of the limbs of the crossroad.]

21 Application made to Somerset County Council on 22 Sep 2008. Their reference 573M.

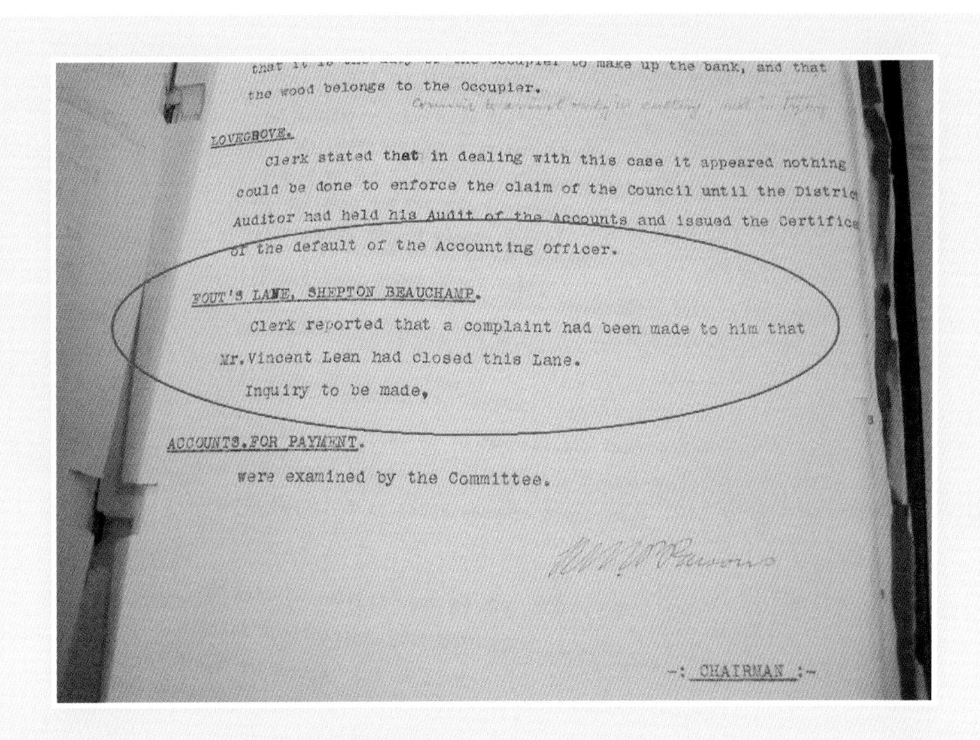

the wood belongs to the Occupier.

LOVEGROVE.

Clerk stated that in dealing with this case it appeared nothing could be done to enforce the claim of the Council until the Distric Auditor had held his Audit of the Accounts and issued the Certifica of the default of the Accounting Officer.

FOUT'S LANE, SHEPTON BEAUCHAMP.

Clerk reported that a complaint had been made to him that Mr. Vincent Lean had closed this Lane.

Inquiry to be made.

ACCOUNTS FOR PAYMENT.

were examined by the Committee.

-: CHAIRMAN :-

Figure 32: Extract of Chard Rural Highway Board Minutes, page 15, 14 March 1924

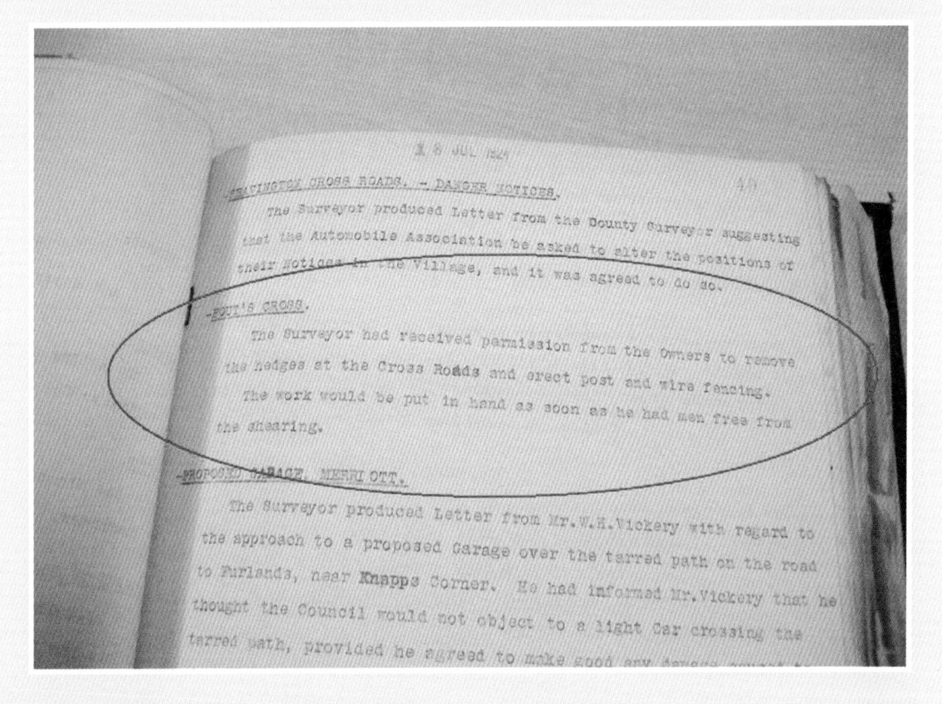

18 JUL 1924

CROSS ROADS. - DANGER NOTICES.

The Surveyor produced Letter from the County Surveyor suggesting that the Automobile Association be asked to alter the positions of their Notices in the Village, and it was agreed to do so.

FOUT'S CROSS.

The Surveyor had received permission from the Owners to remove the hedges at the Cross Roads and erect post and wire fencing.

The work would be put in hand as soon as he had men free from the shearing.

PROPOSED GARAGE, MERRIOTT.

The Surveyor produced Letter from Mr. W.H. Vickery with regard to the approach to a proposed Garage over the tarred path on the road to Furlands, near Knapps Corner. He had informed Mr. Vickery that he thought the Council would not object to a light Car crossing the tarred path, provided he agreed to make good any

Figure 33: Extract of Chard Rural Highway Board Minutes, page 39, 18 July 1924

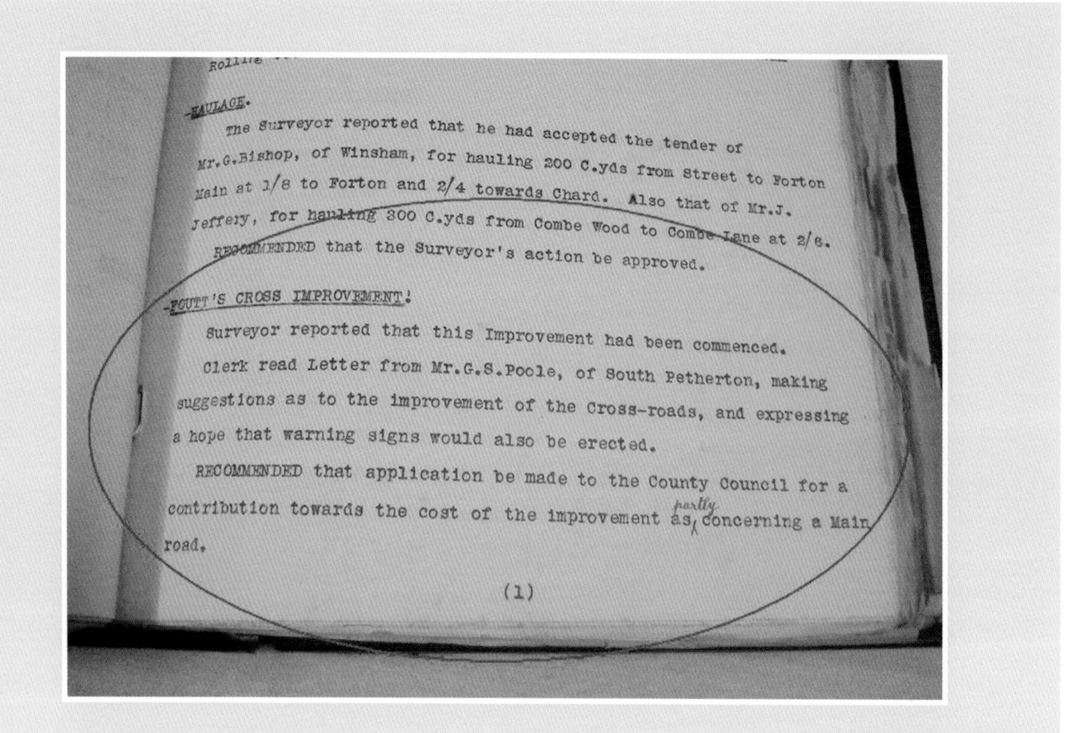

HAULAGE.

The Surveyor reported that he had accepted the tender of Mr.G.Bishop, of Winsham, for hauling 200 C.yds from Street to Forton Main at 1/8 to Forton and 2/4 towards Chard. Also that of Mr.J. Jeffery, for hauling 300 C.yds from Combe Wood to Combe Lane at 2/6.

RECOMMENDED that the Surveyor's action be approved.

FOUTT'S CROSS IMPROVEMENT.

Surveyor reported that this Improvement had been commenced.

Clerk read Letter from Mr.G.S.Poole, of South Petherton, making suggestions as to the improvement of the Cross-roads, and expressing a hope that warning signs would also be erected.

RECOMMENDED that application be made to the County Council for a contribution towards the cost of the improvement as partly concerning a Main road.

(1)

Figure 34: Extract of Chard Rural Highway Board Minutes, page 44, 15 August 1924

The document in the above example is worth four stars (for an application at byway status) because there had been a complaint that the route had been closed, the highway authority had investigated, and the route was reopened. The discussions continued over several meetings, so the risk of undiscovered error is low.

Example for use in an application

15. Chard Rural District Highway Board Minutes (12 November 1926)

a. [Introduction about highway boards as in Example 13 above]

b. The Chard Rural Highway Board minutes are held by the Somerset Heritage Centre under reference D/R/Ch 3/3/1.

c. This minute records that the Surveyor considered some district roads (that is, roads maintained by the District Highways Board) as 'district roads unnecessary for public use'. The inference is that they were public highways maintainable at public expense, but which the District Surveyor considered it unnecessary to spend on because of the volume of use.

d. Under the common law maxim 'once a highway always a highway', these routes retain their highway status unless it can be shown that there is a specific legal event removing the public rights.

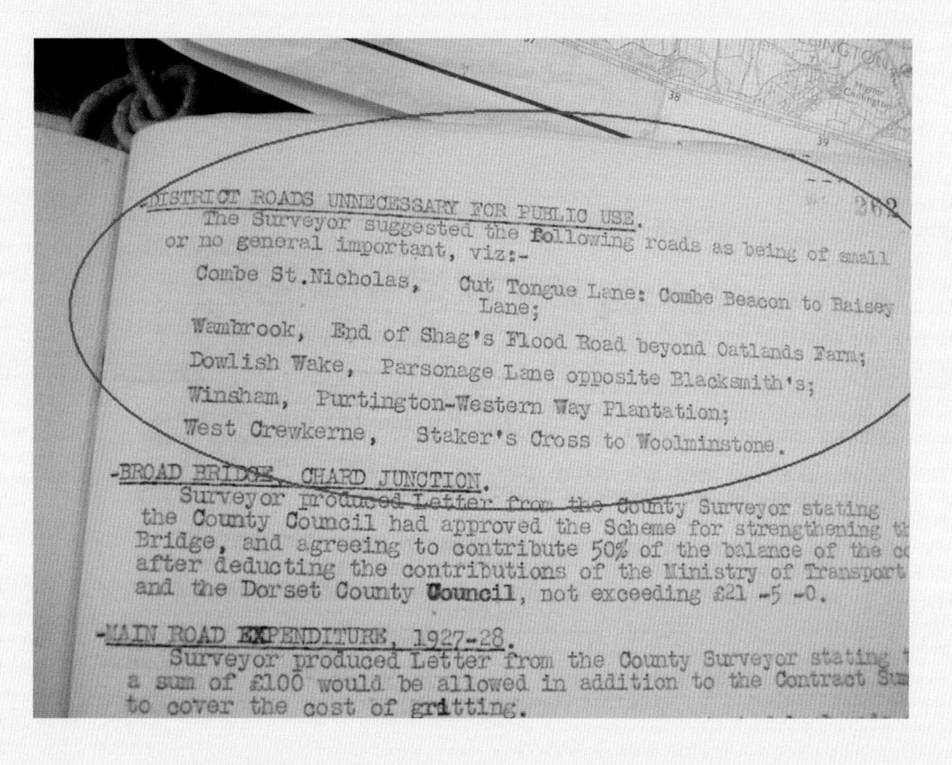

262

-DISTRICT ROADS UNNECESSARY FOR PUBLIC USE.
The Surveyor suggested the following roads as being of small or no general important, viz:-
Combe St.Nicholas, Cut Tongue Lane: Combe Beacon to Raisey Lane;
Wambrook, End of Shag's Flood Road beyond Oatlands Farm;
Dowlish Wake, Parsonage Lane opposite Blacksmith's;
Winsham, Purtington-Western Way Plantation;
West Crewkerne, Staker's Cross to Woolminstone.

-BROAD BRIDGE, CHARD JUNCTION.
Surveyor produced Letter from the County Surveyor stating the County Council had approved the Scheme for strengthening the Bridge, and agreeing to contribute 50% of the balance of the c[ost] after deducting the contributions of the Ministry of Transport and the Dorset County Council, not exceeding £21 -5 -0.

-MAIN ROAD EXPENDITURE, 1927-28.
Surveyor produced Letter from the County Surveyor stating [that] a sum of £100 would be allowed in addition to the Contract Sum to cover the cost of gritting.

Figure 35: Chard Rural District Highways Board Minutes dated 12 November 1926

The document in the above example is worth two stars (for an application at byway status) because the Surveyor recommended to the highway authority that the routes were unnecessary for public use. This would not have been necessary had they not been highways. Had there been positive identification of the status of the routes, or had reference been given in more than one set of the minutes then a third or fourth star could be awarded.

If subsequent minutes show that the route was stopped up, then all earlier stars are removed, but if they only showed that spending on maintenance ceased, the points would remain intact and an additional star awarded for multiple mentions reducing the likelihood of error.

Example for use in an application[22]

16. Chard Rural District Council Minutes Book from 1900 to 1903

a. The Chard Rural District Council was created under powers in the Local Government Act 1894 and took over many of the highways functions of the former Highways Board.

b. It was created under statutory authority to execute statutory powers, and so its records have more evidential weight than completely private documents.

c. The Chard Rural District Council minutes are held by the Somerset Heritage Centre under reference D/R/Ch 2/2/2.

d. The minutes for a meeting dated November 1864 contain an entry for Broadenham Lane which recorded that the parish council believed the route to be a cartway, but not one maintainable by the rural district council.

e. As a statement by the highway authority, this is good evidence that vehicular rights existed over the cartway. It further supplies evidence of bridleway status for a route from the farm to Winsham.

22 Application made to Somerset County Council on 12 Mar 2009. Their reference 596M.

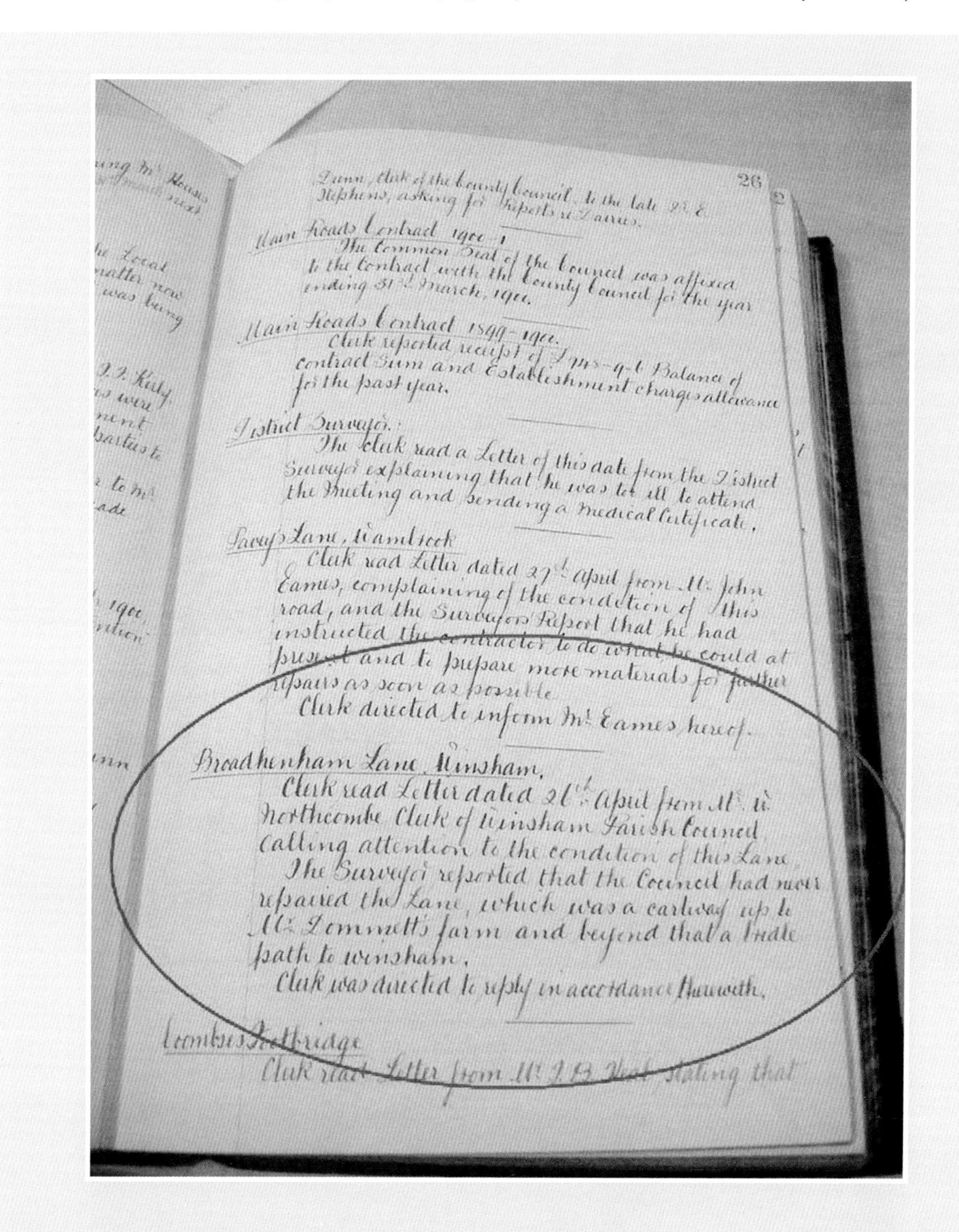

26

Dunn, Clerk of the County Council to the late [illegible] Stephens, asking for Reports re Dams.

Main Roads Contract 1900.

The Common Seal of the Council was affixed to the Contract with the County Council for the year ending 31st March, 1901.

Main Roads Contract 1899–1900.

Clerk reported receipt of £[illegible] Balance of contract sum and Establishment charges allowance for the past year.

District Surveyor.

The Clerk read a Letter of this date from the District Surveyor explaining that he was too ill to attend the Meeting and sending a Medical Certificate.

Savey's Lane, Wambrook

Clerk read Letter dated 27th April from Mr John Eames, complaining of the condition of this road, and the Surveyors Report that he had instructed the contractor to do what he could at present and to prepare more materials for further repairs as soon as possible.

Clerk directed to inform Mr Eames hereof.

Broadhenham Lane, Winsham.

Clerk read Letter dated 26th April from Mr W. Northcombe Clerk of Winsham Parish Council calling attention to the condition of this Lane.

The Surveyor reported that the Council had never repaired the Lane, which was a cartway up to Mr Dommett's farm and beyond that a bridle path to Winsham.

Clerk was directed to reply in accordance therewith.

Coombses Footbridge

Clerk read Letter from Mr J. B. [illegible] stating that

Figure 36: Chard Rural District Highways Board Minutes page 26 dated 14 May 1900

The document in the above example is worth four stars (for an application at byway status for the cartway section and bridleway status for the continuing route to Winsham) because there had been a complaint from the parish council about the route's condition; the highway authority had investigated, determined the status, and repaired the lane. Expenditure would have been unlawful had the route not been a highway.

Example for use in an application[23]

17. Chard Rural District Council Minutes Book from 1900 to 1903

a. [Para a–c are the same as in Example 16]

d. The minutes for a meeting dated November 1901 contain an entry for Coombses to Blackland Road which recorded that, subject to specified works taking place, the road should be taken over by the Rural District Council.

e. This statement is only the movement of maintenance responsibility from one body to another. As such it shows both the parish and rural district councils considered the route to have public highway status, regardless of whether the actual works were undertaken.

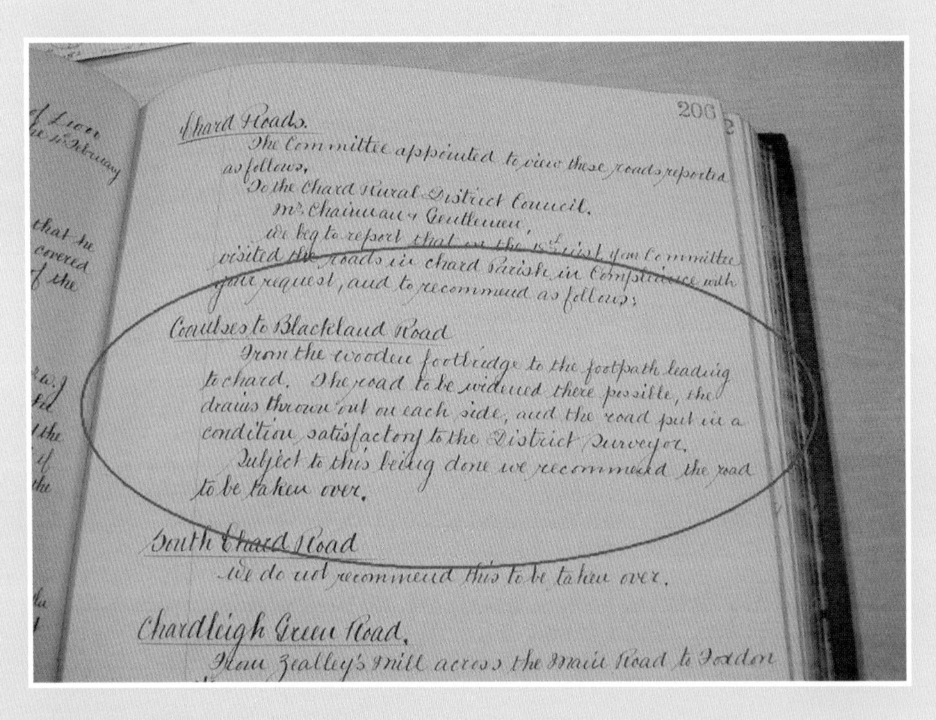

206

Chard Roads.
The Committee appointed to view these roads reported as follows,
To the Chard Rural District Council.
Mr Chairman & Gentlemen,
We beg to report that on the [illegible] your Committee visited the roads in Chard Parish in compliance with your request, and to recommend as follows;

Coombses to Blackland Road
From the wooden footbridge to the footpath leading to Chard. The road to be widened where possible, the drains thrown out on each side, and the road put in a condition satisfactory to the District Surveyor.
Subject to this being done we recommend the road to be taken over.

South Chard Road
We do not recommend this to be taken over.

Chardleigh Green Road.
From Zealley's Mill across the Main Road to [illegible]

Figure 37: Chard Rural District Highways Board Minutes page 206 dated 25 November 1901

23 Application made to Somerset County Council on 12 Dec 2008. Their reference 515M.

The document in the above example is worth three stars (for an application at byway status) because this is the takeover by a highway authority of a route, it is referred to as a road and so is distinguished from footpaths. Expenditure would have been unlawful had the route not been a highway. A contemporary map showing the footbridge and footpath referred to would enable precise identification of the section of road, and would allow the awarding of the fourth star for this document.

Further Reading

The Planning Inspectorate (2011) *Definitive Map Orders: Consistency Guidelines.*

Webb, S & B (1913) *English Local Government: The Story of the King's Highway,* Volume V, Longmans, Green & Co.

Many parish councils have old minute books, and these can show similar records where a complaint is made when a right of way is blocked. Some of these records are now in County Record Offices.

3.11.3 Parish Highway Maintenance Records

From 1835, elected Surveyors of Highways, sometimes unpaid and often unqualified, were responsible for organising highway maintenance. Returns were made by the Surveyor of Highways to the magistrates showing what works had been carried out and what costs (labour and materials) had been incurred. Where they survive, these records are evidence that public money was spent on a particular route. It may be deduced that routes on which money was spent must have been highways, since there was no authority for expenditure on private routes.

These records should be found in county record offices and are returns from the surveyors of highways detailing moneys spent on the roads within their jurisdiction, typically a parish.

Star Rating	4 (provided the route can be identified well enough)
Held at	County Record Offices
Coverage	Individually records will be for a parish or tithing. Overall the coverage should be wide, but many records may not have survived
Appearance	Probably varies, sometimes sheets of A4 buff paper
Shape	Usually by parish or tithing
Date	Mid-1800s
Locating	Ask at county archive offices, possibly catalogued under the petty sessions references and the parish or tithing name.
Interpretation	These records give details of the general condition of the roads, the amount spent on labour and materials, and the length of the roads maintained. When a particular route is named or described, it is proof that public money was spent on that route.
Caveats	Many of these records will not have survived so coverage may be sparse. Many of the returns only list the amount spent on labour and materials for that jurisdiction (parish or tithing), and possibly the total length of roads repaired, rather than individual names of routes. These records do not usually give the status of the road, but the authors believe the records refer to cart tracks and roads unless they say otherwise.

Example for use in an application[24]

18. Petty Sessions Records, 31 March 1848

a. The Petty Sessions records were a record of the returns by the Surveyor of Highways to the Magistrates. They are evidence that public money was spent on a route.

b. This Petty Sessions record is held by the Somerset Heritage Centre under the reference D/PS/Ilm 8/4, and is dated 31 March 1848.

c. The record shows that the Surveyor of Highways spent public money, for labour and materials, on repairing part of Broadenham Lane in Winsham. This would have been *ultra vires* if the route had not been a public highway.

d. The conclusion is that this is good evidence that the route was a public road.

24 Application made to Somerset County Council on 12 Mar 2009. Their reference 596M.

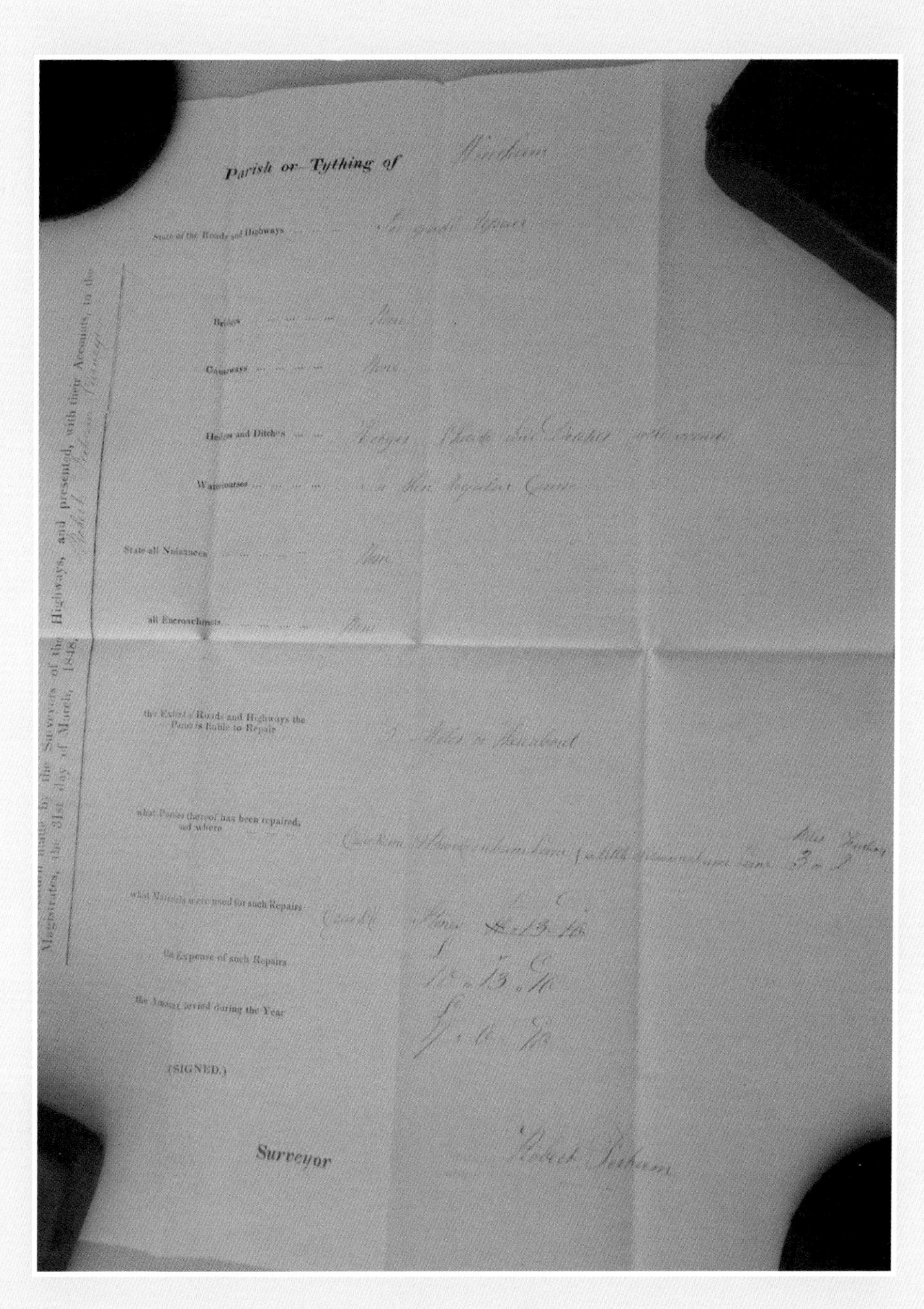

Parish or Tything of

State of the Roads and Highways — In good repair

Bridges — None

Causeways — None

Hedges and Ditches

Watercourses

State all Nuisances — None

all Encroachments — None

the Extent of Roads and Highways the Parish is liable to Repair

what Portion thereof has been repaired, and where

what Materials were used for such Repairs

the Expense of such Repairs

the Amount levied during the Year

(SIGNED.)

Surveyor

... made by the Surveyors of the Highways, and presented, with their Accounts, to the Magistrates, the 31st day of March, 1848.

Figure 38: Petty Sessions Records, 31 March 1848

The document in the above example is worth four stars (for an application at byway status) because it shows that an authorised public official reported the spending of public funds on a route in his report to the Magistrates.

3.11.4 Successor Authorities

When examining records for highway boards be aware that other local government changes may have caused successive records to be in different locations. For example, in Somerset, the Crewkerne Highway Board was formed in 1862. Its minutes are in the records of the Chard Rural District Council from 1862 to 1895. The Crewkerne Urban District Council was formed in 1895 and the later highway records then move to that council's record set.

The archive office staff are usually knowledgeable about how these records were catalogued, and sometimes, but not always, Kelly's Directories for the various years can indicate whether the records might be found in highway, rural, urban or parish committee minutes. It is worthwhile establishing which committees, boards and councils were responsible for highways during which periods, and thus make a chronological list of the documents required. In the example for Crewkerne the directory shows that the records changed from a rural to an urban council around 1895.

Further Reading

Kelly's Directories Ltd, Kelly's Directory of <placename>, various dates.

University of Leicester, http://www.historicaldirectories.org/hd/findbykeyword.asp, provides a searchable record of Kelly's directories. Just enter 'Kelly' as the key word and perform a search for the area in question.

3.11.5 County Bridges

Originally the public highways would have had few bridges and the travelling public would have used fords. The Romans constructed some bridges and many bridges were constructed by private benevolence or by religious orders with, quite possibly, a chapel alongside. More bridges were built in the fourteenth century, some charging a toll or 'pontage', possibly time limited for up to a few years. There may have been an Act of Parliament for a particular bridge.

Where a bridge had been constructed on a public road it obviously became of benefit to the travelling public. Its existence altered the character of the highway and the ford itself perhaps disappeared or an ancient ferry would have been discontinued. Hence should the bridge fail to be maintained, the highway may have effectively been stopped up. Thus the maintenance of bridges became a duty as they formed part of the public highway, regardless of by whom they had been constructed. The general rule of the Common Law was that, in default of any special liability, the County was responsible for the maintenance of public bridges within its area. Some of the major bridges, such as London Bridge, were maintained out of income from lands given or left for the purpose.

The quarter sessions records can hold many entries relating to bridges, concerning both money for their construction and for their maintenance. Many bridges were constructed from the middle of the eighteenth century, because there was a steady increase in carriage traffic that could not conveniently ford streams or use the packhorse bridges. Records of bridges should be found in the Highway District Board records after their formation in1862. It is also probable that any bridge with a name printed on the County series Ordnance Survey maps will have the maintenance responsibility noted in the Ordnance Survey Object Names Books (section 3.15).

Further Reading

Webb, S & B (1913) *English Local Government: The Story of the King's Highway*, Volume V, Longmans, Green & Co.

3.12 Main Road Orders

Under the Highways and Locomotives Act 1878, a highway authority could apply to the county authority to have a highway declared to be a 'main road' if it led between important places or led to a railway station. The county council would then inspect the route and if the route was in sufficient state of repair, it would make an order to take over the road. The order had to be placed on public deposit, and had to be confirmed by the county council for the maintenance responsibility to move to the county. Even if the county council did not confirm its order, it remains good evidence that the parish and county councils both considered the route to be a public highway.

Star Rating	5
Held at	Some county record offices and some council legal departments.
Coverage	Main Roads Orders will be local to the appropriate county, although neighbouring areas may need to be checked as a result of local government reorganisations over the years.
Appearance	The orders themselves are likely to be foolscap or quarto in size, and may have been bound into volumes.
Shape	Usually filed in date order. It is worth asking the archivist whether there is an index system. Hertfordshire, for example, has an index map that relates routes to entries in the index book. The index book gives the date of the order, which can then be located. Other areas may vary.
Date	From 1878 onwards.
Locating	Check the relevant county record office in the first instance. If this fails, ask the county (or unitary) authority's legal department.
Interpretation	All routes listed in a main road order should be considered to be vehicular highways.

Example for use in an application[25]

19. Hertfordshire Highways (Main Roads) No.3 Order 1898

a. Under s.15 Highways and Locomotives Act 1878, a highway authority could apply to the county authority to have a highway declared to be a 'main road' by reason of it being 'a medium of communication between great towns, or a thoroughfare to a railway station, or otherwise'. The county authority would then inspect the route and if it agreed with the application, make an order designating the highway a main road. The order had to be deposited with the Clerk of the Peace of the County for public inspection, and would only come into effect if confirmed. As such, although the 1878 Act did not define the term 'main road', this is excellent evidence of vehicular rights.

b. The 1898 order was held by Hertfordshire County Council legal department and, more latterly, Hertfordshire Archives and Local Studies centre. The application route is listed at item 40 in the Schedule as reproduced below. The order was made on 18 July 1898 and confirmed on 24 October 1898.

THE SCHEDULE ABOVE REFERRED TO (CONTINUED).

Names of Highway Authorities by whom application made. (1)	Name of Highway District. (2)	Length of Highway in District of applying Authority, being a part or the whole of the Road described in the 4th column of this Schedule. (3)	General Description of Road by the above Order declared to be a Main Road. (4)
40. The Surveyor of Highways for the Parish of St. Stephen.	Parish of St. Stephen.	2 0	So much of the Highway leading from Radlett and Aldenham to Bricketwood Station as is situate in the Parish of St. Stephen, commencing at its junction with the road from Aldenham to Colney Street and St. Albans, near Kemprow Farm, passing by Blackbird's Farm and Munden House, crossing Bricketwood Common, and terminating at its junction with the road from Abbots Langley to Bricketwood Station, near Nottler's Wood, but omitting the portion, if any, in such Parish hitherto repaired by Mr. Holland-Hibbert.
41. The Surveyor of Highways for the Parish of St. Stephen.	Parish of St. Stephen.	0 4¼	The Highway leading from Bricket Village to Bricketwood Station, commencing at the South end of the Village, crossing Bricketwood Common, and terminating at its junction with the road from Aldenham to Bricketwood Station.
42. The Surveyor of Highways for the Parish of Flamstead.	Parish of Flamstead.	1 5	The Highway from Studham to Redbourn, commencing at the boundary between the Counties of Bedford and Hertford, near Clement's End, passing along Gaddesden Row, and by Corner Farm and Heavensgate Farm, and terminating at its junction with the Main Road from Redbourn to Hemel Hempstead, at Church End.
The Surveyor of Highways for the Parish of Great Gaddesden.	Parish of Gt. Gaddesden.	2 7	
The Surveyor of Highways for the Parish of Redbourn.	Parish of Redbourn.	0 3¼	
		12 - 2½	

Figure 39: Extract from the Hertfordshire Highways (Main Roads) No. 3 Order 1898

25 Application made to Hertfordshire County Council on 1 Jan 2010. Their reference HTM/184.

c. The application route is part of the route shown as number 40 in the schedule to the order. The description is good enough to be certain of the route. The unrecorded part of the route is treated the same way as the part that is today a metalled public road.

d. The other routes described in the order are public vehicular highways today.

e. The applicant concludes that this route carried vehicular rights at the time of the order.

[Note: the whole order would be attached to the modification order application, so that the extract could be seen in context, and the surveying authority could verify the details.]

The document in the above example is worth five stars (for an application at byway status) because this is the takeover by the county authority of a route put forward by a district highway authority; it is from a confirmed order, so there was an opportunity for objection; the description is good enough to clearly identify the route being considered; and other routes listed are acknowledged today as having public vehicular rights.

3.13 Quarter Sessions Records

These records started in Tudor times and continued until replaced by the County Court by the Courts Act 1971, however, highways functions have gradually diminished over the centuries.

They cover a multitude of subjects including highways.

Star Rating	10 if the order relates to the path in question 5 for other paths referred to in the order
Held at	County Record Offices
Coverage	England and Wales
Appearance	Large bound volumes with separate rolls as the original documents. Typically the bound volumes will be produced, and the relevant roll as a separate document, usually ordered separately.
Shape	Bound volumes summarizing the original documents which are in the original rolls. The exact shape varies from place to place.

Figure 40: Quarter Sessions Proceedings containing the original documents, Somerset, 1878 to 1891

Shape

Figure 41: Quarter Sessions Roll containing the original documents, Somerset, 1878 to 1891

Date

From the late 1500s to 1971.

Locating

Varies from county to county. These volumes were in chronological order and so only useful when they have been catalogued. When cataloguing, it is worth noting the relevant session as the original rolls will probably be stored according to the session (Michaelmas, Hilary, Easter and Trinity).

Interpretation

Descriptions are given when the Justices of the Peace have agreed to a highway being stopped up, diverted, substituted, or created.

Parishes could be indicted for not keeping highways in the parish up to a suitable standard. Quarter Sessions records will show which routes these were, and this is good evidence that they were public.

Caveats

These records are extremely useful, however, unless they have been catalogued, any potentially unrecorded or under-recorded routes are unlikely to be found by chance. Cataloguing these is a project in itself, and many counties have already done so. Check with the county archive office.

Example for use in an application[26]

20. Quarter Sessions Records

a. Highway functions were discharged by Justices of the Peace in Quarter Sessions before powers were gradually handed over to what are now the highway authorities. Court records provide conclusive proof of the matters on which decisions were made.

b. Quarter Sessions papers for Somerset for the period from Epiphany 1878 to Spring 1891 are held at the Somerset Heritage Centre under reference Q/SO 26.

c. The entry for the Michaelmas Session 1880 on pages 136 to 148 has been photographed. It records that on 8 September 1880, a certificate was signed by two Justices of the Peace for the area. The certificate is noted as having included the relevant recitals:

(1) On 27 June 1880 notice of the proposed diversion of the foot and halter paths had been affixed to the doors of the parish church and the congregational chapel.

(2) On 3 July 1880 the inhabitants in vestry assembled approved unanimously that the change should be approved and that the highway board should be asked to make the alteration.

(3) On 5 August 1880, two Justices of the Peace viewed the foot and halter paths and resolved that they should be stopped up, turned and diverted as applied for.

(4) On 5 August 1880, the owner of the land crossed by the new route (Thomas Henry Methuen) consented in writing to the path passing over his land.

(5) That notices dated 7 August 1880 were affixed to each end of the old and new routes for four successive weeks saying that application would be made to the Justices in Quarter Sessions on 19 October 1880 for the change to be made.

(6) That a copy of the notice was published in 'a certain newspaper published and generally circulated in the said county of Somerset' for four successive weeks.

(7) On 8 September 1880 proof had been given to the Justices that these activities had all happened in the manner and style required by statute.

d. The entry then records that no person had appealed against the certificate within four weeks, and that the court ordered that the old line of the foot and halter paths was to be turned and diverted as described in the certificate, and that when the new route was certified as made and put into a good state of repair, a further certificate of two Justices of the Peace would stop up the old line of the paths.

e. The further certificate is given on pages 154–5 of the Quarter Sessions Proceedings. This records that on 4 November 1880, the two Justices of the Peace viewed the new foot and halter path and found it to be in good condition and repair.

f. The photographs and transcript are at Annex A.

g. As a court order, this is a legal event providing conclusive proof of the diversion of the route.

26 Application made to Somerset County Council on 2 Apr 2009. Their reference 646M.

The following Annex would then be enclosed with the application, and listed on the order application form. It does not need to be included in the middle of the proof of evidence. Photographs of the entry in the bound volume and the documents in the roll would also be attached to the application, but for reasons of space they are not all reproduced here.

Annex A – Transcript of Quarter Sessions Proceedings

"Abbas and Temple Combe

WHEREAS by a certificate bearing date the eight day of September in the year of our Lord one thousand and eight hundred and eighty under the hands of Dalton Foster Grant Dalton and Thomas Marriott Dodington esquires, two of her majesty's justices of the peace of and for the county of Somerset and acting in and for the said county and in and for the Petty Sessional Division of Wincanton within which the parish of Abbas and Temple Come in the said county is situated AFTER RECITING that on the third day of July last the inhabitants of the said parish of Abbas and Temple Come were then and there duly assembled in vestry in the said parish in pursuance of a notice signed by the churchwardens of the said parish duly given and affixed on the notice board upon the principal door of the parish church of the said parish of Abbas and Temple Combe and also on the door of the congregational chapel at Temple Combe in the said parish before the commencement of divine service on Sunday the twenty seventh day of June last for the purpose of considering proposals for the alterations of certain foot and halter paths in the said parish of Abbas and Temple Combe AND RECITING that at the said vestry the following resolutions were passed by the inhabitants in vestry then and there assembled. The vestry having had laid before them an application made by Thomas Henry Methuen Bailward esquire to the Highway Board of Wincanton District to stop up certain footpaths and halter paths leading from Lily Lane to Stowell, and which footpaths and halter paths pass over certain closes of land numbered respectively on the tithe apportionment map of the said parish 157, 158, 159, 160A, 101, 104, 94B, 110, 109, 108, 107 and 102 and stating that he proposed to make a footpath and halter path in lieu thereof through and over certain other closes of land and numbered respectively on such map 94B, 105B, 107, 108, 109, 110, 111, 112, 113, 114, 115, 116, 117, and 118 as shown on the plan then before the vestry. It was proposed by Mr. Thomas Young and seconded by Mr. [Page 138] Samuel Worthy Bassey and carried unanimously that this vestry approve of the proposed alterations and desire the Highway Board to take steps to carry out the alteration the same being nearer and more commodious to the public, Mr. Bailward having undertaken to discharge all and every expense attending the same, and the vestry request the Highway Board to make application to two justices to view the proposed alterations AND ALSO RECITING that the chairman of the said vestry meeting by an order in writing under his hand on the third day of July one thousand and eight hundred and eighty directed the Surveyor of Highways of the District of Wincanton in the said County to apply to two of her majesty's justices of the peace of and for the said county of Somerset to view the said foot and halter paths so resolved to be stopped up turned and diverted as aforesaid and the line of the new foot and halter path so resolved to be made in lieu thereof as aforesaid in pursuance of the statue in such case made and provided AND ALSO RECITING that in pursuance of an application of the said Highway Board in that behalf made unto them the said justices THEY the said justices on the fifth day of August in the year of our Lord one thousand and eight hundred and eighty together and in the presence of each other at the same time viewed the said public foot and halter paths thereinbefore mentioned and so resolved to be entirely stopped up turned or diverted as aforesaid AND the lines of the said new foot and halter paths proposed to be made in lieu thereof as aforesaid and which are wholly situated in the said parish of Abbas and Temple Combe [Page 139] aforesaid and were more particularly described in the notice thereinafter set forth and delineated in the plan annexed to the said certificate and marked "A" AND ALSO RECITING that upon such view so made on the application of the said Highway Board as aforesaid it appeared to them the said justices that the said public foot and halter paths so resolved to be stopped up turned or diverted as aforesaid might be stopped up turned or diverted so as to make the same nearer and more commodious to the public by stopping up turning or diverting the same as aforesaid and by making in lieu thereof the said proposed new foot and halter path thereinbefore mentioned AND ALSO RECITING that the said Thomas Henry Methuen Bailward had by writing under his hand bearing date the said fifth day of August one thousand eight hundred and eighty consented to the said foot and halter path being made through his lands and grounds as thereinbefore mentioned AND ALSO RECITING that they the said justices on the said fifth day of August last did direct the said Highway Board of Wincanton and their Surveyor Walter Dyke to affix and in pursuance of such directions in that behalf the said Highway Board for four successive weeks next after they the said justices so viewed the said public foot and halter paths thereinbefore mentioned namely on the eight day of August last and the twenty ninth day of August last respectively affixed a notice to the effect of schedule number 19 annexed to the said statue in that case made and provided in legible characters at the place and by the said of each end of the said public foot and halter paths thereinbefore mentioned and resolved to be [Page 140] stopped up turned or diverted as aforesaid and also at each end of the said new public foot and halter path so proposed to be made in lieu thereof as aforesaid and thereby gave notice that on the nineteenth day of October next application would be made to her Majesty's justices of the Peace assembled at Quarter Sessions in and for the County of Somerset at Wells in the said county for an order for stopping up the said public foot and halter path so resolved to the stopped up turned or diverted as aforesaid and for making in lieu thereof the said new public foot and halter path thereinbefore mentioned and that the certificate of two justices having viewed the same and the proposed stopping up turning and diversion thereof and that such proposed new public foot and halter path would be nearer and more commodious to the public than the foot and halter paths so proposed to be stopped up turned and diverted as aforesaid and that proof had been given to the satisfaction of them the said justices that the several notices required by the statue had been duly published with the plan of the old foot and halter paths and of the proposed stopping up turning and diversion thereof and also of the new foot and halter path would be lodged at Wells with the clerk of the Peace for the said county on the thirteenth day of September then instant AND ALSO RECITING that the said Highway Board in pursuance of the said direction prepared and issued that following notice: "Notice is hereby given that on the nineteenth day of October next application will be made to Her Majesty's Justices of the Peace assembled at Quarter Sessions in and for the County of Somerset at Wells in the said County of Somerset for an order for stopping turning [Page 141] and diverting certain public foot and halter paths respectively situate in the parish of Temple and Abbas Combe in the said County of Somerset and to make a certain public foot and halter path in lieu thereof to wit the following

"Public foot and halter paths to be stopped"

The public foot and halter path leading from A the west end of Lily Lane along the east side of a close of land called Great Lily and numbered 157 on the tithe apportionment map for the said parish or Temple and Abbas Combe to B thence under the north hedge of the same close to a point C thence under the south hedge of a close of land called Wood Piece and numbered 159 on the said map to a point D from thence under the south hedge of a close of land (grubbed) called North Side Wood and numbered 160 on the said map to a point E and from thence across a close called Great Surts numbered 101 on the said map to F the south east corner of a close called Steps Ground numbered 104 on the said map from thence through the last named close to G and from thence across the north part of a close called Great Quarry Ground numbered 94b on the said map to the point H a gate leading into a field in the parish of Stowell called Home Ground numbered 120 on the said map being the boundary between the parishes of Temple and Abbas Combe and Stowell and measuring between the extremes points A and H (and passing through points B,C,D,E,F and G) one thousand five hundred and sixteen yards 2. A public foot and halter path leading from A to the west end of Lily Lane under the south hedge of Great Lily to V thence under the south hedge of Lily Corn Ground to W the south west corner of the same close thence under the north hedge of Jams(?) Lily and [Page 142] Higher Jams(?) Lily formerly divided into two closes and numbered 110 and 109 on the said map but now in one close to X thence through a close of land called Lane numbered 108 on the said map to a point Y thence through a close called Hop Yard numbered 107 on the said map to a point J thence along the west side of the same close to the south east corner of Stowell Wood thence along the west side of Long Close numbered 102 on the said map to the before mentioned close called Great Surts numbered 101 on the said map and thence along the west side of Great Surts to the before mentioned point F the north east corner of Stowell Wood where it meets the first above mentioned foot and halter path and measuring between the extreme points A to F (passing through the points V, W, X, Y, and J) one thousand one hundred and twenty two yards.

The following new foot and halter path to be in lieu and substitution of those to be stopped as aforesaid.

A public foot and halter path leading from A the west end of Lily Lane under the north hedge of a close called Eight Acres numbered 118 on the said map and under the north hedge of a close called Little Lily numbered 117 on the said map under the north hedge of a close called Lilly numbered 116 on the said map under he north hedge of a close called Poors Lily numbered 115 on the said map under the north hedge of a close called Ellins Orchard numbered 114 on the said map thence under the north hedge of a close called Little Lily formerly in three closes and numbered 112, 12 and 111 on the said map but now together with the said closes numbered 118, 117 116, 115, [Page 143] and 114 in one close to a point N thence under the north hedge of the before mentioned close called Jams Lily numbered 110 on the said map to a point M thence under the north hedge of the before mentioned close called Higher Jams Lily numbered 109 on the said map to a point L thence through the before mentioned close called Lane numbered 108 on the said map to a point R thence through the before mentioned close called Hop Yard numbered 107 on the said map to the before mentioned point J a culvert over a brook thence across the north east corner of a close formerly part of West Wood but now grubbed numbered 105a on the said map and thence under the north hedge of the same close to a point I a gate leading into a close called Great Quarry Ground numbered 94b on the said map thence through the last named close to the before mentioned point H where it meets the first above named foot and halter path and measuring between the extreme points A and H (passing through the points U,T,S,R,Q,P,O,N,M,L,K,J and I) one thousand five hundred and seven yards AND that the certificate of two justices having viewed the same and the proposed stopping turning and diversion thereof and that such proposed new foot and halter path will be nearer and more commodious to the public and of proof having been given to their satisfaction of the several notices required by the statue having been duly published with the plan of the old foot and halter paths and of the new proposed stopping turning and diversion thereof and also of the new foot and halter path will be lodged at Wells with the clerk of the Peace for the said County on the thirteenth day of September one thousand eight hundred and eighty.

The cost of the whole of the above works will be borne [Page 144] by Thomas Henry Methuen Bailward esquire.

Charles Barton Chairman of Wincanton Highway Board

James Lancaster, clerk of the said Board

Walter Dyke, Surveyor of the said Board

Dated 7th. August 1880"

AND ALSO RECITING that the said Highway Board in pursuance of the like directions of them given in that behalf by them the said justices for four successive weeks next after they the said Justices so viewed the said public foot and halter paths thereinbefore described namely on the thirteenth day of August last the twentieth day of August last the twenty seventh day of August last and the third day of September then instant respectively inserted the same notice as last aforesaid and the same notice for the said four successive weeks appeared in a certain newspaper published and generally circulated in the said county of Somerset and also on four successive Sundays next after the making of such

Gazette then and at the date of the said certificate still being a newspaper published and generally circulated in the said county of Somerset and also on four successive Sundays next after the making of such view by the said justices as aforesaid namely on Sundays the eight day of August last the fifteenth day of August last the twenty second day of August last and the twenty ninth day of August last the said Highway Board caused to be affixed a like notice as last aforesaid on the two entrance doors of the parish church of Abbas and Temple Combe aforesaid AND ALSO RECITING that proof had that day been there given to and before and to the satisfaction of them the said justices as well by the evidence of witnesses upon oath as otherwise that the said several notices and resolution of vestry thereinbefore [Page 145] mentioned had been respectively given made agreed to affixed and published in the manner and at the times and places thereinbefore particularly mentioned and recited and in manner and form as by the said statute in such case made and provided is required and that a plan had then at the same time been there delivered to them the said justices particularly describing the said old and the said proposed new foot and halter paths by metes(?) bounds and admeasurements thereof and which said plan was thereunto annexed marked A and had then that day been there verified to and before them the said justices by the evidence upon oath of the said Walter Dyke a competent surveyor THEY the said justices in pursuance of the aforesaid statute in such case made and provided DID THEREBY CERTIFY that on the fifth day of August one thousand eight hundred and eighty they together and in the presence of each other at the same time viewed the said foot and halter paths so proposed to be stopped up turned and diverted as aforesaid and also the said new foot and halter path so proposed to be made in lieu thereof as aforesaid and that upon such view they found that the said foot and halter paths proposed to be stopped up turned and diverted as aforesaid might be stopped up turned and diverted as aforesaid and that he said proposed new foot and halter path would be nearer and more commodious to the public than the said foot and halter path so proposed to be stopped up turned and diverted as aforesaid AND they the said Justices DID THEREBY FURTHER CERTIFY that upon such view they found that the said proposed new foot and halter path colored red on the said plan would be nearer for the public and all persons using and travelling along the same with or without horses from the point marked A to the extreme [Page 146] point marked H on the said plan that the said foot and halter paths so proposed to be stopped up turned and diverted as aforesaid as to the said foot and halter path numbered 1 in the said published notice passing through the points B,C,D,E,F and G on the said plan and thereon colored blue by nine yards and as to the and foot and halter path numbered 2 in the said published notice passing through points V,W,X,Y,J,F and G on the said plan and thereon also colored blue by one thousand and ten yards AND that the reasons why the said proposed new foot and halter path would be more commodious to the public were as follows that was to say because the same would be wider more level and less circuitous than the said foot and halter paths so proposed to be stopped up turned and diverted as aforesaid AND they the said justices further certified that the foot and halter paths so proposed to be stopped up as aforesaid would become unnecessary as the new foot and halter path so proposed to be made as aforesaid from the points A to H on the said map and thereon colored red would afford ample accommodation to the public travelling between the said points WHICH said certificate and plan particularly describing the said foot and halter path so proposed to be stopped up turned and diverted as aforesaid and also the said new foot and halter path so proposed to be made in lieu thereof as aforesaid together with the accompanying proofs having been lodged with the clerk of the Peace for the said County and the certificate having been read in open court by the said clerk of the Peace at the present Session (this being the next Quarter [Page 147] Session held after the expiration of four weeks from the day of the said certificate having been lodged with the said clerk of the Peace) And which said certificate together with the proofs and plan as aforesaid as well as the consent in writing of the said Thomas Henry Methuen Bailward the owner of the lands over and through which the said proposed new foot and halter path passes are enrolled by the said clerk of the Peace amongst the records of this session and no person having appealed against the said certificate THIS COURT DOTH ORDER that the said foot and halter path mentioned and described in the said certificate and particularly delineated in the said plan as lying between the points marked with the letter A and H and passing through the points marked with the letters B,C,D,E,F and G and the said foot and halter path mentioned and described in the said certificate and particularly delineated in the said plan as lying between the points A and F and passing through the points marked with the letters V,W,X,Y and J and respectively colored blue on the said plan be respectively turned and diverted as proposed and the a the said proposed new foot and halter path mentioned and described in the said certificate and particularly delineated in the said plan as lying between the points marked with the letters A and H and passing though the points marked with the letters U,T,S,R,Q,P,O,N,M,L,K,J and I and therein colored red be substituted in lieu thereof And that when the said proposed new foot and halter path shall be made and put into good condition and repair and so certified by two justices of the Peace acting in and for the said County upon view thereof pursuant to the statue in that case made and [Page 148] provided the said foot and halter paths so respectively ordered to be turned and diverted as aforesaid be entirely stopped up.

[Page 154]

Temple Combe A certificate of which the following is a copy (that is to say):

[Page 155] Somerset to wit: In the matter of an order made at the General Quarter Sessions of the Peace in and for the County of Somerset held at Wells on the nineteenth day of October one thousand eight hundred and eighty on the application of Thomas Henry Methuen Bailward esquire of Horsington in the said county for the diversion of certain foot and halter paths in the parish of Abbas and Temple Combe in the said County

We the undersigned two of Her Majesty's Justices of the Peace in and for the said County acting in and or the division of Wincanton in the said County (and being the Justices who viewed the said foot and halter paths prior to the making of the above mentioned order as therein recited) DO HEREBY CERTIFY that we have this day together viewed the new foot and halter path laid out and made by the said Thomas Henry Methuen Bailward esquire in the parish of Abbas and Temple Combe aforesaid particularly described in the above mentioned order and in the plan therein referred to and leading from the west end of Lily Lane in the said parish of Abbas and Temple Combe on or towards the parish of Stowell in the said county And upon such view this day made by us we found such new foot and halter path to be made and completed and put into good condition and repair.

Witness our hands this fourth day of November one thousand eight hundred and eighty at Wincanton in the county aforesaid

Witness to both signatures

Having been returned to the clerk of the Peace is by him [Page 156] enrolled amongst the records of this session.

Figure 42: Transcript of Quarter Sessions Proceedings

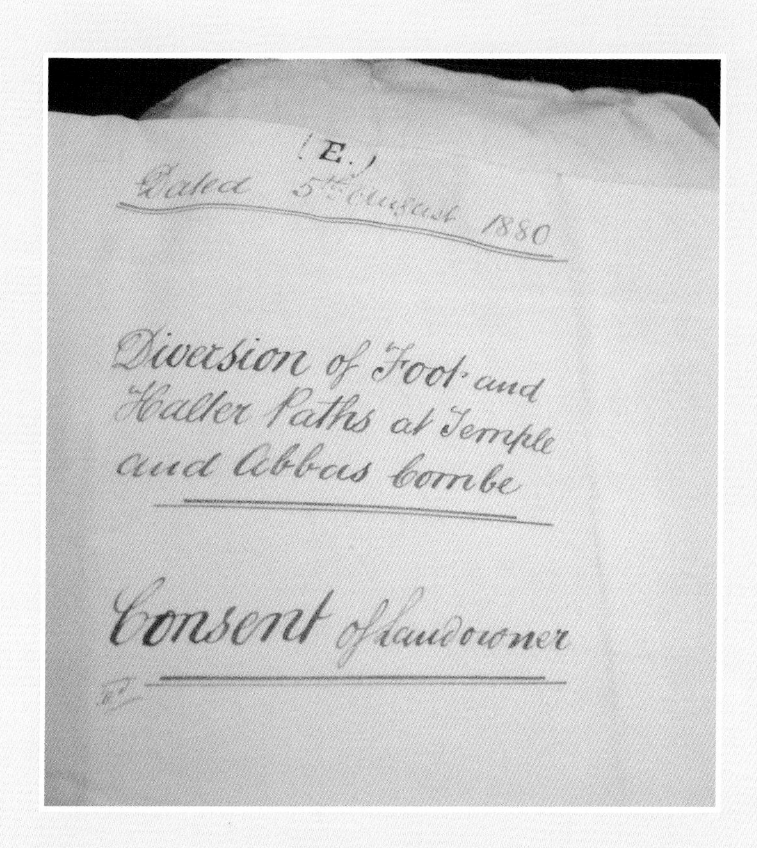

(E.)

Dated 5th August 1880

Diversion of Foot and Halter Paths at Temple and Abbas Combe

Consent of landowner

Figure 43: Photograph of roll containing the Consent of the Landowner

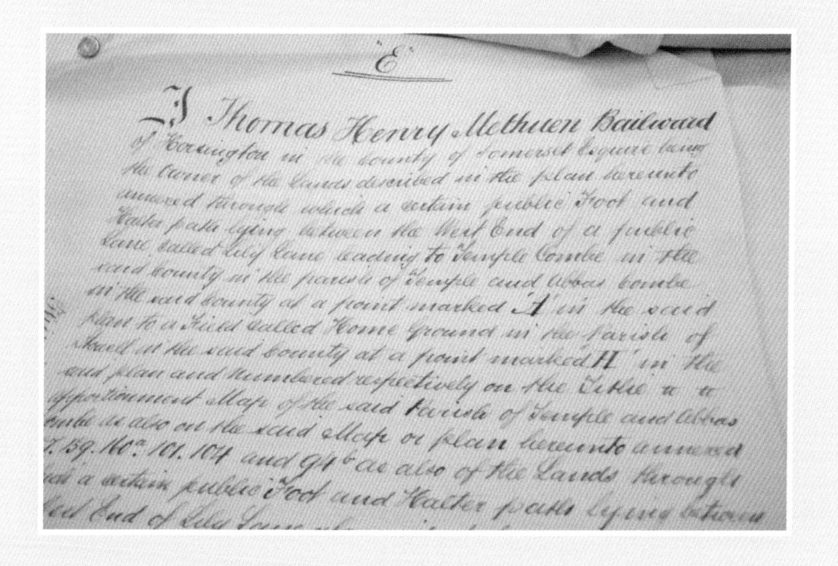

"E"

I Thomas Henry Methuen Bailward of Horsington in the County of Somerset Esquire being the Owner of the Lands described in the plan hereunto annexed through which a certain public Foot and Halter path lying between the West End of a public Lane called Lily Lane leading to Temple Combe in the said County in the parish of Temple and Abbas Combe in the said County at a point marked "A" in the said plan to a Field called Home Ground in the parish of [illegible] in the said County at a point marked "H" in the said plan and numbered respectively on the Tithe [illegible] Apportionment Map of the said Parish of Temple and Abbas Combe as also on the said Map or plan hereunto annexed [illegible]7. 59. 100a. 101. 104 and 94b as also of the Lands through [illegible] a certain public Foot and Halter path lying between [illegible] End of Lily Lane [illegible]

Figure 44: The landowner's consent – Part 1

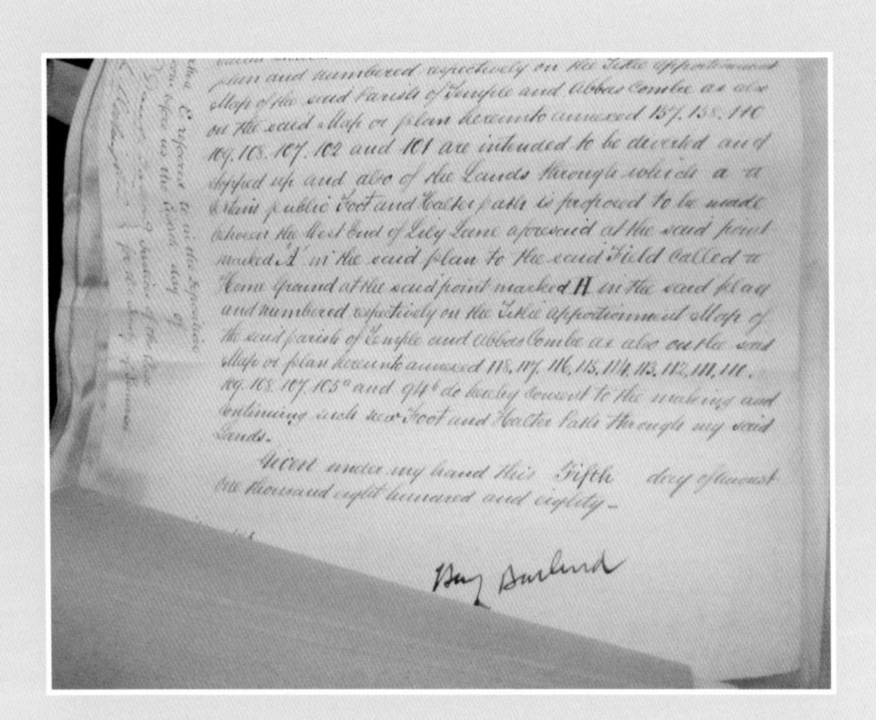

plan and numbered respectively on the Tithe Apportionment
Map of the said Parish of Temple and Abbas Combe as also
on the said Map or plan hereunto annexed 157. 158. 110
109. 108. 107. 102 and 101 are intended to be diverted and
stopped up and also of the Lands through which a
certain public Foot and Halter path is proposed to be made
between the West End of Lily Lane aforesaid at the said point
marked "A" in the said plan to the said Field called the
Home Ground at the said point marked H in the said plan
and numbered respectively on the Tithe Apportionment Map of
the said parish of Temple and Abbas Combe as also on the said
Map or plan hereunto annexed 118. 117. 116, 115. 114. 113. 112, 111, 110,
109. 108. 107. 105a and 94b do hereby consent to the making and
continuing such new Foot and Halter path through my said
Lands.

Given under my hand this Fifth day of August
One thousand eight hundred and eighty -

Figure 45: The landowner's consent– Part 2

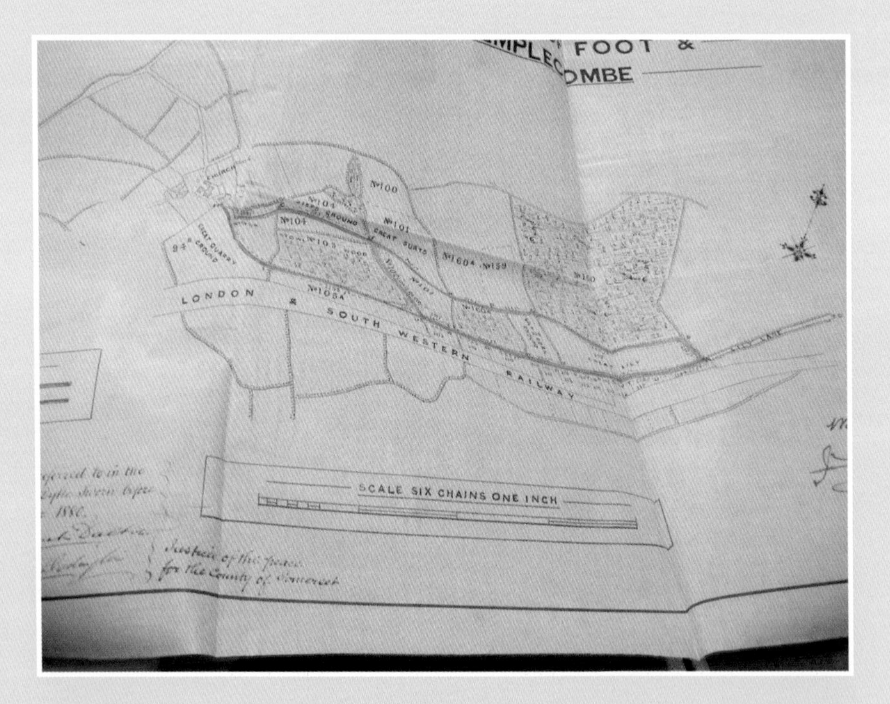

Figure 46: Photograph 1 of the Plan contained in the Quarter Sessions Roll

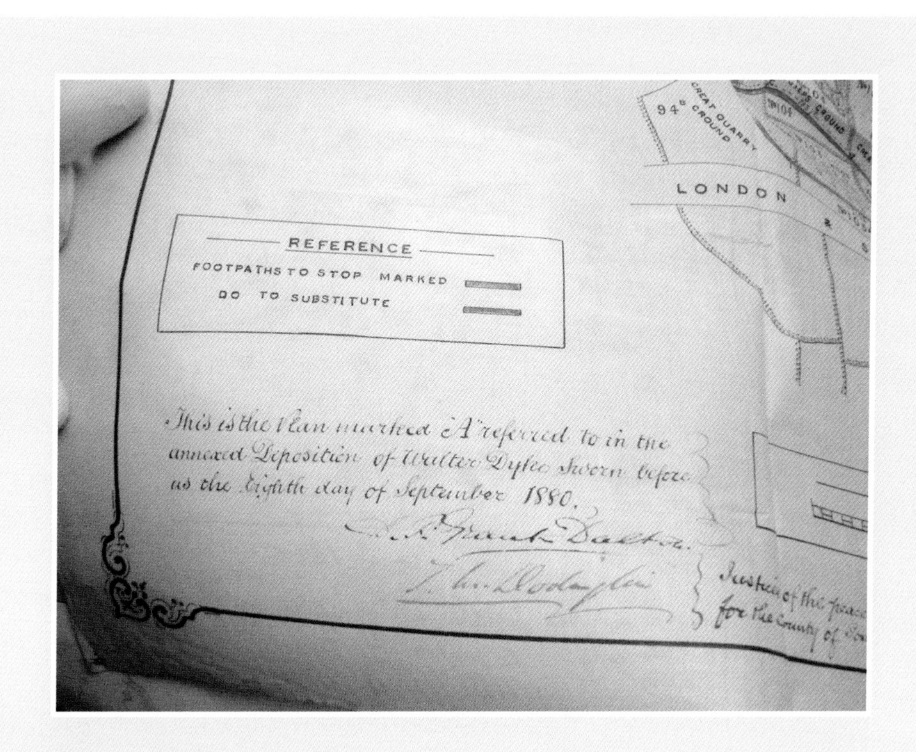

Figure 47: Photograph 2 of the Plan contained in the Quarter Sessions Roll

The document in the above example is worth ten stars (for an application at bridleway status) because this is a court order setting out the route at the defined status.

3.14 Ordnance Survey Boundary Records

The Ordnance Survey was given the duty of ascertaining and recording all public boundaries by the Ordnance Survey Act 1841. The Act allowed the Ordnance Survey to summon the Clerk of the Peace and any books, maps, papers or other documents he held, and provided that it was an offence to obstruct or hinder the Ordnance Survey surveyor. The production of the Boundary Sketch Map was advertised and the map was open to public inspection.

The Boundary Remark Books were prepared by meresmen, a representative from each of the parishes, who walked and agreed the boundary and noted the landmarks on the boundary. As with any 'OS' class of documents, it was not created to annotate rights of way.

Three records are relevant: the Boundary Remark Books which show specific sections of a boundary, the Boundary Sketch Maps which will typically show a whole parish or group of parishes, and the Journals of Inspection. Where the boundary runs along or crosses a highway, it is often noted.

The 'Journal of Inspection' often covered several districts, for example, one journal might cover 4 or 5 districts containing over 75 parishes. This document shows where the boundary book was made available for public inspection and the press notices used to advertise this fact. It contains a map and an index which lists each parish and the Boundary Remark Book number. Then there are sheets which list the comments, generally two parishes to a page. There are rarely any more comments other than 'I agree with the boundaries as shown', however, there are occasionally some useful comments on which parish or parishes paid for the repair of a particular road.

3.14.1 Boundary Remark Books

Star Rating	Up to 5
Held at	The National Archives, class/series OS 26
Coverage	England and Wales
Appearance	Boundary Remark Books are notebooks sized about three inches by five inches. This example shows the OS26/4973 reference, and the original Ordnance Survey Boundary Remark Book reference 3353, both circled. It will be important to note that these two alternative numbering systems are used for different purposes.

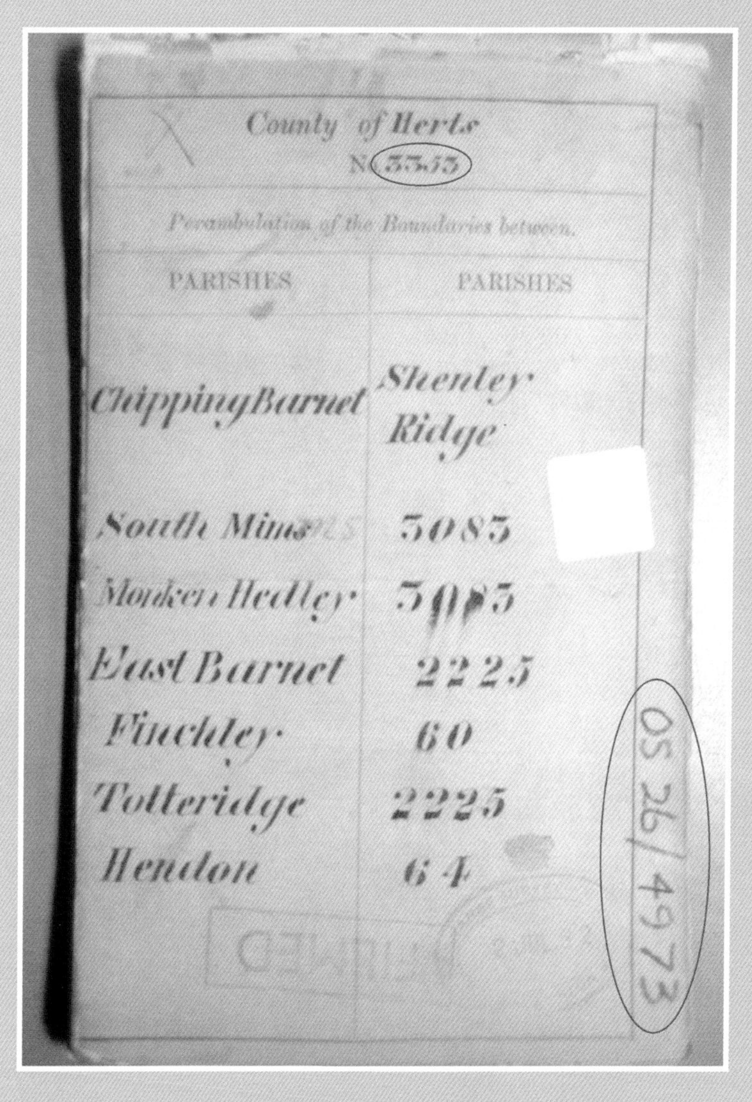

Figure 48: An Ordnance Survey Boundary Remark Book

Shape Parish system

The Boundary Remark Books show the parish boundary as a linear route – from one side of the page to the other with the parish names at the top and bottom of the pages, and no reference to north or south.

Alternatively, they show the parish boundary marked on a section of an Ordnance Survey map pasted onto the page. In these cases, the map at the front of the book, after the index, will show which page to look at.

Date circa 1880 to 1885

Use with OS 27 Boundary Sketch Maps and OS 29 Journals of Inspection

Locating Using the online catalogue (http://www.nationalarchives.gov.uk/catalogue/), type the parish name in the top line and OS 26 in the third line.

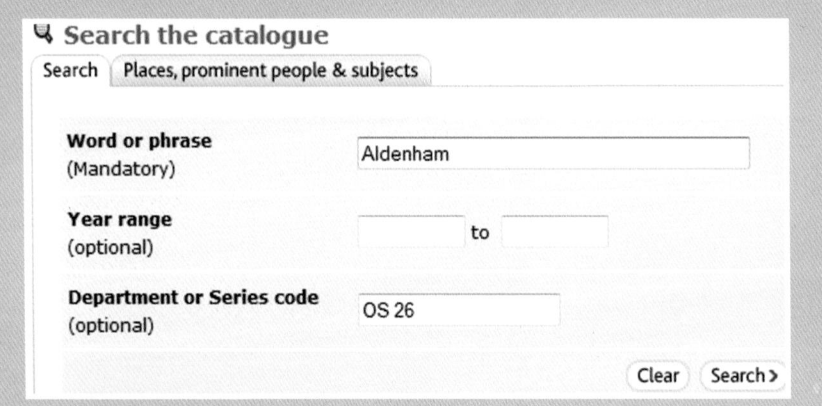

Figure 49: TNA search for OS26 records

The result will be a list of books that show any boundary with the required parish. Note down the numbers.

Catalogue:

Sort by: Catalogue reference | Former reference | Date range | Relevance ranking

Catalogue Reference	Title/Scope and Content
OS 26/4976	Hertfordshire: Aldenham
OS 26/4976	Hertfordshire: Aldenham Abbey
OS 26/6578	Hertfordshire: Aldenham
OS 26/4977	Hertfordshire: Aldenham
OS 26/6579	Hertfordshire: Aldenham

Figure 50: TNA search for OS26 records – results

Now repeat the search using the name of the adjoining parish. The boundary books of interest will be the ones whose numbers appear in both sets of results.

For parishes whose name includes the word 'Saint' or 'St', note that either form may have been used in the indexing, so it may be necessary to try both variations. In addition, one form may have been used to index records in OS 26 and the other in OS 27.

The alternative method is to look up the Boundary Remark Book number shown against the relevant boundary on the OS 27 Boundary Sketch Map. The only way to translate the original Boundary Remark Book number into the new The National Archives' OS 26 computer reference number is to use the paper catalogues at The National Archives. These ring binders are on the shelves in the Map Room and also in the shelves in first floor reading room (only the ones on the first floor are updated). In these files the references are listed within the OS 26 series by parish within the county. The old Boundary Remark Book number is on the right-hand column and the new OS 26 number is in the left-hand column.

Interpretation

The book starts with a list of adjoining parishes followed by a diagram of the outline of the parish with the section covered by the Boundary Remark Book highlighted.

The maps are only of use for highways that cross or run along a public boundary (parish, division or hundred). Where this occurs, the map and books can provide strong evidence of reputation depending on how they are shown. Sometimes routes are shown through the parish which suggests that they were major routes.

For example, they can show a 'halter path' or 'carriage road' crossing a boundary, or 'to/from a place name'. It is unlikely that a destination would be given if the route did not have some public status.

In some books there is a note of which parish is responsible for maintenance on some sections of the roads which would indicate that they were highways maintainable at public expense. There may be comments about other maintenance responsibilities and boundary discrepancies on pages after the maps, and these can be helpful, so it is sensible to look at the whole book, not just the pages relevant to a particular highway crossing. Where the maintenance of a bridge is documented (e.g. 'kept in repair by the county council') it might help, particularly if it refers to the type of bridge: a plank bridge would be adequate for a footpath, but a stone or arched bridge should, logically, indicate a higher status.

Caveats

Boundary Remark Books (OS 26) and Boundary Sketch Maps (OS 27) do not exist for some counties/areas. There may be OS 33 records (which appear as small sections of Ordnance Survey maps on card) which were compiled in the 1930s to replace the Boundary Remark Books and Boundary Sketch Maps but the authors have found these of little use.

Example for use in an application[27]

21. Ordnance Survey Boundary Remark Books

a. The Ordnance Survey was given the duty of ascertaining and recording all public boundaries by the Ordnance Survey Act 1841. The OS Boundary Remark Books, held at The National Archives in series OS 26, are the results of the Ordnance Survey's checking of the boundaries with the meresmen from the parish on each side.

b. The National Archives document OS 26/4976 is the Boundary Remark Book for the parish of Aldenham. The boundary survey, which was approved by representatives from each parish, shows the application route as a physical feature in the same way as other roads at that time. It is also named 'Malt Lane' indicating that the route was of some significance at the time. It is considered unlikely that a purely private route would be named.

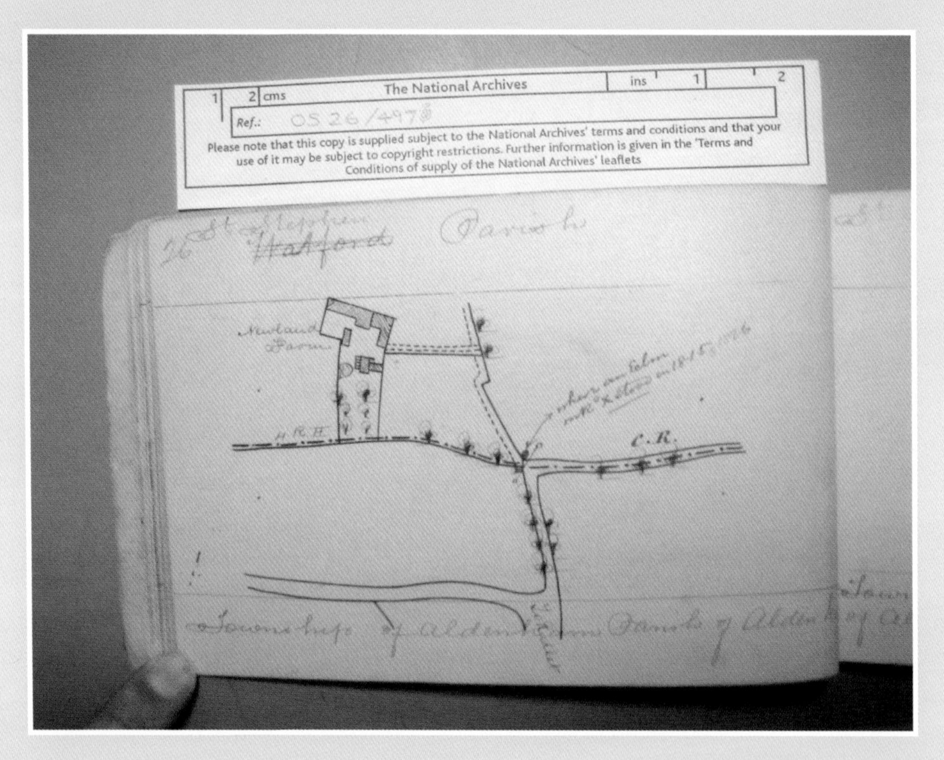

Figure 51: Extract (p26) from the OS Boundary Remark Book for Aldenham Parish

27 Application made to Hertfordshire County Council on 1 Jan 2010. Their reference HTM/184.

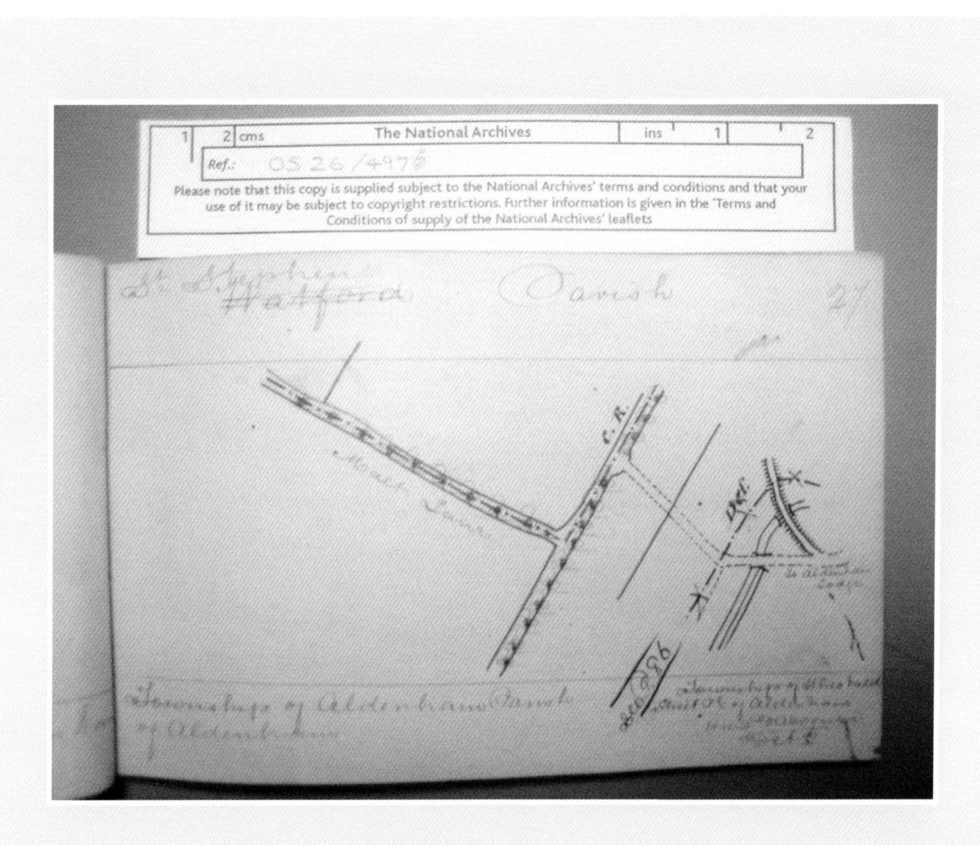

Figure 52: Extract (p27) from the OS Boundary Remark Book for Aldenham Parish

The document in the above example is worth four stars (for an application at byway status) out of a maximum five because it was produced under statutory requirement; the contents were agreed with two independent meresmen (so allowing a degree of scrutiny); and the drawing is good enough to clearly identify the route being considered. It does not actually give the status of the route (sometimes 'road to …' is found on boundary books).

Example for use in an application

22. Ordnance Survey Boundary Remark Books

a. [Introduction as in Example 21].

b. The National Archives document OS 26/9379 is the Boundary Remark Book for the parish of Kingsbury Episcopi in Somerset. The entry on page 15 refers the reader to a note on page 49 detailing maintenance responsibility for various sections of the roads on the parish boundary indicating that it was maintained at the expense of the two adjoining parishes.

c. The fact that the route from A to B is maintainable by the parishes means that it is a highway maintainable at the public expense.

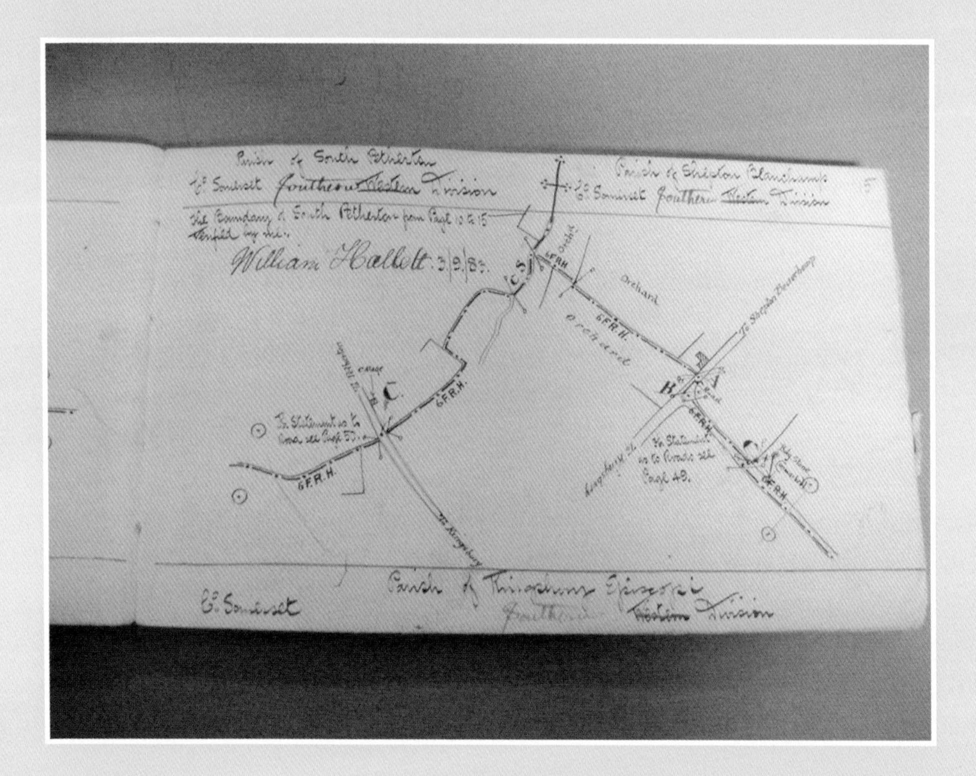

Figure 53: Extract (p15) from the OS Boundary Remark Book for Kingsbury Episcopi Parish

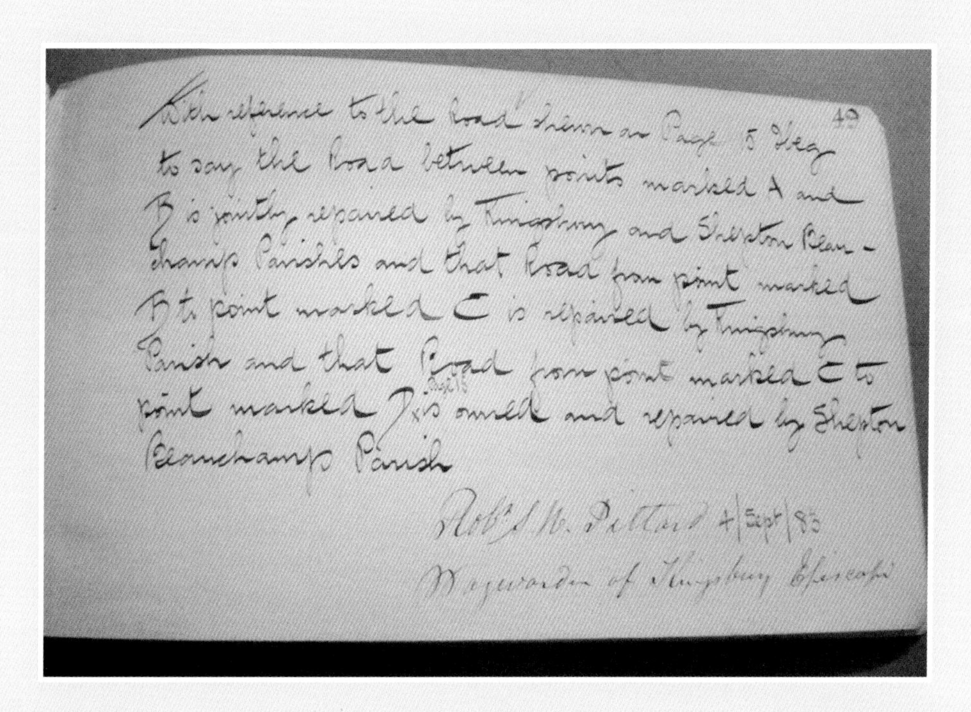

49

With reference to the road shewn on Page 15 beg
to say the Road between points marked A and
B is jointly repaired by Kingsbury and Shepton Beau-
champs Parishes and that Road from point marked
B to point marked C is repaired by Kingsbury
Parish and that Road from point marked C to
point marked D is owned and repaired by Shepton
Beauchamps Parish

Robt M. Pittard 4/Sept/83
Waywarden of Kingsbury Episcopi

Figure 54: Extract (p49) from the OS Boundary Remark Book for Kingsbury Episcopi Parish

The document in the above example is worth five stars (for an application at byway status) out of a maximum five because it was produced under statutory requirement; the contents were agreed with independent meresmen (so allowing a degree of scrutiny); and the drawing is good enough to clearly identify the route being considered. The meresmen have accepted that their parishes are responsible for maintenance. While it does not actually give the status, both ends of the route show where the route goes, which is unlikely to be shown in this way if the route were only a footpath or bridleway. (Note this route is a public road today.)

3.14.2 Boundary Sketch Maps

Star Rating	Up to 3
Held at	The National Archives, class/series OS 27
Coverage	England and Wales
Appearance	Boundary Sketch Maps are folded maps on linen sections (approx 11in x 9in) They may be as few as 6 sections or as many as 20.
Shape	Parish system The Boundary Sketch Maps show one or more parishes together and north is at the top of the always folded, linen backed map.
Date	circa 1880 to 1885
Use with	OS 26 Boundary Remark Books and OS 29 Journals of Inspection
Locating	Using the online catalogue (http://www.nationalarchive.gov.uk/catalogue/), type the parish name in the top line and OS 27 in the third line.

Search the catalogue
Search | Places, prominent people & subjects

Word or phrase (Mandatory) — Aldenham
Year range (optional) — to
Department or Series code (optional) — OS 27

Clear | Search >

Figure 55: TNA search for OS27 records

The result will be a list of one or more Boundary Sketch Maps that show any boundary with the required parish. Note down the numbers.

Now repeat the search using the name of the adjoining parish. The Boundary Sketch Map of interest will be the one whose number appears in both sets of results.

Catalogue:

Sort by: Catalogue reference ∨ | Former reference ∨ | Date range ∨ | Relevance ranking ∨

Catalogue Reference	Title/Scope and Content
OS 27/2450	*i* Hertfordshire: Aldenham
OS 27/2450	*i* Hertfordshire: Aldenham Tp
OS 27/2489	*i* Hertfordshire: Aldenham (Det)
OS 27/2489	*i* Hertfordshire: Aldenham Tp (Det)
OS 27/2502	*i* Hertfordshire: Aldenham Abbey

Figure 56: TNA search for OS27 records – results

Interpretation — As for OS 26 Boundary Remark Books, but sometimes routes will be shown across the parish.

Caveats — Boundary Remark Books (OS 26) and Boundary Sketch Maps (OS 27) do not exist for some counties/areas. There may be OS 33 records (which appear as small sections of Ordnance Survey maps on card) which were compiled in the 1930s to replace the Boundary Remark Books and Boundary Sketch Maps but the authors have found these of little use.

Example for use in an application[28]

23. Ordnance Survey Boundary Sketch Map

a. The Ordnance Survey was given the duty of ascertaining and recording all public boundaries by the Ordnance Survey Act 1841. Of particular value for determining highway status are the Boundary Sketch Maps (OS 27) and Boundary Remark Books (OS 26). These were produced under Parliamentary authority (the 1841 Act), with the power to summon the Clerk of the Peace and any books, maps, papers or other documents he held (s.5 of the 1841 Act) and under provisions that an offence be committed for obstructing or hindering the surveyor appointed under the 1841 Act (s.8 of the 1841 Act). The Boundary Sketch Map was advertised for public inspection. The records have been held in official custody, firstly by the Ordnance Survey, and latterly by The National Archives.

b. The OS Boundary Sketch Maps in The National Archives series OS 27 show the whole of a parish (sometimes a group of parishes), and indicate which of the Boundary Remark Books is needed to look at a specific section of the parish boundary.

28 Application made to Hertfordshire County Council on 1 Jan 2010. Their reference HTM/184.

c. The Boundary Sketch Map for Aldenham, held as The National Archives document OS 27/2450 shows, at its southern end, the boundary with St Stephen's parish. The application route forms part of the boundary, and was considered by the surveyors to be of sufficient importance to be named on the boundary map. It is submitted that it must have been a route of more than purely private significance in order to be named on the OS 27 records.

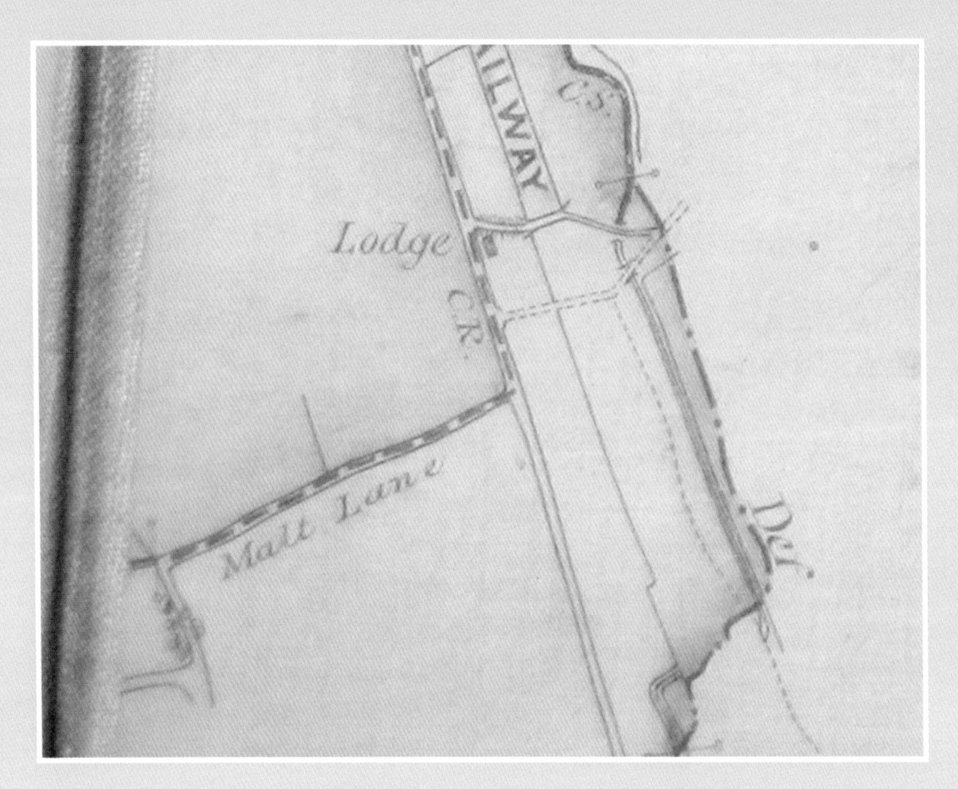

Figure 57: Extract from the OS Boundary Sketch Map for Aldenham Parish

The document in the above example is worth no stars because it is simply repeating the information in the Boundary Remark Book. If the Boundary Remark Book had gone missing (and so no stars were awardable), then this document would have provided one out of a maximum of three stars (for physical presence), with a second or third star awardable only if additional useful information had been put on the map.

3.14.3 Journals of Inspection

Star Rating	Up to 4
Held by	The National Archives, class/series OS 29
Coverage	England and Wales
Appearance	These are about A2 size, with a dark buff coloured cover
Shape	District systemt The Journals of Inspection contain a map showing the area with the district and parish boundaries marked.
Date	circa 1880 to 1885
Use with	OS 27 Boundary Sketch Maps and OS 26 Boundary Remark Books.
Locating	Using the online catalogue (http://www.nationalarchives.gov.uk/catalogue/), type the parish name in the top line and OS 29 in the third line.

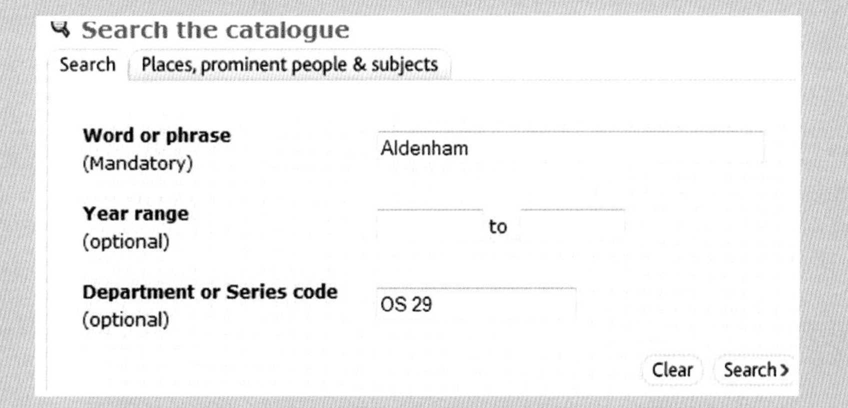

Figure 58: TNA search for OS29 records

The result will be the Journal of Inspection for the area around and books.

Catalogue:

Sort by: Catalogue reference | Former reference | Date range | Relevance ranking

Catalogue Reference	Title/Scope and Content
OS 29/134	Aldenham (and Det part), Hertfordshire
OS 29/134	Aldenham Park (Extra Parochial), Hertfordshire

Figure 59: TNA search for OS29 records – results

Interpretation	The Journals of Inspection contain copies of press advertisements announcing that the boundaries had been ascertained and inviting inspection by the public. They also contain a record of the comments made by anyone who inspected the boundary maps. These are often signed by prominent landowners or their agents. These can be useful, not only for refuting any idea that this process was conducted in private, but also because there could be comments from landowners and their agents providing details about the ownership and maintenance of a road which runs along a parish boundary. The journals can include extracts from local papers advertising a forthcoming opportunity for public examination and comment. These may be used to refute any notion that the process was closed to landowner comment.

3.15 Ordnance Survey Object Names Book

When the Ordnance Survey were collecting information to put on their second series of published maps, they were most keen to ensure the accuracy of the information printed, not just on the alignment of physical features, but also the names that were to be recorded on the maps. In order to ensure accuracy, their surveyors recorded the names of anything that was to be shown on a map. The Ordnance Survey Object Names Book for an area records these names, the description of the item named, and the local person attesting to the name. The instructions to the Ordnance Survey staff were to be careful only to take names or spellings from the well-educated who have been in the district for some time, to make sure that good information was obtained. Many old roads had names, and the description of these provides evidence of the reputation of the named route. Often the names will be attested to by owners or estate agents, clergy, postmasters, overseers, or road surveyors.

Star Rating	Up to 4
Held at	The National Archives, class/series OS 35
Coverage	England and Wales, although some were destroyed during the War The following counties have OS 35 coverage: OS35s exist for: Bedfordshire, Berkshire, Brecknockshire, Buckinghamshire, Cambridgeshire, Cardiganshire, Cheshire, Cornwall, Cumberland, Denbighshire, Derbyshire, Devonshire, Dorset, Durham, Essex, Flintshire, Glamorganshire, Gloucestershire, Hampshire, Herefordshire, Hertfordshire, Huntingdonshire, Kent, Lancashire, Leicestershire, Lincolnshire, Merionethshire, Middlesex, Monmouthshire, Montgomeryshire, Norfolk, Northamptonshire, Northumberland, Nottinghamshire, Oxfordshire, Pembrokeshire, Rutland, Shropshire, Somerset, Staffordshire, Suffolk, Surrey, Sussex, Warwickshire, Westmorland, Wiltshire, Worcestershire, Yorkshire.
Appearance	Buff files approximately, 50cm x 30cm, held with a pair of treasury tags containing anything from several to 50 pages. There is an index at the front and usually some pages of authorising signatures at the end, or occasionally interspersed with the record pages.

Shape	Grid system. Many books cover a quarter of the Ordnance Survey county series sheet number, i.e. four smaller maps: NW is maps 1, 2, 5 & 6; NE is maps 3, 4, 7 & 8; SW is 9, 10, 13 & 14; and SE is maps 11, 12, 15 & 16. In some areas, a book may cover just one or two of the sixteenths of the grid, for example maps 3 and 7.

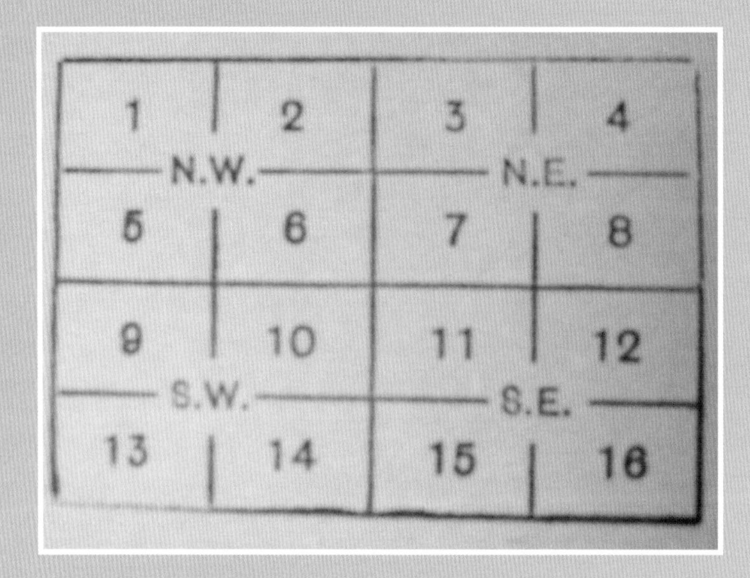

Figure 60: Ordnance Survey County Map Grid System

Date	Most were originally compiled around 1900 to 1905. Revisions were made some years later by annotating the original records in coloured ink.
Use with	County Series Ordnance Survey maps. (These were the map base for the Inland Revenue valuations, so those records provide a convenient way of accessing the data.)
Locating	Although compiled on the grid system, they are indexed at The National Archives by parish. There is currently no means of typing in a grid / map number and finding the OS 35 computer reference; however, it is sometimes possible to work out the grid of OS 35 numbers gradually from the parish map numbers. They are in the OS class of documents, and the series is OS 35. The piece number is generally a four figure number. Using The National Archives' online catalogue (http://www.nationalarchives.gov.uk/catalogue/), type the parish name in the top line and OS 35 in the third line.

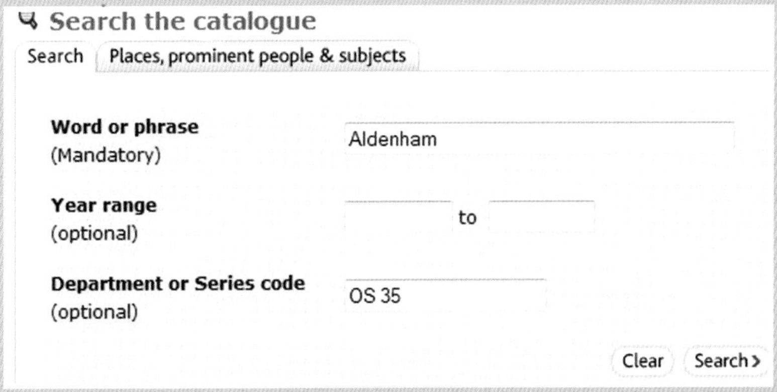

Search the catalogue

Search | Places, prominent people & subjects

Word or phrase (Mandatory): Aldenham

Year range (optional): to

Department or Series code (optional): OS 35

Clear Search >

Figure 61: TNA search for OS35 records

The result is usually a few references.

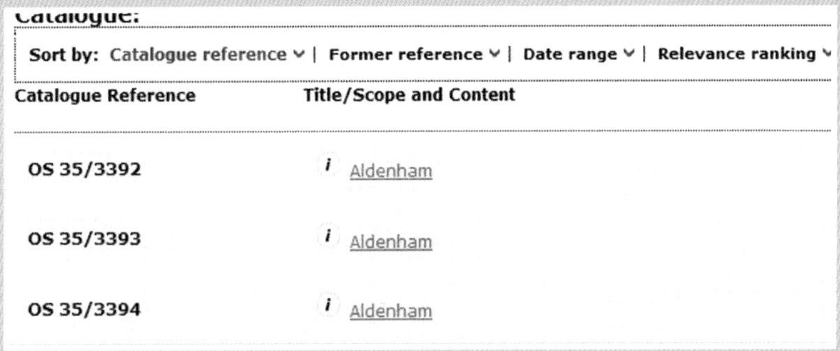

Catalogue:

Sort by: Catalogue reference | Former reference | Date range | Relevance ranking

Catalogue Reference	Title/Scope and Content
OS 35/3392	Aldenham
OS 35/3393	Aldenham
OS 35/3394	Aldenham

Figure 62: TNA search for OS35 records – results

Check each document's online description in turn to find out which quarter of the grid is covered. If more than one document is shown for the same quarter, then both books need to be obtained to find out which one is relevant.

Where a named route passes from one map to another and is printed on both maps, it will be recorded in the object names book for each of the maps.

Interpretation

The descriptions usually state where the road started and finished, and frequently describes the route as a road, lane or drove, and often as a public, district or parish, or occupation road. It is worth checking routes that connect to the one under investigation, as their description may indicate that they joined a district or parish road, so providing additional information. Descriptions of bridges often include information about who owned them or who maintained them. This can provide evidence of public maintainability and hence of highway status. The signature confirming or authorising the name is usually the owner where the entry is private, and is typically the district surveyor or overseer for public roads. Examples can often be found where a road that is not public is listed, and these add weight to the public nature of the other roads listed, as shown in the example.

Example for use in an application[29]

24. Ordnance Survey Object Name Book

a. The Ordnance Survey needed a reliable way of determining the names put on their maps. They recorded the authority for the names and the modes of spelling. Their record books give other information.

b. The Object Name Book for map Hertfordshire XXXIX 12, held as The National Archives document OS 35/3393 records the name of the application route as Malt Lane. The description given is 'A lane extending from Darnels to the main road between Radlett and Park Street.'

c. The second extract from the same Object Name Book gives the entry for Beech Avenue. This one is described as 'A private road extending from The Avenue to its junction with the Drive ... The property of the Radlett Park Building Estate.'

d. The fact that the Ordnance Survey drew a distinction between 'lanes' and 'private lanes' leads to the conclusion that Malt Lane was not considered to be private at the time of the name determination. In other words, it was considered to be public.

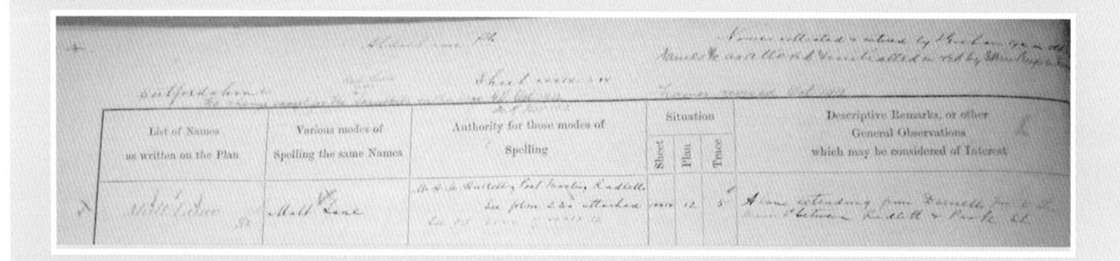

List of Names as written on the Plan	Various modes of Spelling the same Names	Authority for those modes of Spelling	Situation: Sheet	Situation: Plan	Situation: Trace	Descriptive Remarks, or other General Observations which may be considered of Interest
Malt Lane	Malt Lane	[illegible]	[illegible]	12	5	A lane extending from Darnells [illegible] between Radlett & Park St.

Figure 63: Extract 1 from the OS Object Name Book OS35/3393

Figure 64: Extract 2 from the OS Object Name Book OS35/3393

29 Application made to Hertfordshire County Council on 1 Jan 2010. Their reference HTM/184.

The document in the above example is worth the full four stars (for an application at byway status) because it was produced by a public body (the OS); the contents were agreed by notable people in the locality; a comparison with this route and a private route enables this one to be confirmed as public; and it can be related to an exact route because this document was compiled to verify the description of the wording/names printed on the OS county series map.

Further Reading

Seymour, WA (ed.), *A History of the Ordnance Survey*, ISBN 978-0-7129-0979-2, Wm Dawson & Sons, 1980 (see p. 176 on determining names of objects).

3.16 Ordnance Survey Published Maps

The Ordnance Survey started compiling maps for the South East of England when there was a fear of invasion from France in the late 1790s. Since then the Ordnance Survey has been surveying and printing maps continually at various scales. In some cases they were printing maps of one series for one part of the country whilst starting on a new edition or series for another part of the country. The terminology can be confusing as they have produced series, editions, and revisions at various scales and times. Thus all dates shown in this book will be approximate and will vary depending on which part of the country is referred to and whether the reference is to the survey, the revision, or the publication. Also, some maps were re-scaled from other surveys.

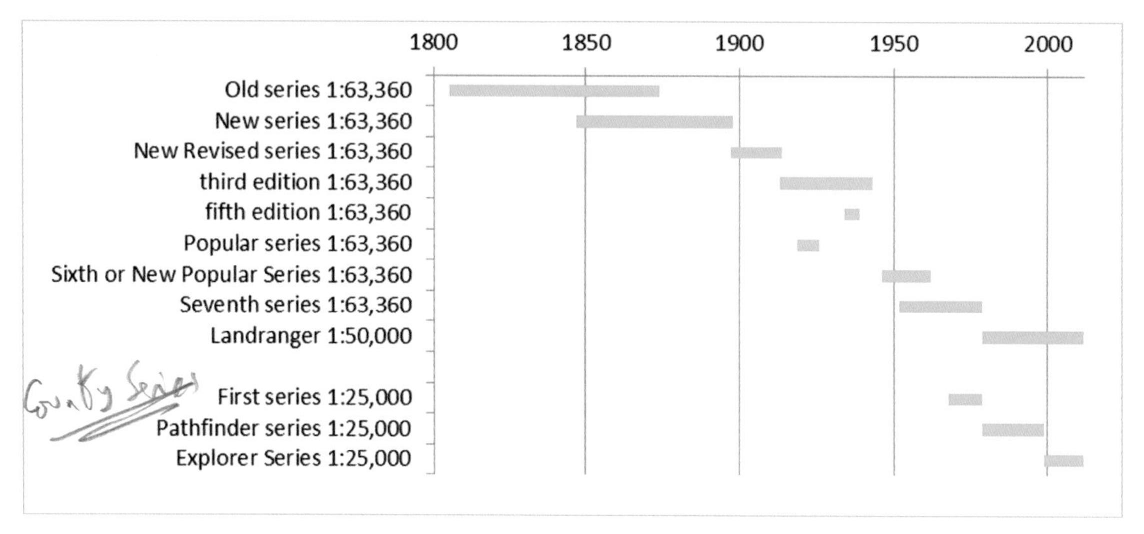

Figure 65: OS published maps and the years of production

For rights of way research purposes, it is perhaps easiest to work with three scales: Landranger, Explorer and County. The Landranger and Explorer maps are presented on a national grid system, while the County series are on a county grid system.

The current Landranger Series (1:50,000) was preceded by several editions, revisions and series at the scale 1:63,360. The Old Series (1805 to 1874), the New Revised Series (1897 to 1904), and the Popular Series (1919 to 1926) have all been re-projected and re-scaled to 1:50,000 and are now published by Cassini Publishing Ltd (previously Timeline Maps Ltd). These are readily available and help show when a route physically existed.

The key to earlier maps of the 1:63,360 'New Popular Edition' is peculiar in that it shows various categories of 'roads', and 'footpaths', but no mention is made of bridleways. In later maps of the same edition, the key has been changed to put 'footpaths and bridleways' against the notation previously labelled 'footpaths'. If a map is being used as evidence that a route is a footpath and not a bridleway, the key must be checked. If it is the older key where bridleways are not mentioned at all, it can be argued that either the key is wrong, or that bridleways had to be shown as something, that the Ordnance Survey wouldn't have wished to overstate the status, and hence that footpath was the only notation left to them. Either way, the map is silent on the question of bridleway rights rather than evidence that such rights did not exist.

The current Explorer Series (1:25,000) was preceded by the Provisional series (1943 to 1968), renamed the First Series (1968 to 1979), and rebranded as 'Pathfinder' in 1979. Pathfinders were gradually replaced by Explorer maps between 1994 and 2003. In some parts of the country, the Explorer map is called an Outdoor Leisure map. This is a good scale to use as a research map and is sufficient for use in modification order applications.

The 1:2,500 scale is usually referred to as the County Series. Old maps of this scale are not generally on sale to the public, although some, particularly for urban areas, have been reprinted by Alan Godfrey Maps. It was the scale at which the country was surveyed, and many maps printed at larger scales have been derived from these maps. For research purposes the County Series are used for more detailed work. As the name suggests, each county had its own set of maps. These are detailed black and white maps which show field boundaries, field numbers, and the later ones showed field acreages. The early ones which did not show acreages had 'area books' published, by parish, containing this and additional information (see section 3.10). The County Series were used as the base maps for the 1910 Finance Act information (see section 3.17). The names printed on them are verified in the Object Names Books (see section 3.15). They are currently used by the Land Registry and by conveyancing solicitors.

Each county has its own set of maps and these are numbered from the top of the county, from left to right, with each full sheet containing 16 (4 x 4) maps/individual sheets. The numbering of these individual sheets is illustrated in section 3.15. Each county is separate and where a map covers the area around a county boundary, the individual sheet number for both counties will be printed on the top right corner of the map. Each county will only put on the information relating to that county and will leave the rest unmarked. In the example here the same individual sheet is numbered Dorset VI 7 (6–7) and Somerset LXXXIV 7 (84–7). As counties are irregular shapes and sizes, the grid numbers do not connect in any pre-definable way.

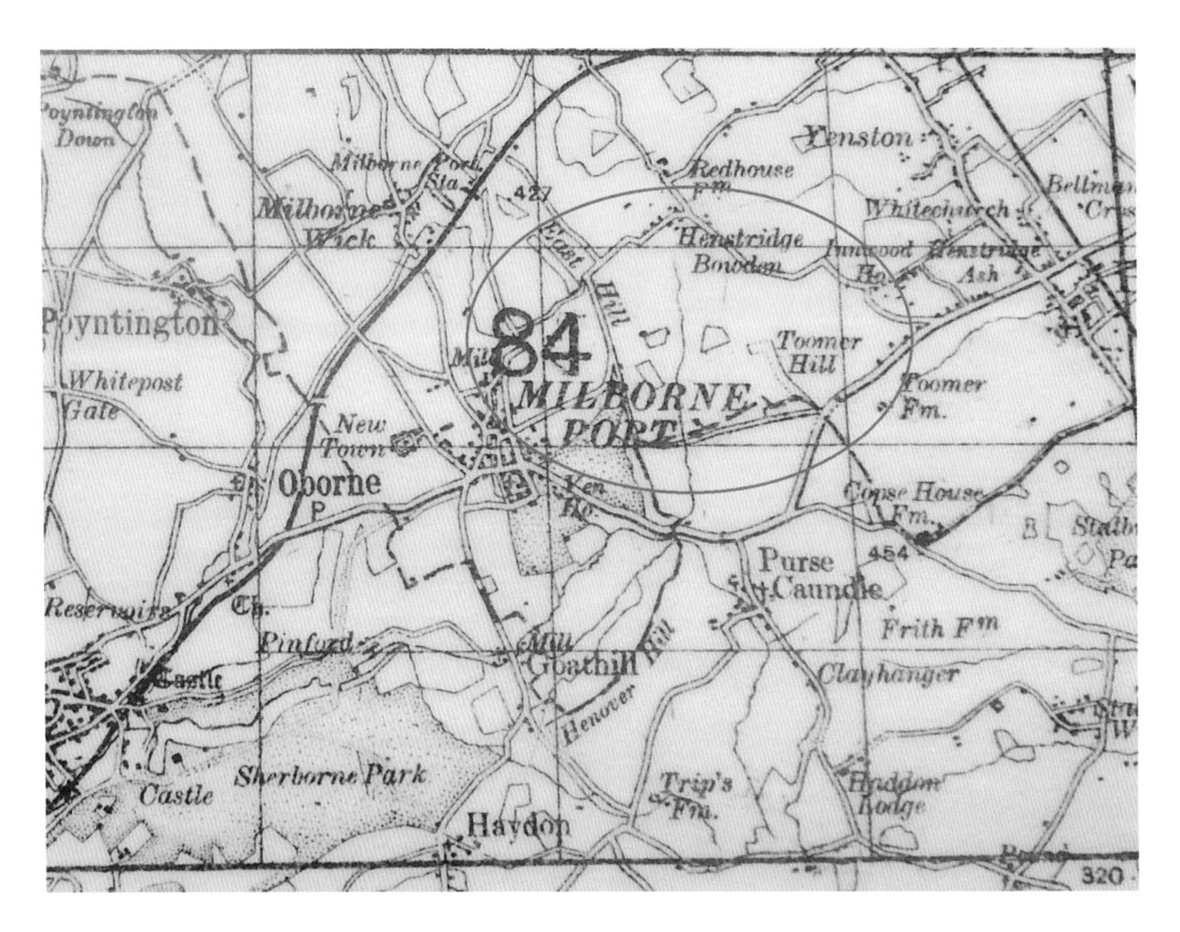

Figure 66 (above and facing page): OS grid of Somerset and Dorset

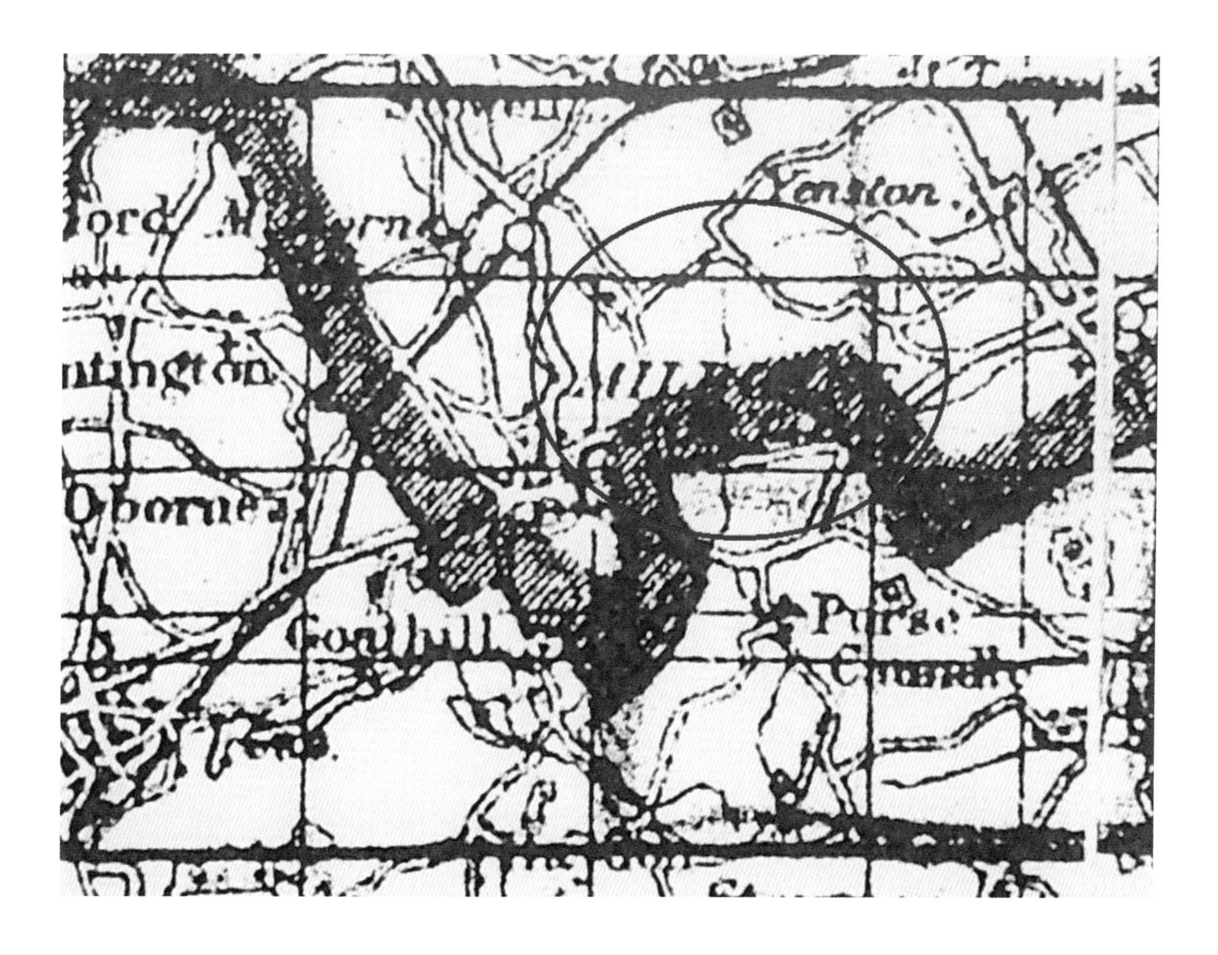

Apart from these three commonly used scales, a researcher may come across other Ordnance Survey maps being given in evidence in connection with modification order applications. These can generally be interpreted as for those cited above.

Star Rating	2 if a suitable comparison or argument can be drawn 1 if simply shown as a physical feature Add 1 if 'B.R.' is shown on a route on the 1:2,500 scale, and the route is presently unrecorded or recorded just as a footpath. (While all editions can count in evidence, do not count more than 3 stars from these sources.)
Held at	1:63,369 British Library, TNA, County Record Offices. 1:50,000 Available for purchase (Ordnance Survey, Cassini). 1:25,000 New ones are available for purchase. Older ones can sometimes be found in bookshops, occasionally at auctions or jumble sales or on the internet. 1:2,500 British Library, TNA, County Record Offices.
Coverage	England and Wales. Complete
Appearance	Flat maps, folded
Shape	Grid system
Date	Early 1800s up to today
Locating	Current maps: http://www.ordnancesurvey.co.uk or local book shops. Cassini reprints can be purchased from http://www.cassinimaps.co.uk. Godfrey reprints can be obtained from http://www.alangodfreymaps.co.uk. The sheet number for a County Series map can be obtained from The National Archives' IR valuation office map finder, described in section 3.17.
Interpretation	These are best used for checking that a route existed over a period of time, and hence identifying which other primary sources are likely to show the route, if it carried public rights.
Caveats	Ordnance Survey maps have nearly always carried the disclaimer 'The representation on this map of a Road, Track or Footpath is no evidence of a right of way.' Maps published since the Definitive Map was available carry the disclaimer 'The representation on this map of any other road, track or path is no evidence of the existence of a right of way'. Accordingly, they provide evidence only of physical existence, unless special circumstances allow other inferences to be drawn. 'B.R.' was only used on maps printed between 1884 and the late 1940s. There are numerous books on Ordnance Survey maps and the authors do not attempt to include this information on the background to the maps.

Three examples for use in applications[30,31,32]

25. Ordnance Survey New Popular Edition 1 inch Map for Taunton and Lyme Regis (sheet 177)

a. The Ordnance Survey New Popular Edition map for Taunton and Lyme Regis (sheet 177) at a scale of one inch to the mile printed in 1945 is a full revision from 1930 with later corrections.

b. The extract of this map is taken from a published copy of the Ordnance Survey map which the author purchased in a second-hand bookshop. The letters in red (A to H) have been added by the applicant to enable paths to be identified.

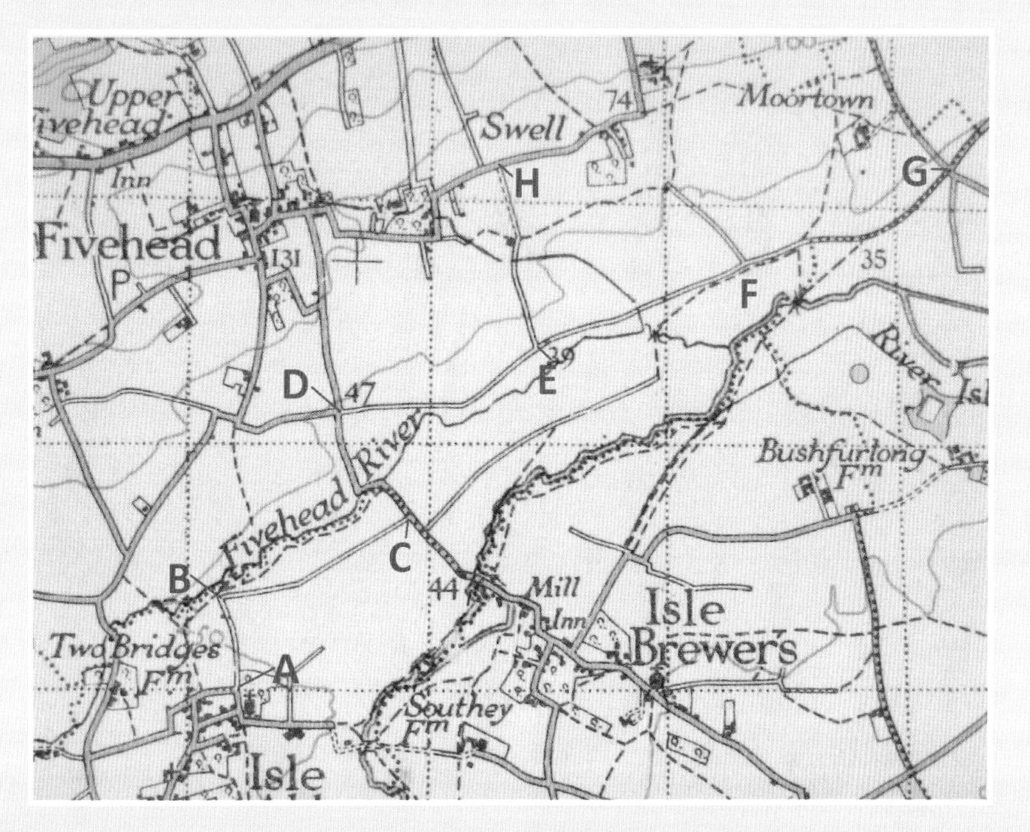

Figure 67: Extract 1 from OS New Popular Edition Map for Taunton and Lyme Regis (sheet 177)

30 Application made to Somerset County Council on 28 Jul 2008. Their reference 538M & 539M.

31 Application made to Somerset County Council on 29 Sep 2008. Their reference 546M.

32 Application made to Somerset County Council on 26 Nov 2011. Their reference 572M.

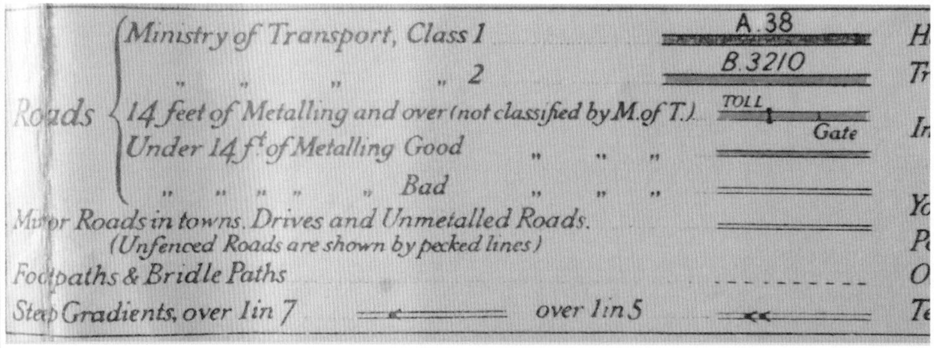

Figure 68: Extract 2 Key from OS New Popular Edition Map for Taunton and Lyme Regis (sheet 177)

c. Extract 1 shows the application route labelled A – B – C. The routes marked D – E – F – G and E–H are currently recorded as bridleways on the definitive map and are shown in the same manner as A – B – C. Currently, A to B is recorded as part of a longer footpath and B to C is unrecorded. All are shown in the manner of 'minor roads, drives and unmetalled roads' according the key in Extract 2. This shows that the unrecorded route appeared on the ground to be similar in physical characteristics as the bridleways. Coupled with other evidence, this supports the assertion that the routes north and east from Isle Abbotts are of the same nature as those bridleways in the adjoining parish (Fivehead).

26. Ordnance Survey New Popular Edition 1 inch Map for Taunton and Lyme Regis (sheet 177)

a. The Ordnance Survey New Popular Edition map for Taunton and Lyme Regis (sheet 177) at a scale of one inch to the mile printed in 1945 is a full revision from 1930 with later corrections.

b. The extract of this map is taken from a published copy of the Ordnance Survey map which the author purchased in a second-hand bookshop. The letters in red (A to E) have been added by the applicant to enable paths to be identified.

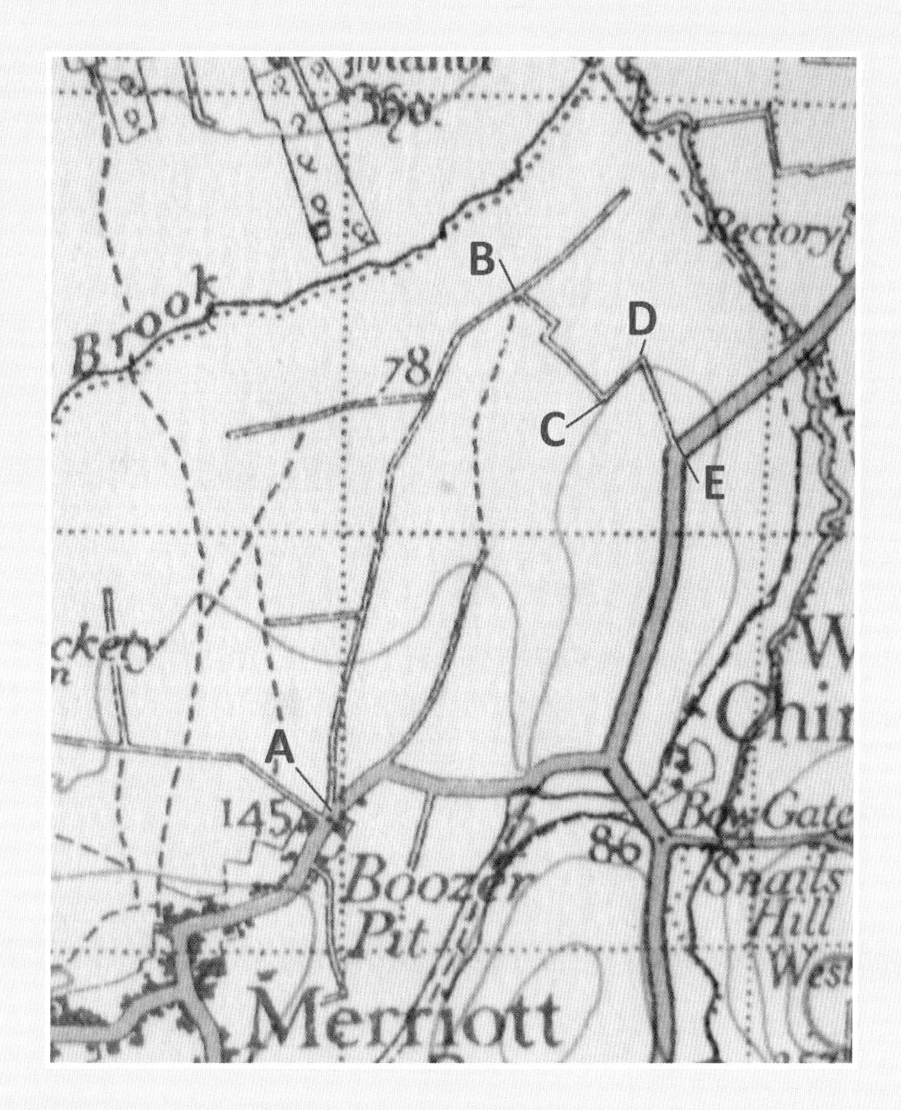

Figure 69: Extract 3 from OS New Popular Edition Map for Taunton and Lyme Regis (sheet 177)

c. This section of map shows the application route A – B – C. This is unrecorded on the present definitive map. The joining route C – D – E is currently recorded as a bridleway. The map shows that there was no barrier between the sections when the map was prepared. The applicant notes that the application route and recorded bridleway form a continuous route, and there is no indication of a place of public resort at the end of the currently recorded bridleway (Point C). The whole of the route A to E is shown in the same way, suggesting that the whole route should have the same status.

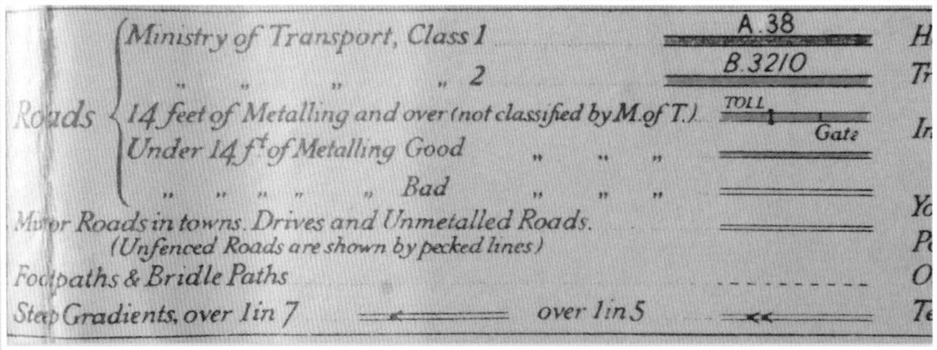

Figure 70: Extract 4 Key from OS New Popular Edition Map for Taunton and Lyme Regis (sheet 177)

The key to the map shows that the whole route A to E is described as 'Minor roads in towns, Drives and Unmetalled Roads'. The applicant believes that this route is being shown as an unmetalled road, and so immediately prior to the commencement of the Natural Environment and Rural Communities Act 2006, had full vehicular rights.

27. Ordnance Survey First Series Map for Blackdown Hills East

a. The Ordnance Survey First Series Map for Blackdown Hills East (Sheet ST21) at a scale of 1:25,000 was printed in 1959 from surveys from 1901–29 and partial systematic revision.

b. The extract of this map is taken from a published copy of the Ordnance Survey map which the author purchased from a second-hand bookshop. It has not been altered or modified.

c. All the uncoloured routes shown on this map extract in Bickenhall parish are currently recorded as bridleways on the definitive map and statement for the area. The route in Ashill parish which runs from Barrington Hill Road in the south east of the map going up to Forest Drove is depicted on the map in the same way but is not recorded on the definitive map. The identical depiction shows that the unrecorded route would have been capable of taking the same public traffic as the recorded bridleways. Coupled with other evidence, this is consistent with the belief that the unrecorded route was missed out by Ashill parish when the definitive map was compiled.

Figure 71: Extract from Ordnance Survey First Series 1:25000 Map ST21

The document in example 25 is worth two stars (for an application at bridleway status) because comparison argument relates it to routes currently recorded as bridleways. It could also be used as two stars towards byway status based on the key to the map (but then route D – E – F would also need to be considered for upgrade). The comparison and key arguments shows that example 26 is worth two stars for bridleway (A–C) or byway (A–E) status in the same way. The comparison argument provides two stars in example 27 for bridleway status as the application route is shown in the same way as definitive bridleways to which it connects.

Further Reading

Harley, JB (1975) *Ordnance Survey Maps – A descriptive manual*, Oxford University Press, ISBN 978-0-319-00000-7.

Higley, Chris (2011) *Old Series to Explorer – A Field Guide to the Ordnance Map*, The Charles Close Society, ISBN 978-1-870598-30-9.

Hewitt, Rachel (2010) *Map of a Nation*, Granta Publications, ISBN 978-1-84708-254-1.

Hinks, Arthur R (1942) *Maps and Survey*, Cambridge University Press, 4th edn.

Hodson, Yolande (December 2002) *Ordnance Survey and the Definitive Map of Public Rights of Way in England and Wales*, The Cartographic Journal, Vol 39 No 2 pp 101–24.

Hodson, Yolande (September 2005) *Coloured Roads on Ordnance Survey First Edition*, The Cartographic Journal, Vol 42 No 2, pp 85–110.

Hodson, Yolande (1999) *Popular Maps, The Ordnance Survey Popular Edition One Inch Map of England and Wales, 1919 to 1926*, The Charles Close Society ISBN 978-1-870598-15-6

Oliver, Richard (2005) *Ordnance Survey Maps, a concise guide for historians*, The Charles Close Society, ISBN 978-1-870598-24-8.

Seymour, WA (ed.) (1980) *History of the Ordnance Survey*, Wm Dawson & Sons Ltd, ISBN 978-0-7129-0979-2.

3.17 Inland Revenue Valuation Records – Finance (1909–10) Act 1910

The Finance (1909–10) Act 1910 caused every property in England and Wales to be valued. The purpose was to charge a tax on any increase in value when the property was later sold or inherited. The valuation involved complicated calculations which are not relevant for highway purposes. However, two features do affect highways: public vehicular roads were usually excluded from adjoining landholdings, and discounts could be requested for land crossed by footpaths or bridleways. These features are provided by different sections of the legislation, and result in different ways of using the records as noted under 'Interpretation' below.

The exclusion of vehicular roads from valuation stems from section 35 of the Finance (1909–10) Act 1910 which provided:

> No duty under this Part of this Act shall be charged in respect of any land or interest in land held by or on behalf of a rating authority.

A highway authority was a rating authority.

The discount for footpaths and bridleways is given in section 25:

> The total value of land means the gross value after deducting the amount by which the gross value would be diminished if the land were sold subject to any fixed charges and to any public rights of way or any public rights of user, and to any right of common and to any easements affecting the land, and … [other exclusions.]

Star Rating	5 for white roads and for deductions on a route that can be defined. 3 for routes where a deduction for footpath or bridleway was allowed but the route is not certain from the IR documentation.
Held at	The National Archives, class/series IR 124 to IR 135 for maps, and IR 58 for field books. Some County Record Offices.
Coverage	England and Wales, although a small number were destroyed by enemy action during the War.

Appearance	These records are in two parts: maps and field books (but see also section 3.17.1 for an alternative to field books). The information on the maps is coloured onto the second edition county series Ordnance Survey maps which are flat maps approximately 3ft 3in x 2ft 3in (1m x 70cm) and cover an area about 2 km x 1.5 km. Each landholding is coloured or has the boundary coloured and there will be a handwritten number, usually in red, for each landholding.

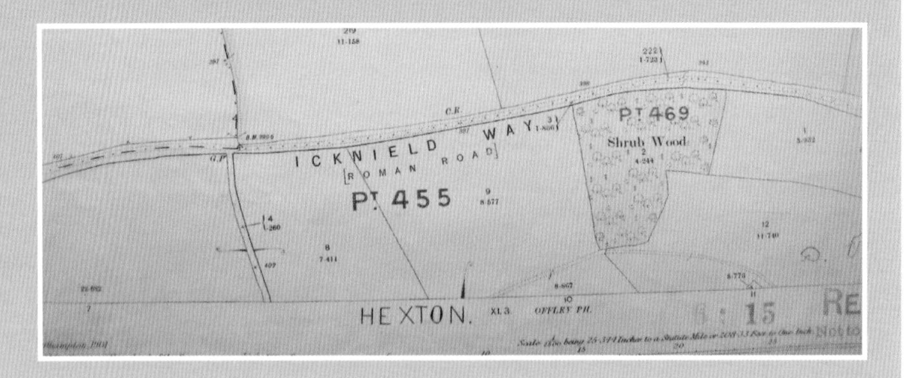

Figure 72: Extract from Inland Revenue Valuation Office Plan

In this extract of Hertfordshire VI 15 (IR 126/4/39) from The National Archives, the income tax parish boundary is shown in yellow. The income tax parish name is given in red (but only if it differs from the actual parish name) as are the hereditament numbers.

The field books are brown bound volumes approximately 20cm x 15cm and contain information on up to (usually) 100 landholdings (called 'hereditaments').

Shape	Grid system for the valuation maps, and Inland Revenue parish system for the land parcel valuation records (field books). The Inland Revenue parish may not be the same as the local government parish.
Date	1910 or shortly thereafter.
Use with	Use IR 58 with IR 124 to 135.
Locating	Using the online catalogue (http://www.nationalarchives.gov.uk/catalogue/), type the county and map number (in Roman numerals for the large sheet number and the Arabic number for the individual sheet number, for example Dorset XXIV 5) in the top line and IR in the third line.

Search the catalogue

Search | Places, prominent people & subjects

Word or phrase (Mandatory): Dorset XXIV 5

Year range (optional): to

Department or Series code (optional): IR

Clear | Search

Figure 73: TNA search for IR Valuation Records

The computer will show a list of all valuation maps for the entry given.

Catalogue:

Sort by: Catalogue reference | Former reference | Date range | Relevance ranking

Catalogue Reference	Title/Scope and Content
IR 125/2/239	OS Sheet Reference: Dorset XXIV 5

Figure 74: TNA search for IR Valuation Records – results

If the Ordnance Survey map number is unknown, there is a convenient valuation office map finder tool available at http://labs.nationalarchives.gov.uk/maps/valuation.html. This tool enables searching by place name, and shows the modern Ordnance Survey Explorer map with the Ordnance Survey county series grid overlay. Selecting a grid square reveals the county series name number and the IR reference for use at The National Archives.

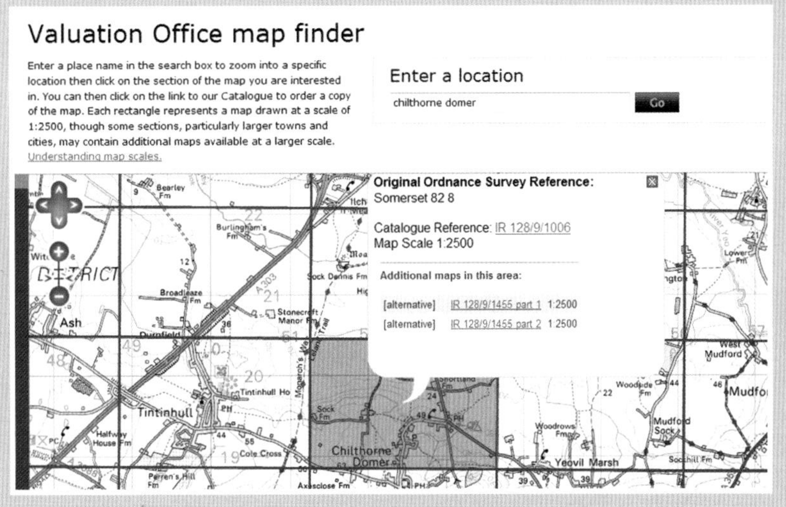

Figure 75: TNA graphical search for IR Valuation Office maps

Once a hereditament of interest has been identified on the map (shown with (usually) a red number), note the Inland Revenue parish name (also shown in red). Using The National Archives' online catalogue, type the Inland Revenue parish name in the top line and IR 58 in the third line. This will give you the reference numbers for all the field books in that parish, typically four or five.

Sometimes the field book entries for one parish will be combined with the field books for an adjacent or nearby parish. If so, check the field books for adjacent parishes with a name beginning with a letter earlier in the alphabet. Those parishes which do include other entries for other parishes are likely to have more field books than average. If identifying a field book is a frequent problem, it may be worthwhile to check the listings for the whole of that district and seeing which parishes have an unusually high number of field books for their size and number of properties. Another way would be to consult the Duties on Land Values Books (see section 3.17.1) which will give the name of the leading parish.

Interpretation

(1) Public vehicular highways were usually excluded from adjoining land parcels ('hereditaments') and so appear as 'white roads'. If the same landowner owns land on each side of the white road, there may be a red brace joining the two sections together. While in some areas, the individual land holdings are shaded (as in the first application example below), in others only the edge of a holding is coloured in (as in the second application example). In the second situation, sometimes a 'white road' will be detected only from the presence of occasional red braces indicating, by a gap between the two parts of the brace, that the road is not part of the surrounding hereditament. For white roads, there will be no entry in the IR 58 field books and so these need not be consulted.

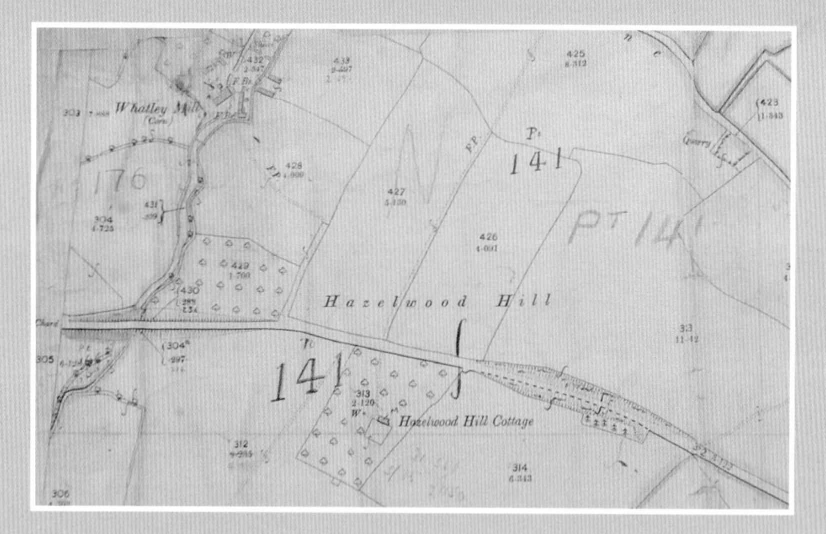

Figure 76: Example of open red brace showing presence of a white road IR128/9/1125

(2) Footpaths and bridleways may be shown on the underlying base map, but are rarely shown annotated by the Inland Revenue. Their existence would entitle the landholder to claim a deduction on his land value. If the discount was claimed, a note of this will appear in the field book (IR 58 series). However, it may not say the status (footpath or bridleway), and it may not indicate where in the hereditament the highway runs. For large landholdings this is unhelpful, and is resolved by taking the evidence into account with other evidence of a route's existence. The second example below is helpful in that the additional information is given. IR 58 field book extracts are essential if relying on deductions to indicate highway status.

Caveats

There was no obligation on a landholder to claim any deduction for rights of way, but there were severe penalties (hard labour) for falsely claiming a deduction. It follows that, unless there is evidence of prosecution, all deductions should be treated as evidence of a right of way. The field book will give more information, but unfortunately may not say exactly where the footpath or bridleway ran. It is most effective if linked to other records that provide evidence of the route. A road that was a public vehicular highway but which provided for example a grazing crop because it was lightly used may be coloured in as part of the neighbouring land.

Typically, Crown land (including land held for a government department or ministry) was left uncoloured even though it was not highway land.

The lack of a deduction for rights of way does not imply the absence of such a right; it only means that the landholder chose not to seek any discount.

Note: each county has its own grid and where there is a county boundary the records for each county will appear on an Ordnance Survey second edition county series sheet with a number for that county, leaving the section covering the other county blank.

Example for use in an application[33] – White Road

28. Inland Revenue Valuation

a. The Finance (1909–10) Act 1910 provided for land valuations to take place across the country so that the increase in its value could be taxed. Deductions from the assessable value could be claimed by landowners where the land was crossed by a (public) footpath or bridleway. Where a public vehicular highway crossed land, it was usually omitted from the valuation, excluded from adjacent hereditaments, and shown on the Inland Revenue's plans as a 'white road'. If the route were a private vehicular way, then it could be developed, increase in value and so be taxed. Accordingly, private tracks were not usually excluded from the assessable hereditaments.

b. The extracts below are from the records that were passed from the IR Valuation Offices to The National Archives at Kew.

c. Document IR 126/4/162 has Hertfordshire 20 – 5 as its base map. It clearly shows that the route from Point A westwards to the map edge as a white road, excluded from the valuation. Section 35 of the Finance (1910–11) Act 1910 provided that land owned by a rating authority (here, the highway authority) had to be excluded from the valuation. Had the route been a private track, it could have changed value in the future as a result of development, and so would have needed to have been valued. The applicant therefore draws the conclusion that the application route carried vehicular rights at the time of the survey.

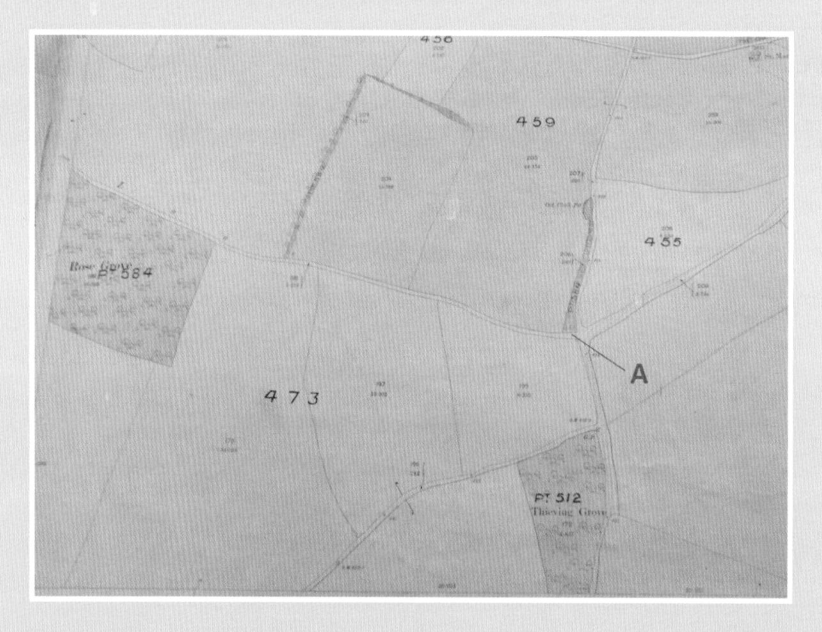

Figure 77: Extract from Inland Revenue Valuation Plan for Hertfordshire 20 – 5

33 Application made to Hertfordshire County Council on 12 Feb 2010. Their reference NH/210.

d. Document IR 126/4/154 has Hertfordshire 19 – 8 as its base map. It shows the continuation of Long Lane, started in IR 126/4/162, as it continues westwards. The route remains shown as a white road, excluded from the valuation, as far west as a field boundary at Point F. The applicant draws the conclusion that the application route carried vehicular rights at the time of the survey. The remainder of the route to the west of Point F is left indistinct, and so no inference can be drawn as there was no obligation on the landowner to claim deductions, only a penalty if he falsely claimed any.

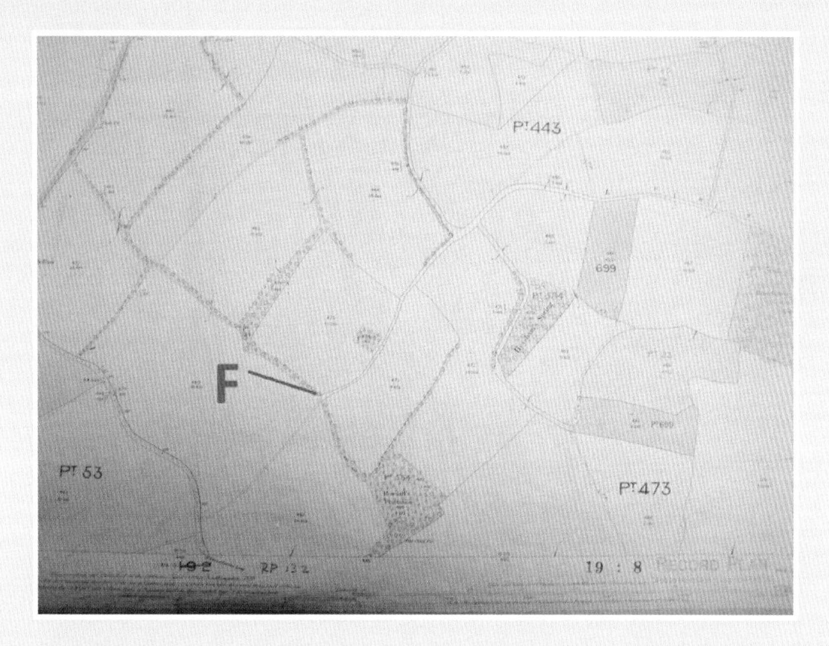

Figure 78: Extract from Inland Revenue Valuation Plan for Hertfordshire 19 – 8

The document in the above example is worth the full five stars (for an application at byway status) because it was produced under statutory authority; the legislation permitted deductions for public highways; deductions would have been resisted by the Inland Revenue, and so would have been checked before being allowed; private routes would have had the capability for future development and so would not have been excluded; the route is easily ascertained from the map.

Example for use in an application[34] – Bridleway

29. Inland Revenue Valuation

a. The Finance (1909–10) Act 1910 provided for land valuations to take place across the country so that the increase in its value could be taxed. Deductions from the assessable value could be claimed by landowners where the land was crossed by a footpath or bridleway. Where a vehicular highway crossed land, it was usually omitted from the valuation, excluded from adjacent hereditaments, and shown on the Inland Revenue's plans as a 'white road'. Footpaths and Bridleways were usually not excluded from the valuation, but a discount was applied.

b. The extracts below are from the records that were passed from the IR Valuation Offices to The National Archives at Kew.

c. Document IR 128/9/1125 has Somerset 92 – 6 as its base map. It clearly shows the route labelled as Broadenham Lane (the application route) running inside the field boundary.

Figure 79: Extract from Inland Revenue Valuation Plan for Somerset 96 – 6

34 Application made to Somerset County Council on 12 Mar 2009. Their reference 596M.

d. The field is part of hereditament number 30. Although this is in the Parish of Winsham, the income tax parish is Cricket St Thomas. The field book entry for Cricket St Thomas 30 is in field book IR 58/82329. Two of the four pages for this entry provide evidence. Page 4 of the field book entry has an entry of £13 for 'Public Rights of Way or User'. This indicates that the landowner claimed, and the valuer accepted, that there should be a deduction for a public highway. Had it been a private route, it would have been listed as an easement.

Less deductions in respect of
Fixed Charges, including—
Fee Farm Rent, rent seck, quit rent, chief rents, rent of Assize ....£
Any other perpetual rent or Annuity...£
Tithe or Tithe Rent Charge..............£ 381
Other Burden or Charge arising by operation of law or under any Act of Parliament£
If Copyhold, Estimated Cost of Enfranchisement ....£
Public Rights of Way or User...........£ 13
Rights of Common..........................£
Easements.......................................£ 5
Restrictions ....£
£ 399
TOTAL VALUE......£ 3876
Less Value attributable to Structures, timber, &c. (as before)..........................£ 1100
Value directly attributable to—
Works executed ....£
Capital Expenditure ....

Figure 80: Extract from Inland Revenue Field Book entry for Cricket St Thomas, hereditament 30, page 4

e. The basis of the calculation is given on page 2 of the field book entry. This shows that the rights of way had the status of bridleway, and that it passed through field numbers 56, 54 and 53. These fields are the three that Broadenham Lane passes through.

Charges, Easements, and Restrictions affecting market value of Fee Simple
Tithe £15. 4. 5 × 25 YP = £381.
Bridle road across 56. 54 & 53. = 10/- p.a. × 25 YP. = £13.
User of Water by 27 from field O.S. No. 380 – say £5

Figure 81: Extract from Inland Revenue Field Book entry for Cricket St Thomas, hereditament 30, page 2

f. The applicant draws the conclusion that this is good evidence that at least bridleway rights existed along the route at the time of the survey.

[Note: although it is convenient to show extracts in the application for a DMMO, all four pages for this hereditament should be copied and sent with the application.]

The document in the above example is worth the full five stars (for an application at bridleway status) because it was produced under statutory authority; the legislation permitted deductions for public paths; deductions would have been resisted by the Inland Revenue, and so would have been checked before being allowed; the status of the public path has been written in as bridleway; while the route is not conclusive, it appears likely on the balance of probabilities to be Broadenham Lane.

3.17.1 Inland Revenue 'Duties on Land Values' Books ('Domesday Books')

Star Rating	2 (but not if stars are taken for a field book entry)
Held at	In places where the records were accepted by the archivists, in county record offices. Records for the City of London and Westminster are held at The National Archives under series IR 91.
Coverage	England and Wales, but not all documents have survived.
Appearance	Approximately A3 sized book.
Shape	Inland Revenue Parish System. The Inland Revenue parish may not be the same as the local government parish.
Date	1910 or shortly thereafter
Use with	IR 58 and IR 124 to 135
Locating	At county record offices, ask the archivist. At The National Archives, browse the IR 91 entries in the catalogue (http://www.nationalarchives.gov.uk/catalogue/) for the Cities of London and Westminster.

Interpretation	The books contain a summary of the entries from the field books (IR 58). In those county record offices that hold the Domesday books, but not the field books, it enables a quick check to be made whether there was any deduction for public rights of way before a visit to Kew to look at the field book is scheduled. It is recommended, however, that where the field book entry can be obtained, it is used in preference to the Domesday Book entry, as the field books contain more information. Domesday books may also be helpful where the county record office does not have the Inland Revenue valuation maps available. This is because the names of the farms are listed against the hereditament numbers, and so can assist in determining whether a visit to Kew is needed.

Example for use in an application[35] – Bridleway

This is how Example 29 would look if there were no field book. Note the weaker conclusion than was made in Example 29 because less information is available to the researcher from this record.

30. Inland Revenue Valuation

a. [Introduction as in Example 29].

b. The Inland Revenue summarised the entries in the field books in 'Duties on Land Values' books, more commonly known as Domesday books. These show the same entries for hereditament number and deductions for public rights of way or user as are given in the field book and so provide useful information in the event that the field book is unavailable.

c. Broadenham Lane was shown on the Somerset 92 – 6 base map passing through hereditament 30 in Cricket St Thomas.

d. The Domesday Book for Cricket St Thomas and Winsham parishes is held at the Somerset Heritage Centre under reference DD/IR/T 12/3. It had previously been held by the Inland Revenue.

e. The Domesday Book has an entry against hereditament 30 of £13 for 'Public Rights of Way or User'. This indicates that the landowner claimed, and the valuer accepted, that there should be a deduction for a public highway. In the Domesday Book extracts below, the hereditament number and deduction have been circled for ease of identification.

35 Application made to Somerset County Council on 12 Mar 2009. Their reference 596M.

f. The applicant draws the conclusion that this is good evidence that highway rights existed along the route at the time of the survey. Unfortunately, it does not indicate the status of the highway (footpath, bridleway, or carriageway) and this must be deduced from other evidence.

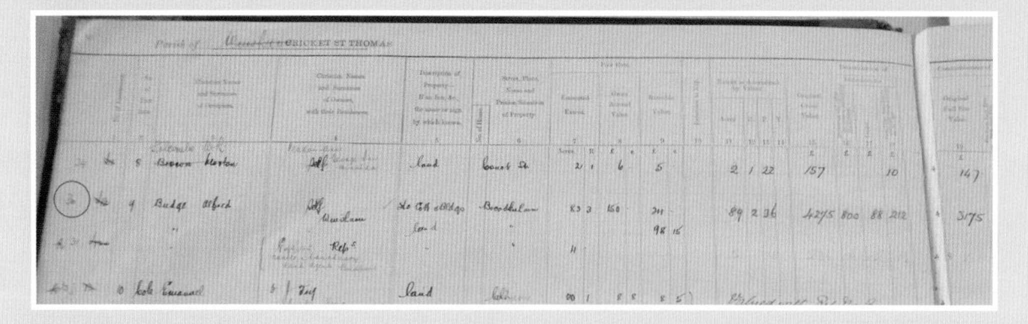

Figure 82: Extract from Domesday Book for Cricket St Thomas and Winsham Parishes (LH page)

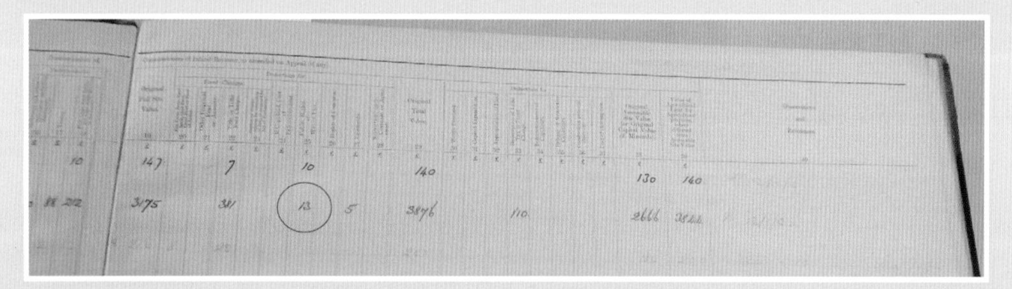

Figure 83: Extract from Domesday Book for Cricket St Thomas and Winsham Parishes (RH page)

The document in the above example is worth two stars if the field book evidence is unavailable and if the route is presently unrecorded because it was produced under statutory authority; the legislation permitted deductions for public paths; and deductions would have been resisted by the Inland Revenue, and so would have been checked before being allowed. However, no status is given, so if Broadenham Lane had been recorded as a footpath, it would be hard to argue that the deduction meant bridleway instead of footpath. The hereditament numbers are not given, so there is more uncertainty over the route that attracted the deduction.

Further Reading

Beech, Geraldine and Mitchell, Rose (2004) *Maps for Family and Local History*, The National Archives, ISBN 978-1-903365-50-2 (although now out of print, there is at least one copy on the shelves in the Map Room)

The Planning Inspectorate (2011) *Definitive Map Orders: Consistency Guidelines*.

3.18 Sales Documents

These were compiled when a public auction took place or public funds were used to buy farms. Although the dates continue to the current day, there were a large number of such sales during and after the First World War when many large estates were broken up. Some auctions sold just one very large estate which had lands in several parishes, while other auctions sold several smaller landholdings.

Star Rating	3
Held at	County Record Offices. (A very small number are held at The National Archives.) The National Monuments Record Centre (see section 7.5) holds some for large estates (for example the Church Commissioners and some universities).
Coverage	Throughout England and Wales, where such sales took place. They were compiled to inform potential buyers of the property available for sale.
Appearance	A variety of auction catalogues, all of which would have had one or more maps either stapled into the catalogue or tucked into the back cover.
Shape	Auction catalogues, usually grouped together as one document with the catalogues from a dozen or more sales.
Date	Various, mainly the first half of the 1900s. Some have been lost.
Locating	The document reference can usually be found via the parish name, sometimes on the computer and sometimes on a card index. If in doubt, ask the archivist for help.
Interpretation	These documents show which parcels of land were included in each lot for sale. They were drawn up by the landowner or his agent. The public roads will have been excluded from such sales and not included in any of the lots. It is safe to assume that the new owner did not buy such excluded land, and equally, that if the seller had owned it, he would have probably sold it. It is also worth checking the description of the lots to see if there is any mention of 'off xxxx lane/drove' and whether this was with an easement. If no easement is mentioned, it is reasonable to assume that none was necessary, and the lane/drove carried public rights. If a lot has an easement or public right of way over it, it is likely to be detailed in the particulars.

Always photograph the description of any lot in an auction catalogue which abuts a possible application route. It will say whether the lot is accessed off the route with an easement over the route, and if there is no easement, it points to the possible application route having public rights.

Land being split into lots would often be divided such that any public rights fell between lots rather than across them, as potential purchasers would be likely to pay more for land free from public access.

Occasionally the roads shown will have 'to xxx' or 'from yyy'.

Example for use in an application[36] – The Somerton Estate

31. Somerton Estate Sales Particulars (1920)

a. The Somerton Estate was sold by auction in 1920. Papers were prepared for prospective purchasers, and these are held at Somerset Heritage Centre under reference DD/KW/3.

b. The route of interest is known as Little Moors Furlong. The Estate Plan contained in the papers shows this route and Ricksey Lane in the same manner. Neither is included in any of the surrounding lots. Today Ricksey Lane is a road (public vehicular highway) and Little Moors Furlong has no recorded status.

c. The applicant draws the conclusion that this is evidence that the owner of the land considered Little Moors Furlong to be similar in status to Ricksey Lane at the time the sale particulars were drawn up. It would have been in the vendor's interest not to admit highways if he could get away with it, to maximise his sale returns.

36 Application made to Somerset County Council on 5 May 2011. Their reference 709M.

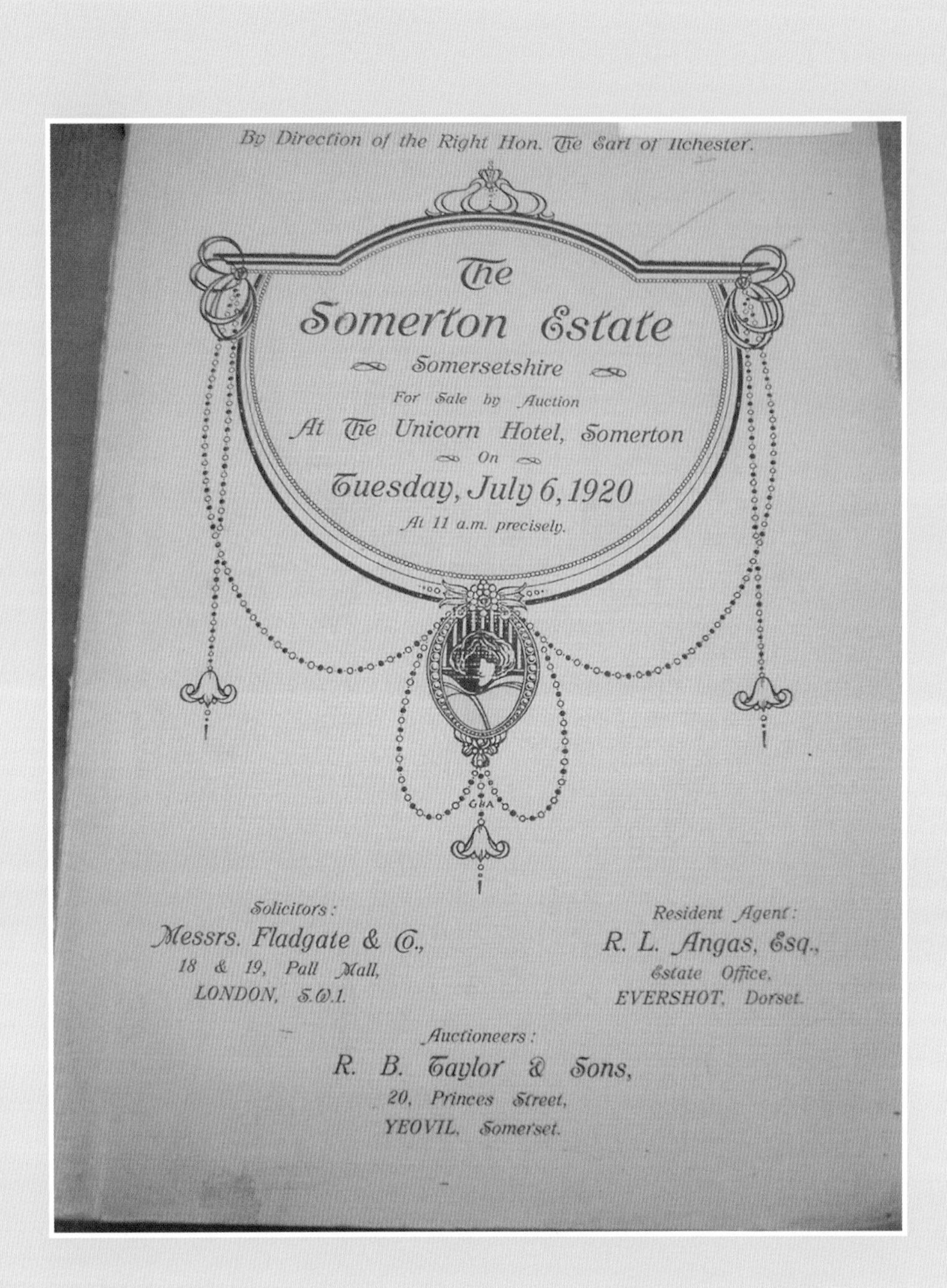
By Direction of the Right Hon. The Earl of Ilchester.

The Somerton Estate

Somersetshire

For Sale by Auction

At The Unicorn Hotel, Somerton

On

Tuesday, July 6, 1920

At 11 a.m. precisely.

Solicitors:

Messrs. Fladgate & Co.,

18 & 19, Pall Mall,

LONDON, S.W.1.

Resident Agent:

R. L. Angas, Esq.,

Estate Office,

EVERSHOT, Dorset.

Auctioneers:

R. B. Taylor & Sons,

20, Princes Street,

YEOVIL, Somerset.

Figure 84: Cover of Somerton Estate Sale Particulars Document (1920)

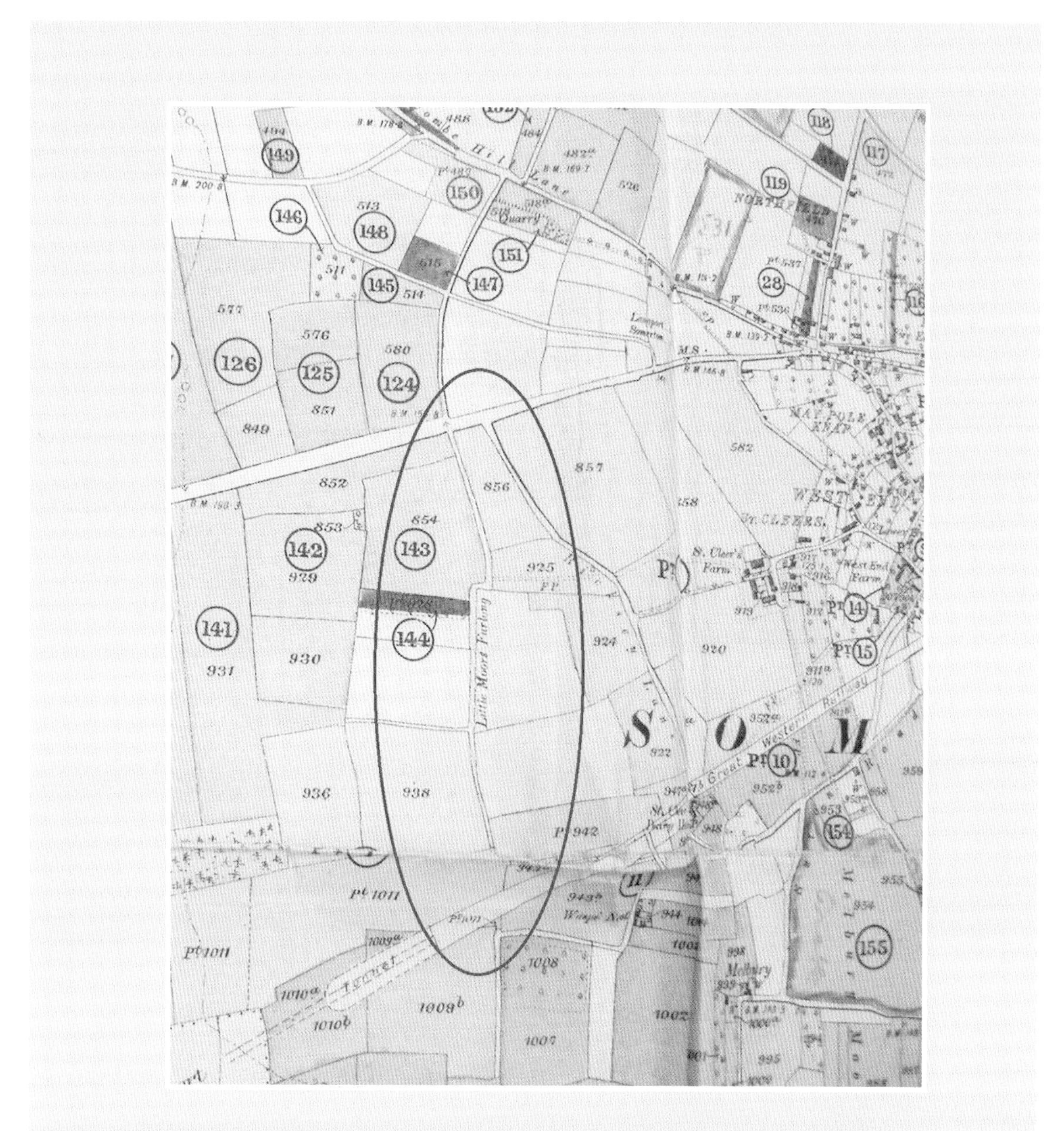

Figure 85: Extract of Somerton Estate Sale Particulars Document (1920)

The document in the above example is worth the full three stars (for an application at byway status) because it was produced for the surrounding landowner; it would have been in the vendor's interest not to disclose public highways; and the comparison argument has been applied between public vehicular routes and the application route.

Example for use in an application[37] – The Cadbury Estate

32. Cadbury Estate Sales Particulars (1877)

a. The Cadbury Estate was sold by auction in 1877. Papers were prepared for prospective purchasers, and these are held at Somerset Heritage Centre under reference DD/SCL/8.

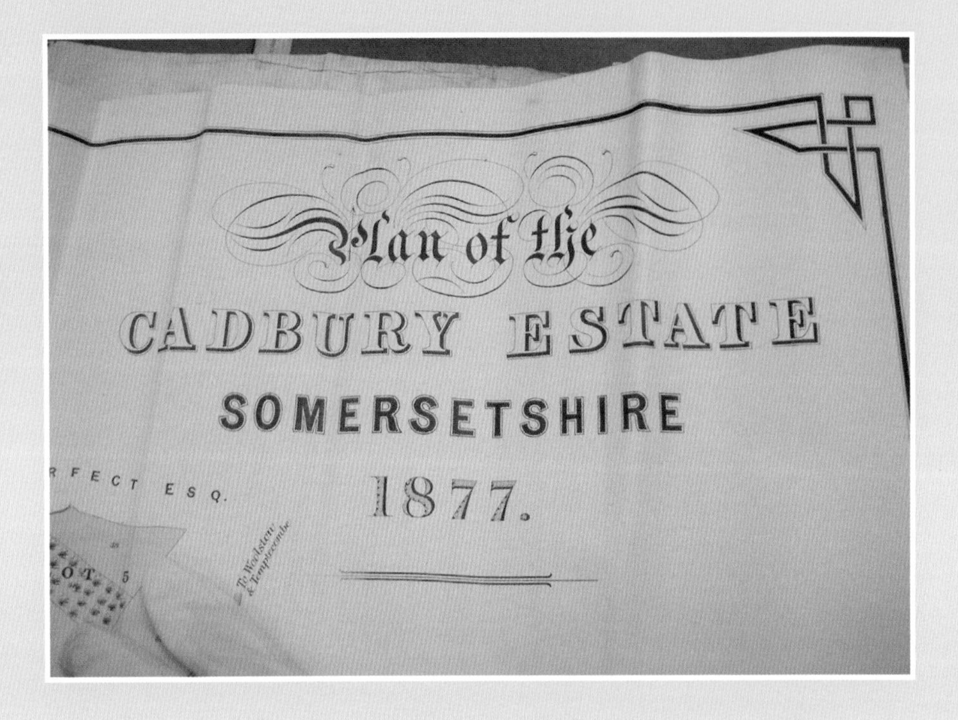

Figure 86: Cover of Cadbury Estate Sale Particulars Document (1877)

b. The route in question has been circled in red on the sales plan in the auction catalogue. This shows a road north of the trees surrounded but not included in lot 1, coloured the same as other tracks which are today public vehicular roads. This indicates that it was not included in the sale, and logically had the same status as the other tracks coloured sienna.

c. The applicant draws the conclusion that this is evidence that the owner of the land considered this route to be similar in status to the other public roads at the time the sale particulars were drawn up. It would have been in the vendor's interest not to admit highways if he could get away with it, to maximise his sale returns.

37 Application made to Somerset County Council on 15 May 2009. Their reference 650M.

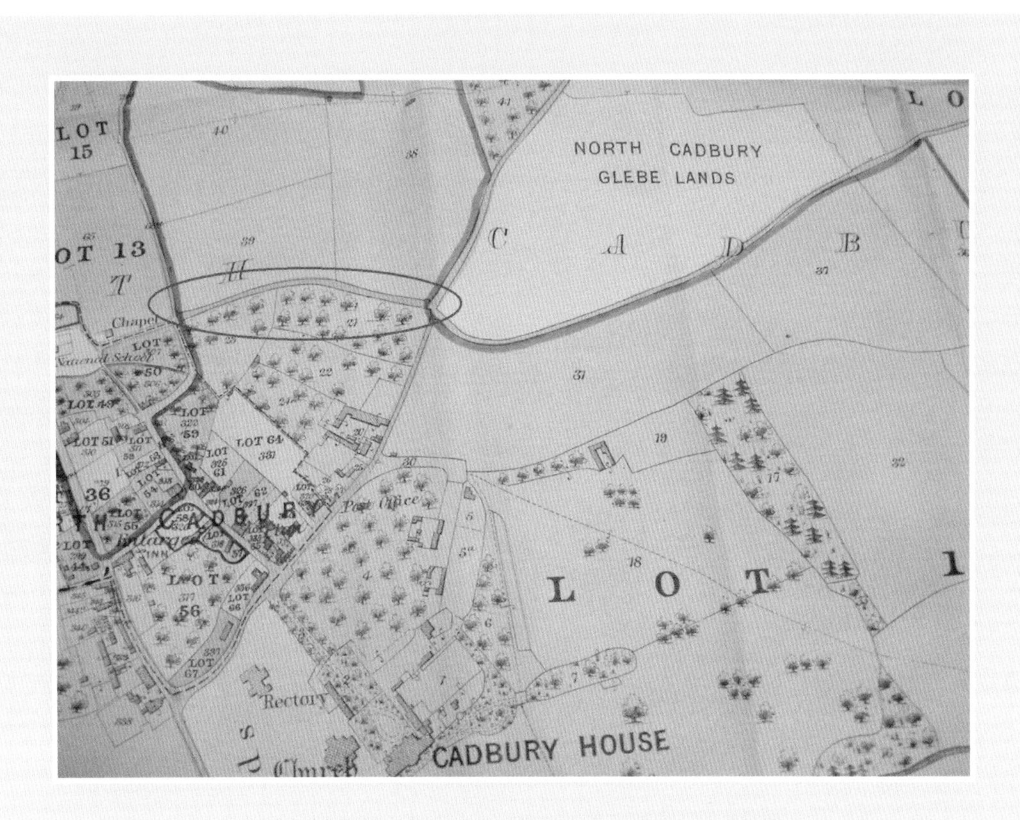

Figure 87: Extract from Cadbury Estate Sales Particulars (1877)

The document in the above example is worth the full three stars (for an application at byway status) because it was produced for the surrounding landowner; it would have been in the vendor's interest not to disclose public highways; and the comparison argument has been applied between public vehicular routes and the application route.

3.18.1 Valuations by the County Valuer

Typically these are records from when the county council purchased or valued holdings directly. They are not auction particulars but they hold similar information. These lands, parcels of land, or possibly smallholdings, were often purchased by the county council to give returning First World War servicemen a business.

Star Rating	3
Held at	County Record Offices
Coverage	Variable
Appearance	Generally a set of A4 pages folded into three, one of which will be a diagrammatic sketch of the land concerned.
Shape	Local to the land in the immediate area
Date	1910s to 1930s and maybe other dates
Locating	County Record Offices, references will be particular to each county
Interpretation	Shows the land to be purchased and gives a good description of it. They were bought with public money and scrutinised by the land agents at that time. [Note: Occasionally these holdings or part of them are sold at auction, and if there is evidence of an unrecorded right of way across the land, it is worthwhile bringing this to the attention of the county council's legal department and the auctioneers before the auction, so giving them the opportunity to dedicate the route.]
Caveats	Only available where such sales took place and the records survive. They were not compiled to show rights of way, however, they will show the network of roads relevant to the parcel(s) of land.

Example for use in an application[38] – The Calder Estate

33. Farm Valuation (1913)

a. The lands of the late Mr William C Calder were sold in 1913. This record is held by the Somerset Heritage Centre under reference number A BNK2-1.

b. Extract 1 shows the cover of the valuation record prepared by the County Valuer. Extract 2 shows the plan contained in the valuation, Extract 3 is text within the valuation document, and Extract 4 shows the valuation and appointment of the surveyor.

c. This document shows that the land, situated in Curry Rivel, Somerset, was accessed from what was recognised as a 'soft lane' and that no easement for access was required. The signatory of the document was the Valuer to the Smallholdings and Allotment Committee of the county council.

d. The fact that no easement was needed to access the land is good evidence that the lane was considered a public vehicular route. As supporting evidence, the applicant notes that other roads shown in a similar way in the document are part of the public road network today.

38 Application made to Somerset County Council on 26 Jun 2010. Their reference 689M.

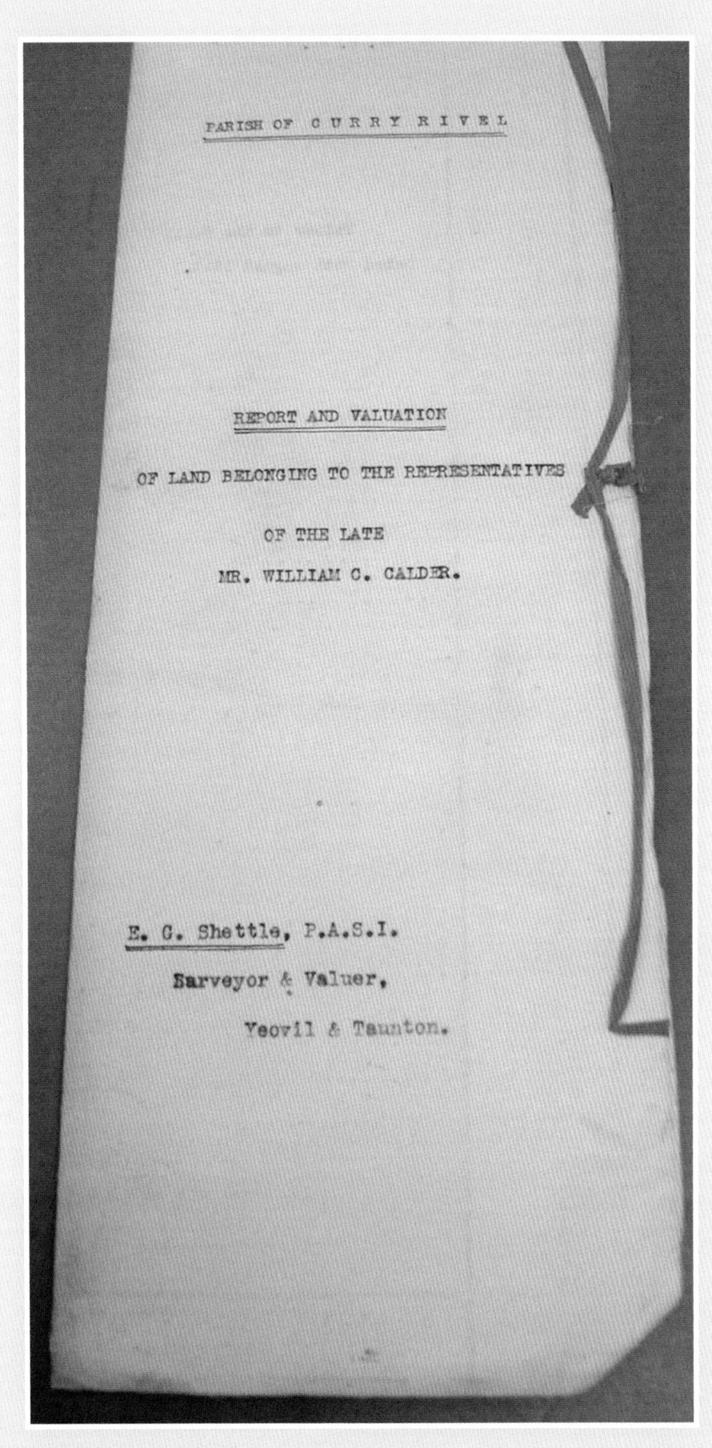

PARISH OF C U R R Y R I V E L

REPORT AND VALUATION

OF LAND BELONGING TO THE REPRESENTATIVES

OF THE LATE

MR. WILLIAM C. CALDER.

E. G. Shettle, F.A.S.I.

Surveyor & Valuer,

Yeovil & Taunton.

Figure 88: Extract 1 of the Report and Valuation by the Surveyor and Valuer for Yeovil and Taunton

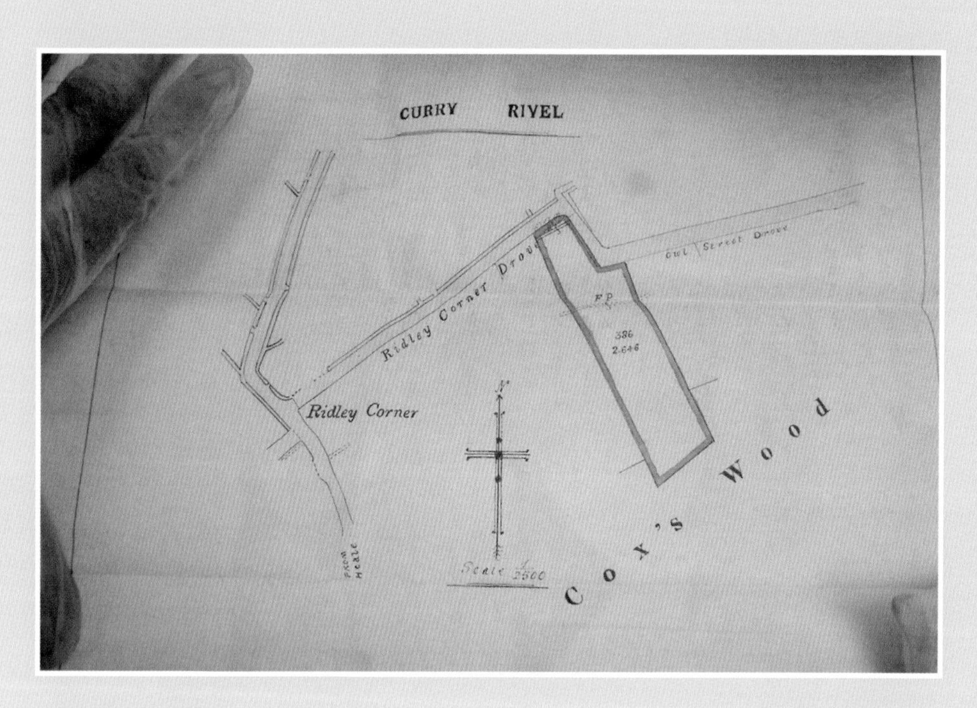

Figure 89: Extract 2 of the Report and Valuation by the Surveyor and Valuer for Yeovil and Taunton

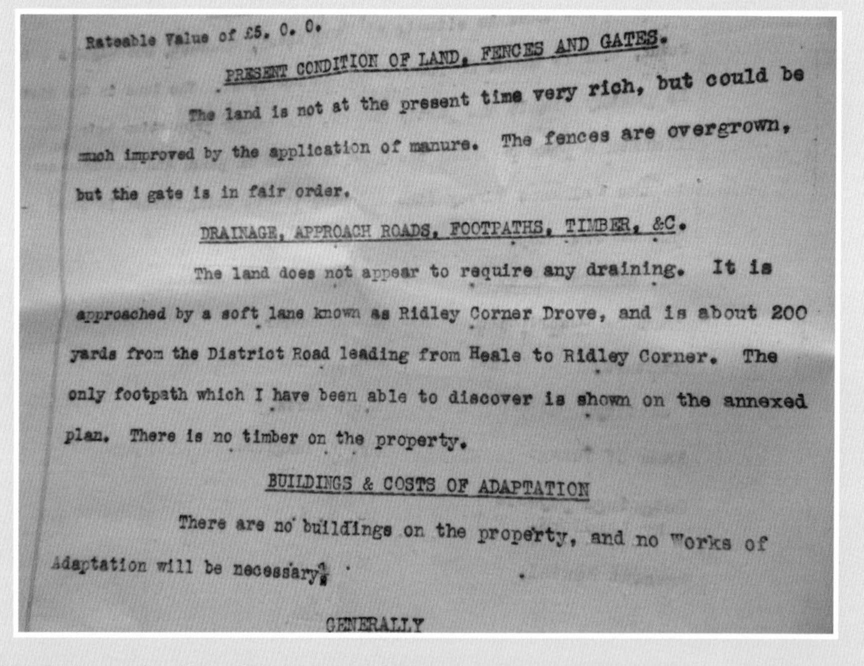

Rateable Value of £5. 0. 0.

PRESENT CONDITION OF LAND, FENCES AND GATES.

The land is not at the present time very rich, but could be much improved by the application of manure. The fences are overgrown, but the gate is in fair order.

DRAINAGE, APPROACH ROADS, FOOTPATHS, TIMBER, &C.

The land does not appear to require any draining. It is approached by a soft lane known as Ridley Corner Drove, and is about 200 yards from the District Road leading from Heale to Ridley Corner. The only footpath which I have been able to discover is shown on the annexed plan. There is no timber on the property.

BUILDINGS & COSTS OF ADAPTATION

There are no buildings on the property, and no Works of Adaptation will be necessary.

GENERALLY

Figure 90: Extract 3 of the Report and Valuation by the Surveyor and Valuer for Yeovil and Taunton

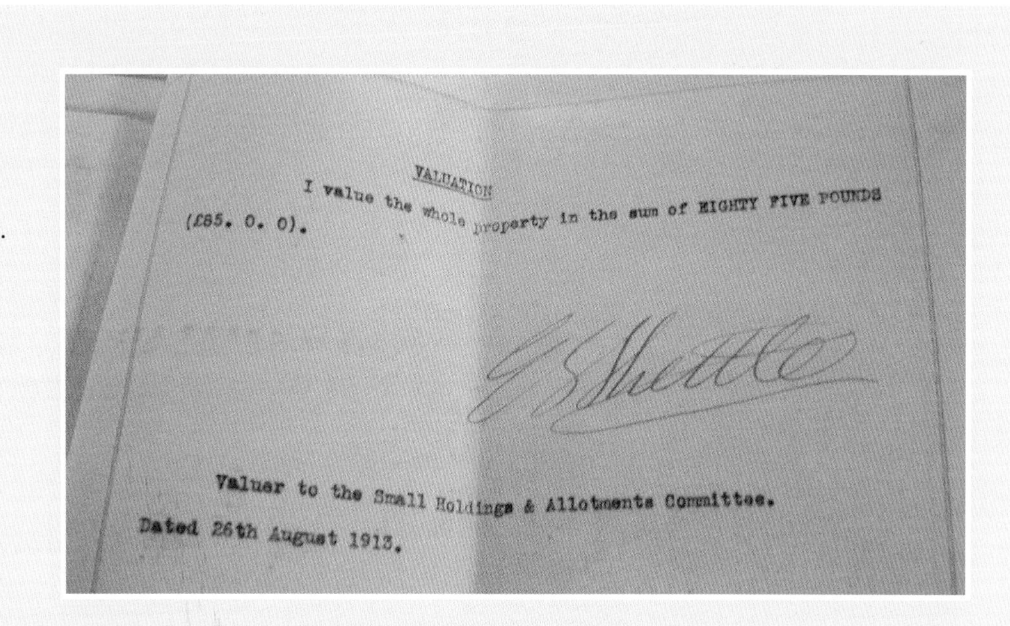

VALUATION

I value the whole property in the sum of EIGHTY FIVE POUNDS (£85. 0. 0).

Valuer to the Small Holdings & Allotments Committee.

Dated 26th August 1913.

Figure 91: Extract 4 of the Report and Valuation by the Surveyor and Valuer for Yeovil and Taunton

The document in the above example is worth the full three stars (for an application at byway status) because it was produced by the county council valuer for a committee decision on purchase; it would have been important for the valuer to have determined means of access, otherwise the valuation would have been vastly reduced; the route of the access highway is clearly shown on the plan.

Further Reading

http://www.english-heritage.org.uk/daysout/properties/national-monuments-record-centre/

National Monuments Record Centre.

3.19 Handover Maps

The Local Government Act 1929 caused county councils to take over highway responsibilities from the rural district councils on 1 April 1930. Many set about creating internal records of the routes for which they had become responsible, based on information supplied by the rural district, and these maps came to be known as 'handover maps'.

The handover map was not open to formal public inspection, although some councils did permit access. The information recorded was whatever the county surveyor found to be helpful in administering the highways. Some chose only to record public carriageways, while others recorded lesser highways via an extended classification system.

Some councils have a list instead of (or as well as) a map.

Star Rating	5
Held at	County Record Offices, County Land Charges departments or County Highways or Rights of Way departments.
Coverage	Variable
Appearance	Varies from county to county
Shape	County or rural district based
Date	1930s
Use with	Maps and schedules should be used together, if available.
Locating	Ask County Record Office, Rights of Way department, or Highways department.
Interpretation	As county surveyors would be unlikely to wish to pick up additional maintenance responsibility unnecessarily, the showing of a route on a handover map is usually good evidence that it existed as a highway maintainable at the public expense with at least the status shown in any key, or most likely vehicular if there was no key (although this ought to be demonstrated by looking for counter examples). Conversely the omission of a route from a handover map, if other evidence is strong, could just indicate omission by error, or from the fact that the surveyor wished to avoid maintaining a route that did not seem to him to be used much or of high value. The interpretation of the evidence will depend on all the circumstances.
Caveats	The handover map was not a public document in the sense that it was not open to public scrutiny. Many have been lost over the years. Those that came with a schedule or list giving more details may have become separated.

Example for use in an application[39] – Route not depicted on handover map

34. Handover Map

a. The highway handover map for Somerset is held in the Somerset Heritage Centre under reference C/S 1 G/370 and was prepared by the county council circa 1930. It comprises a series of Ordnance Survey map sheets covering the county, marked up with the highway information.

b. The handover map comes with a key defining types of highway. Five types are identified: first and second class roads, shown red and blue respectively; then roads carrying through traffic (green), roads of local importance only (brown) and roads of little importance (yellow).

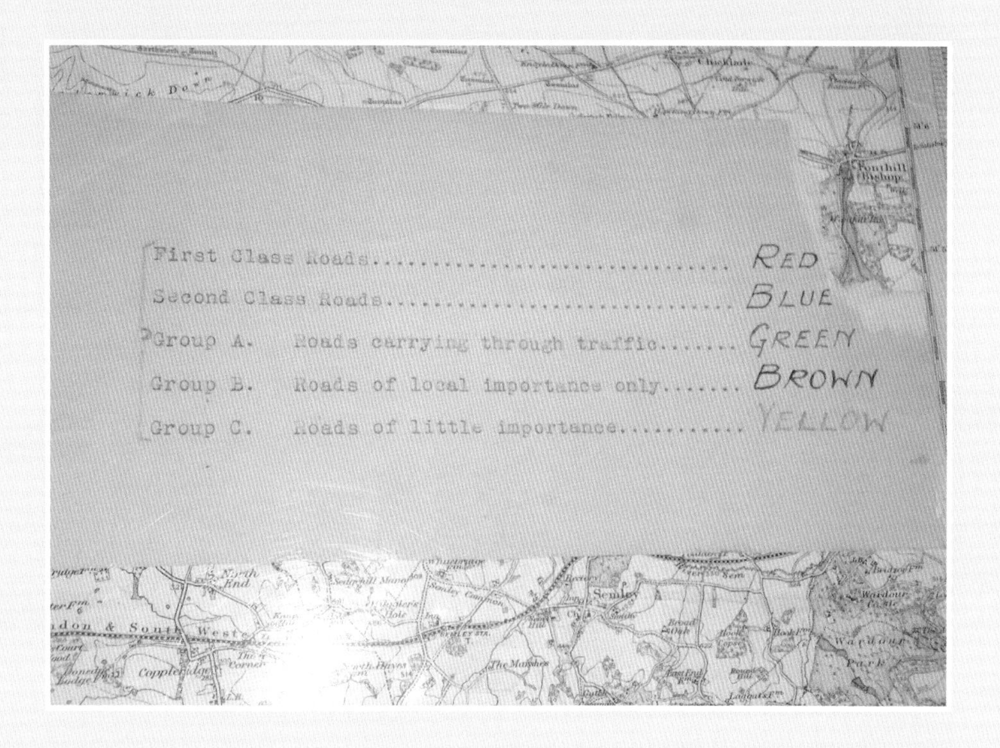

Figure 92: Key to the Somerset Handover Map

c. Broadenham Lane is shown on the Ordnance Survey base map as a well defined route, but is not coloured in, and so does not appear to have been handed over as a carriageway from the district council to the county council under local government reorganisation.

d. The omission of any colouring could be consistent with either a lower status than the handover map is showing, so, for example a footpath or bridleway rather than a carriageway, or it could relate to a vehicular highway that was not recorded by the district council at the time of the handover.

39 Application made to Somerset County Council on 12 Mar 2009. Their reference 596M.

e. Taken with the other evidence, for example the Inland Revenue valuation [see section 3.17], the applicant concludes this route is most likely a bridleway.

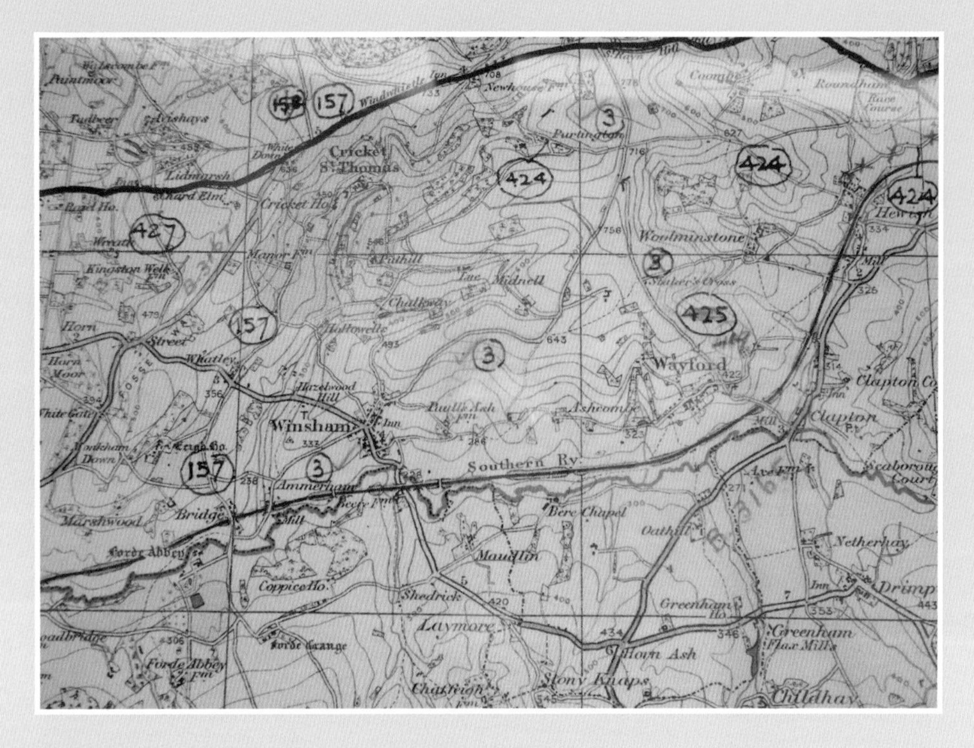

Figure 93: Extract of Handover Map showing Broadenham Lane

The document in the above example is worth no stars (for an application to add a route to the definitive map) because it does not show the route in question as a highway maintainable at the public expense.

Example for use in an application[40] – Route shown coloured on handover map

35. Handover Map

a. [Para a and b and the map key as in Example 34].

c. The application route runs from Moorhayes Farm to Gooselands Farm. It is shown in yellow on the handover map. The Key indicates that this means 'Roads of Little Importance'. Significantly, it was shown as a road, and footpaths and bridleways do not appear to have been coloured on the handover map. The route to the north of the eastern end of the application route is shown in the same colour as the application route, and is today recorded as a restricted byway.

d. The creation of handover maps was conducted by local government bodies in order to fulfil their statutory functions set out by an Act of Parliament. Accordingly the map is good evidence of the matters it shows, as both district and county councils would have had oversight of its contents. The application route is shown in the manner of roads, and footpaths and bridleways are not shown on the map. Accordingly, this is good evidence that the route carried public vehicular rights and hence should be recorded as a byway. Unless any of the exemptions set out in the Natural Environment and Rural Communities Act 2006 apply, this route will today carry restricted byway rights.

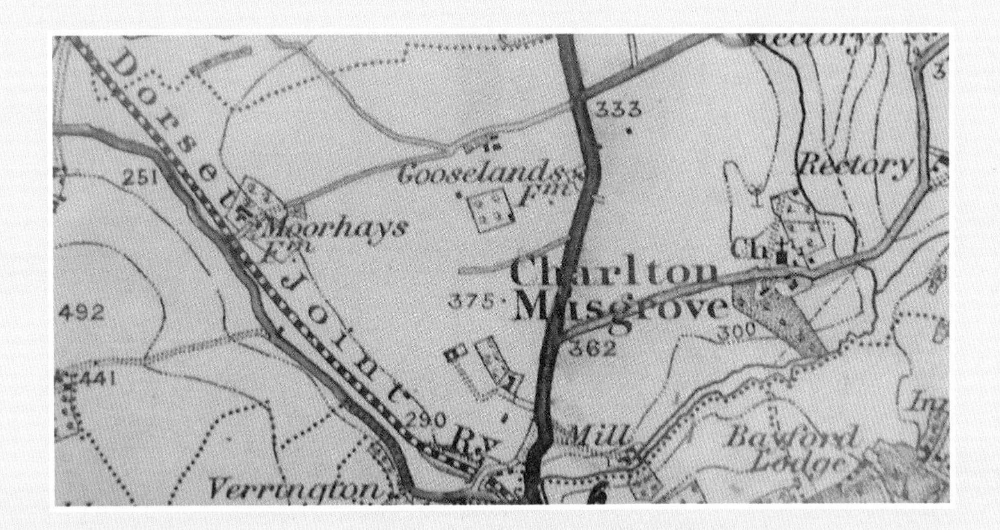

Figure 94: Extract of the Handover Map showing Lane at Moorhays

40 Application made to Somerset County Council on 2 Apr 2009. Their reference 643M.

The document in the above example is worth the full five stars (for an application at byway status) because it was produced by the district council and accepted by the county council for the statutory transfer of highway responsibility; the route is clearly defined; the key to the plan indicates that the route was a road (and there is no indication of handover of any footpaths or bridleways); and other routes shown in the same way on the plan are also recorded as byways today.

Further Reading

Sugden, John (September 1995) 'Highway Authority Records', RWLR 9.1 pp 1–9.

3.20 Stopping Up and Extinguishment Orders

Highway stopping up and extinguishment orders have been made for many years under various pieces of legislation. Many orders have been passed to The National Archives, while others are still held by the Highways Agency, Department for Transport, or county councils.

The first point of particular interest to the researcher is that the title 'stopping up order' is highly misleading. While these orders did stop up highways, they frequently set out replacement routes, and it is only by inspecting the orders that the full information is revealed.

Orders in this class were also used to enable utility companies to retain cables and pipes under highways that may have been installed under temporary War powers. These orders provide good evidence that the affected route was a highway since it would have been *ultra vires* to make a highway order on a route not having that status.

The orders will be a form of delegated legislation known as 'statutory instruments'. Each order or instrument will cite the legislation under which it was made, and which gives it authority. It may be necessary to look at this underlying legislation for a full understanding of the extent of the powers being used.

Regardless of how good any earlier evidence may be for a route having highway status, if it is stopped up, that earlier evidence is of no value. Those seeking to oppose an application to record a route might well wish to check for stopping up orders.

Star rating	10 for stopping up orders where the path is set out as the replacement highway
	5 for stopping up orders where the path is shown but is not the subject of the order
	5 where the path is shown in a retention of cables, mains and pipes order
Held at	The National Archives, series MT 78, and at county record offices.
Coverage	England and Wales – where the order was made, many occurred when land was being used for airfields during the War or developed for building projects, or where utility pipes and cables were being put under a highway.
Appearance	A Statutory Instrument (which will be a light buff coloured A5 document, typically two or three pages) with a map attached.

Shape	Local to the site of the extinguishment and/or creation of the highway concerned.
Date	Mainly 1900s. Many occurred during the War years near airfields. They are also used in association with construction and infrastructure projects, and are still being made today.
Locating	At The National Archives these are catalogued by parish, and the reference can be found by typing the parish name in the first line and MT 78 in the third line of the catalogue search engine (http://www.nationalarchives.gov.uk/catalogue/).

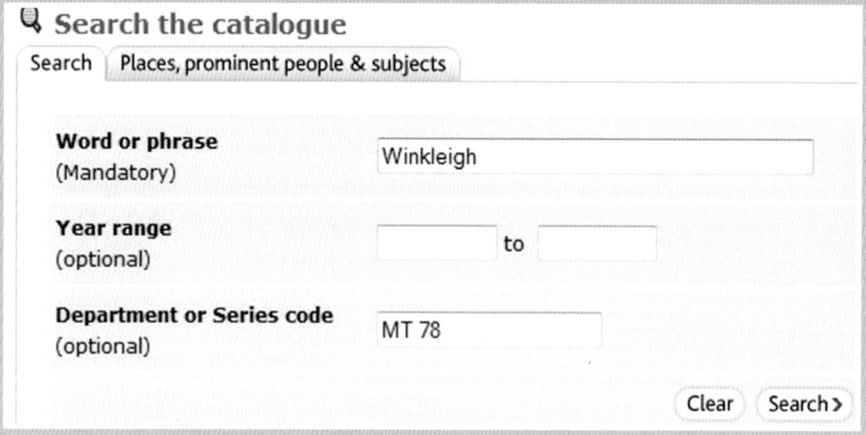

Search the catalogue

Search | Places, prominent people & subjects

Word or phrase (Mandatory): Winkleigh

Year range (optional): to

Department or Series code (optional): MT 78

Clear | Search >

Figure 95: TNA search for MT78 records

The result will show a list of orders affecting that parish. The level of information given is generally good.

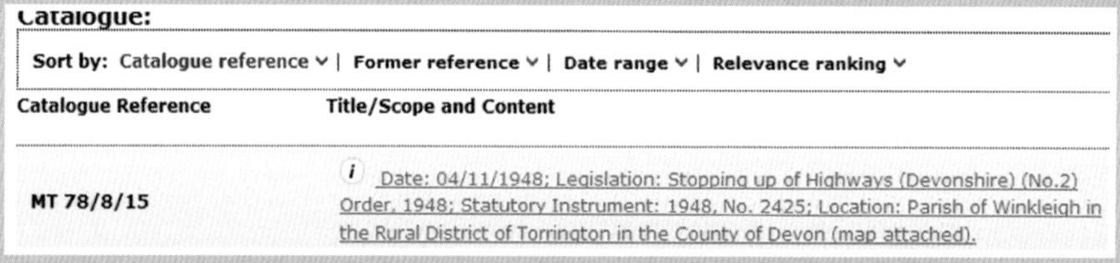

Catalogue:

Sort by: Catalogue reference | Former reference | Date range | Relevance ranking

Catalogue Reference	Title/Scope and Content
MT 78/8/15	Date: 04/11/1948; Legislation: Stopping up of Highways (Devonshire) (No.2) Order, 1948; Statutory Instrument: 1948, No. 2425; Location: Parish of Winkleigh in the Rural District of Torrington in the County of Devon (map attached).

Figure 96: TNA search for MT78 records – results

The catalogue reference indicates that this will be the fifteenth document in a large bundle. The document to be entered into the ordering system is MT 78/8. The county (or borough) name is in the title, and the parish a few short paragraphs further down the first page. Some copies have large red wax seals in the top left-hand corner.

Copies held by county record offices will be referenced differently, possibly under 'stopping up orders', or 'extinguishment orders'.

Interpretation	The descriptions and map will state exactly which highways were to be legally stopped up and which were to be created. The same legal mechanism was used to put public utilities pipelines and cables under roads and where these were done without easements it could be assumed that the highway being dug up was public. Although useful, many are only minor diversions of footpaths in urban areas, and of no relevance to bridleways or restricted byways. Some stopping up orders were time limited (that is, temporary in nature) and once expired, the route will have come back into being.
Caveats	Some councils are reluctant to make a modification order based solely on a stopping up order if the new route is not readily apparent on the ground. It is submitted, however, that a properly made stopping up order constitutes a legal event for the purposes of definitive map modifications.

Example for use in an application – Stopping Up of Highways Order (which creates alternative routes)

36. Stopping Up of Highways Order (1948)

a. The Stopping Up of Highways (Devonshire) (No. 2) Order 1948 is a statutory instrument (number 2425) made pursuant to the Requestioned Land and War Works Act 1948. The Original Order is held by The National Archives under reference MT 78/8/15.

b. The Order provides that an earlier (temporary) stopping up is to be maintained, and that two new highways are to be created in lieu of the old routes.

c. The Order constitutes a legal event, providing very strong evidence that the new routes are vehicular highways.

d. The application route is shown in the manner of roads, and footpaths and bridleways are not shown on the map. Accordingly, this is good evidence that the routes carried public vehicular rights and hence should be recorded as a byway. Unless any of the exemptions set out in the Natural Environment and Rural Communities Act 2006 apply, this route will today carry restricted byway rights.

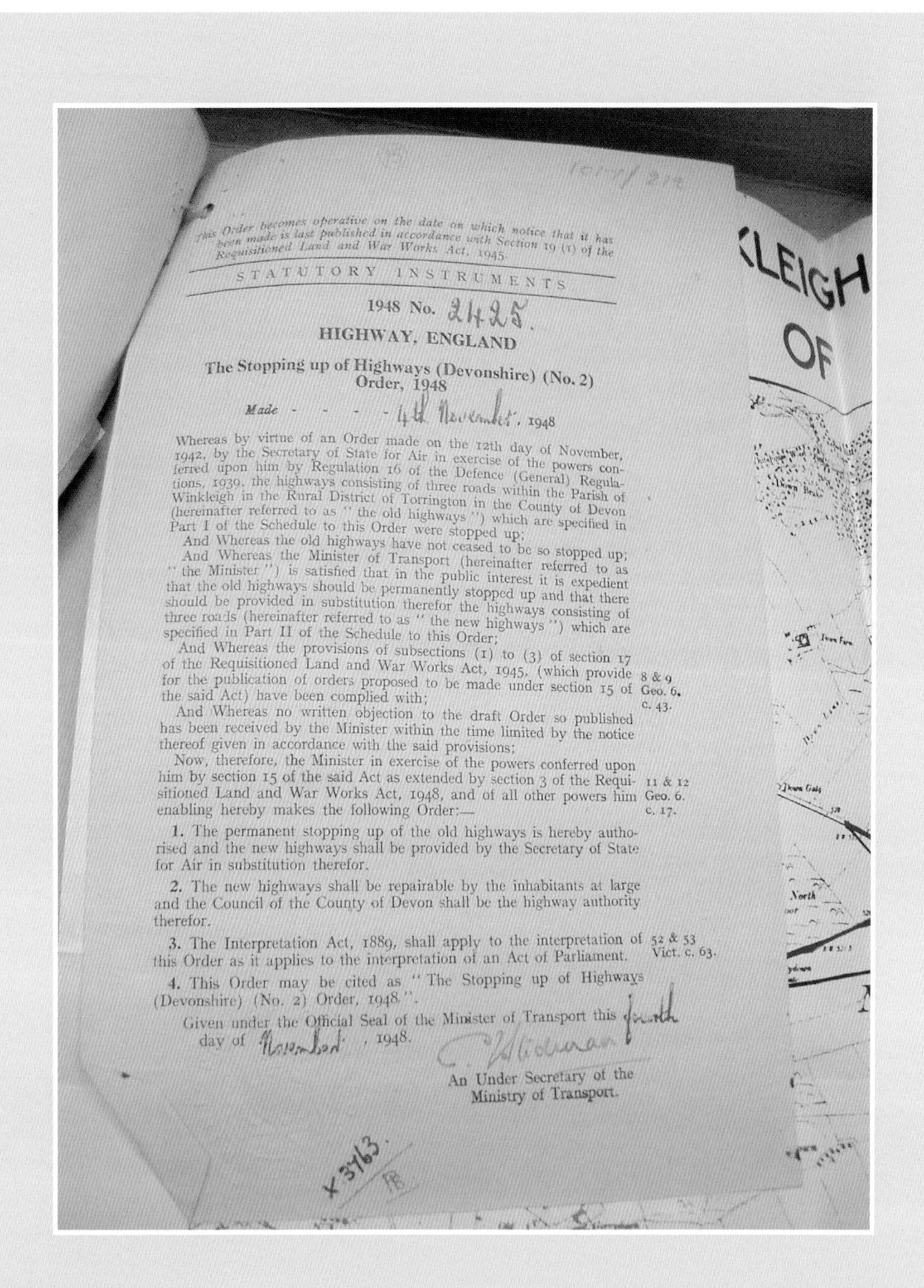

This Order becomes operative on the date on which notice that it has been made is last published in accordance with Section 19 (1) of the Requisitioned Land and War Works Act, 1945.

STATUTORY INSTRUMENTS

1948 No. 2425.

HIGHWAY, ENGLAND

The Stopping up of Highways (Devonshire) (No. 2) Order, 1948

Made - - - - 4th November, 1948

Whereas by virtue of an Order made on the 12th day of November, 1942, by the Secretary of State for Air in exercise of the powers conferred upon him by Regulation 16 of the Defence (General) Regulations, 1939, the highways consisting of three roads within the Parish of Winkleigh in the Rural District of Torrington in the County of Devon (hereinafter referred to as "the old highways") which are specified in Part I of the Schedule to this Order were stopped up;

And Whereas the old highways have not ceased to be so stopped up;

And Whereas the Minister of Transport (hereinafter referred to as "the Minister") is satisfied that in the public interest it is expedient that the old highways should be permanently stopped up and that there should be provided in substitution therefor the highways consisting of three roads (hereinafter referred to as "the new highways") which are specified in Part II of the Schedule to this Order;

And Whereas the provisions of subsections (1) to (3) of section 17 of the Requisitioned Land and War Works Act, 1945, (which provide for the publication of orders proposed to be made under section 15 of the said Act) have been complied with; (8 & 9 Geo. 6. c. 43.)

And Whereas no written objection to the draft Order so published has been received by the Minister within the time limited by the notice thereof given in accordance with the said provisions;

Now, therefore, the Minister in exercise of the powers conferred upon him by section 15 of the said Act as extended by section 3 of the Requisitioned Land and War Works Act, 1948, and of all other powers him enabling hereby makes the following Order:— (11 & 12 Geo. 6. c. 17.)

1. The permanent stopping up of the old highways is hereby authorised and the new highways shall be provided by the Secretary of State for Air in substitution therefor.

2. The new highways shall be repairable by the inhabitants at large and the Council of the County of Devon shall be the highway authority therefor.

3. The Interpretation Act, 1889, shall apply to the interpretation of this Order as it applies to the interpretation of an Act of Parliament. (52 & 53 Vict. c. 63.)

4. This Order may be cited as "The Stopping up of Highways (Devonshire) (No. 2) Order, 1948".

Given under the Official Seal of the Minister of Transport this fourth day of November, 1948.

An Under Secretary of the Ministry of Transport.

Figure 97: The Stopping Up of Highways (Devonshire) (No.2) Order 1948 – Page 1 (MT 78/8/15)

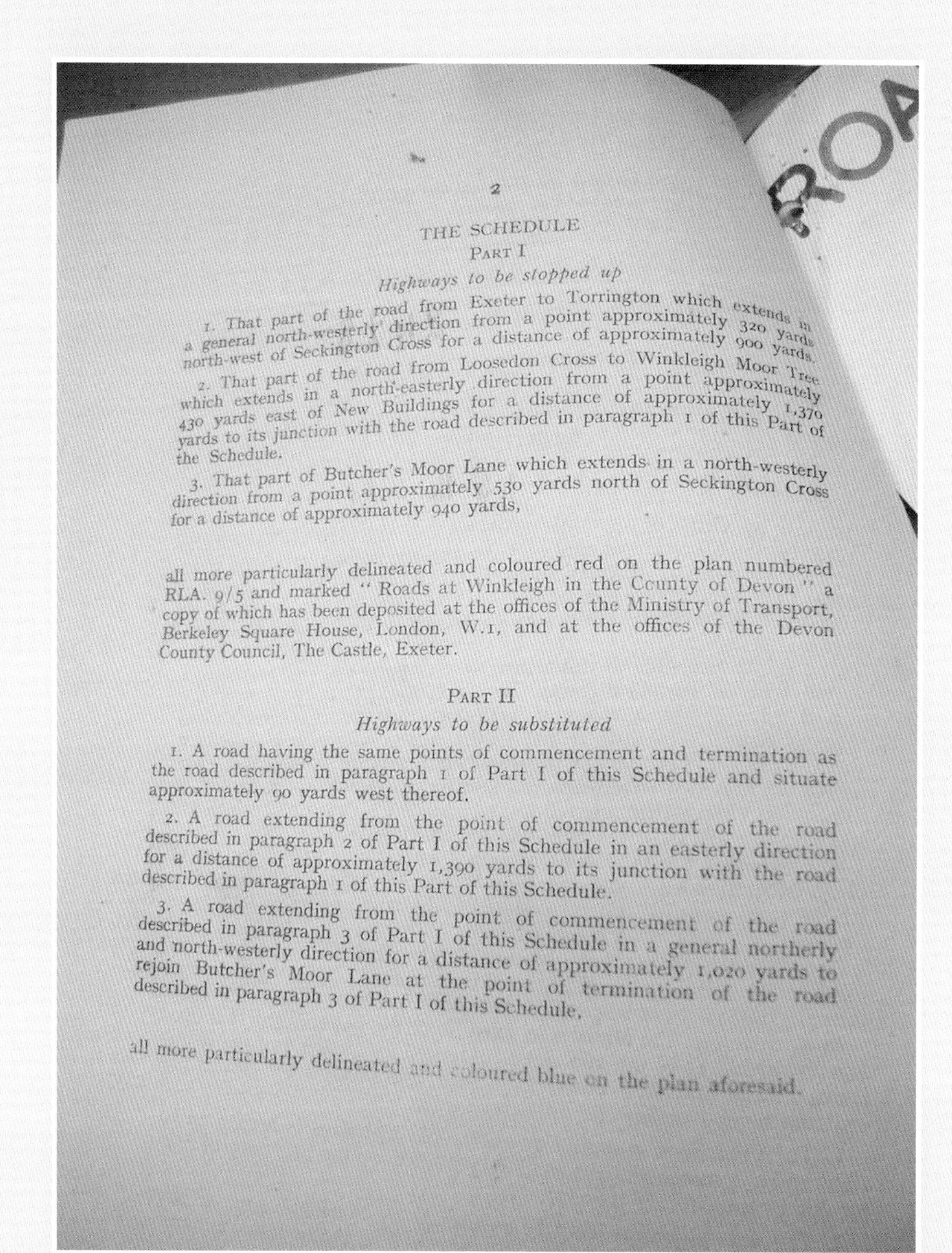
2

THE SCHEDULE

PART I

Highways to be stopped up

1. That part of the road from Exeter to Torrington which extends in a general north-westerly direction from a point approximately 320 yards north-west of Seckington Cross for a distance of approximately 900 yards.

2. That part of the road from Loosedon Cross to Winkleigh Moor Tree which extends in a north-easterly direction from a point approximately 430 yards east of New Buildings for a distance of approximately 1,370 yards to its junction with the road described in paragraph 1 of this Part of the Schedule.

3. That part of Butcher's Moor Lane which extends in a north-westerly direction from a point approximately 530 yards north of Seckington Cross for a distance of approximately 940 yards,

all more particularly delineated and coloured red on the plan numbered RLA. 9/5 and marked "Roads at Winkleigh in the County of Devon" a copy of which has been deposited at the offices of the Ministry of Transport, Berkeley Square House, London, W.1, and at the offices of the Devon County Council, The Castle, Exeter.

PART II

Highways to be substituted

1. A road having the same points of commencement and termination as the road described in paragraph 1 of Part I of this Schedule and situate approximately 90 yards west thereof.

2. A road extending from the point of commencement of the road described in paragraph 2 of Part I of this Schedule in an easterly direction for a distance of approximately 1,390 yards to its junction with the road described in paragraph 1 of this Part of this Schedule.

3. A road extending from the point of commencement of the road described in paragraph 3 of Part I of this Schedule in a general northerly and north-westerly direction for a distance of approximately 1,020 yards to rejoin Butcher's Moor Lane at the point of termination of the road described in paragraph 3 of Part I of this Schedule,

all more particularly delineated and coloured blue on the plan aforesaid.

Figure 98: The Stopping Up of Highways (Devonshire) (No.2) Order 1948 – Page 2 (MT 78/8/15)

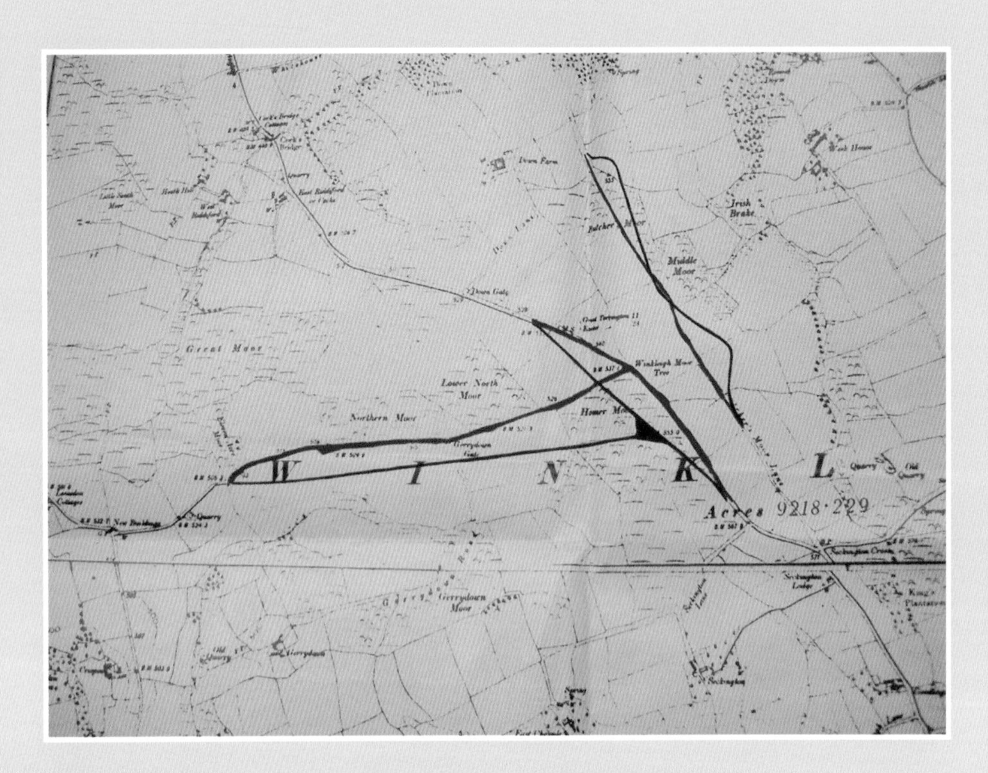

Figure 99: The Stopping Up of Highways (Devonshire) (No.2) Order 1948 – Plan (MT 78/8/15)

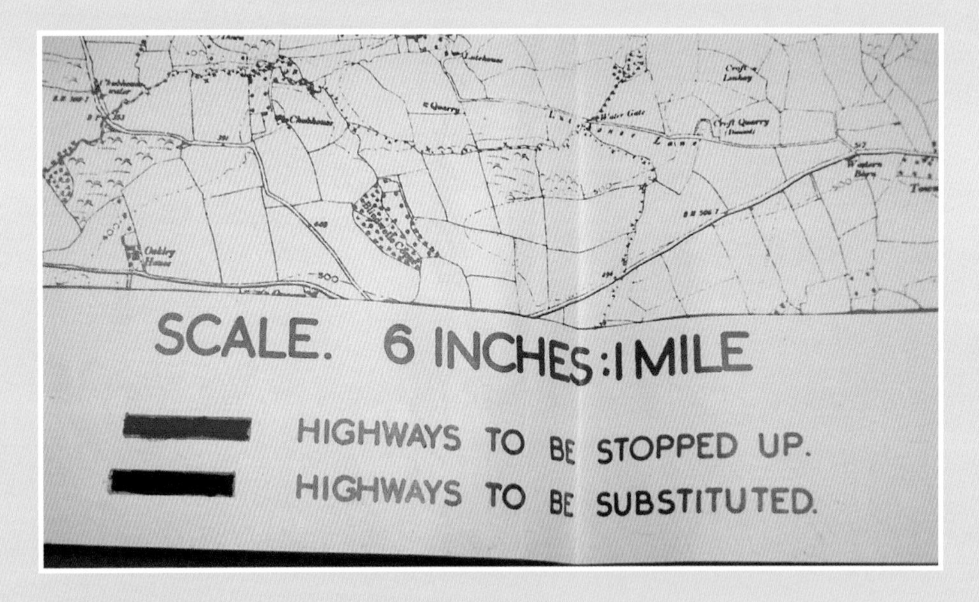

Figure 100: The Stopping Up of Highways (Devonshire) (No.2) Order 1948 – Key to Plan (MT 78/8/15)

The document in the above example is worth the full ten stars (for an application at byway status) because the new highways were set out under statutory powers in a signed and sealed order, which has come into effect. The Order gives the status of the new routes as 'roads'.

Example for use in an application – Retention of Cables etc under Highways Order

37. Retention of Cables Mains and Pipes under Highways (Somersetshire) (No.1) Order 1956

a. The Retention of Cables Mains and Pipes under Highways (Somersetshire) (No.1) Order 1956 is a statutory instrument (number 1395) made pursuant to the Requisitioned Land and War Works Act 1948. The Original Order is held by The National Archives under reference MT 78/42/1.

b. The Order provides that the placing of cables under the listed highways was performed for War purposes, and that it is in the public interest for the rights to retain the cables to be permanent.

c. While the Order does not directly alter highway rights, it requires that the routes were highways in order that the Order could be made at all. This is therefore good evidence of the reputation of the listed highways at the time the Order was made. In addition, it refers to the highways as roads, thus suggesting the presence of vehicular rights.

d. The application route, Rod Lane, has two locations where cables pass under it. These cables are authorised by the Order. Accordingly, this is supporting evidence that the routes carried public vehicular rights. Unless any of the exemptions set out in the Natural Environment and Rural Communities Act 2006 apply, this route will today carry restricted byway rights.

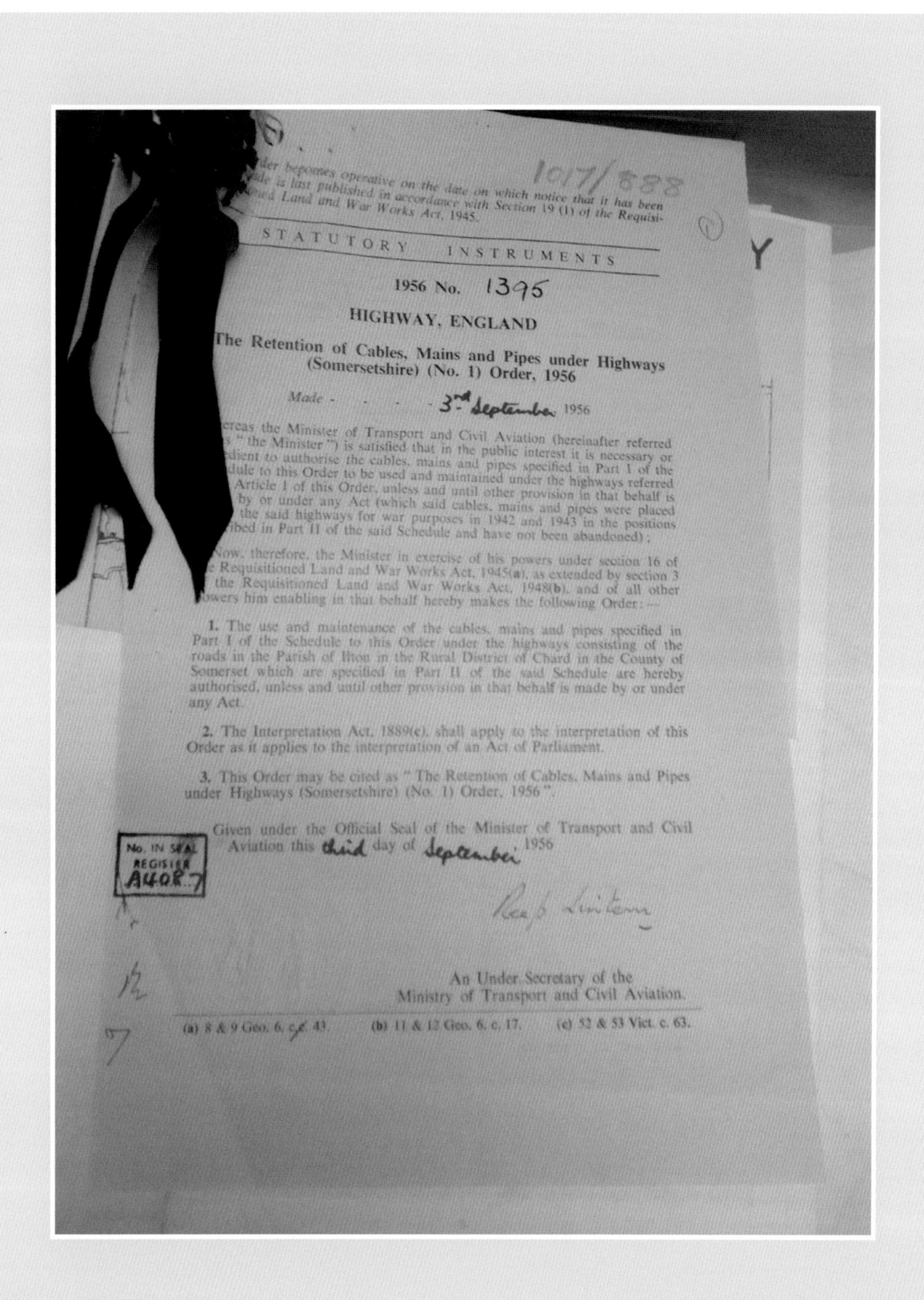

der becomes operative on the date on which notice that it has been
de is last published in accordance with Section 19 (1) of the Requisi-
ned Land and War Works Act, 1945.

1017/888

STATUTORY INSTRUMENTS

1956 No. 1395

HIGHWAY, ENGLAND

The Retention of Cables, Mains and Pipes under Highways (Somersetshire) (No. 1) Order, 1956

Made - - - - 3rd September 1956

ereas the Minister of Transport and Civil Aviation (hereinafter referred s "the Minister") is satisfied that in the public interest it is necessary or dient to authorise the cables, mains and pipes specified in Part I of the dule to this Order to be used and maintained under the highways referred Article 1 of this Order, unless and until other provision in that behalf is by or under any Act (which said cables, mains and pipes were placed the said highways for war purposes in 1942 and 1943 in the positions ibed in Part II of the said Schedule and have not been abandoned);

Now, therefore, the Minister in exercise of his powers under section 16 of e Requisitioned Land and War Works Act, 1945(**a**), as extended by section 3 the Requisitioned Land and War Works Act, 1948(**b**), and of all other owers him enabling in that behalf hereby makes the following Order:—

1. The use and maintenance of the cables, mains and pipes specified in Part I of the Schedule to this Order under the highways consisting of the roads in the Parish of Ilton in the Rural District of Chard in the County of Somerset which are specified in Part II of the said Schedule are hereby authorised, unless and until other provision in that behalf is made by or under any Act.

2. The Interpretation Act, 1889(**c**), shall apply to the interpretation of this Order as it applies to the interpretation of an Act of Parliament.

3. This Order may be cited as "The Retention of Cables, Mains and Pipes under Highways (Somersetshire) (No. 1) Order, 1956".

Given under the Official Seal of the Minister of Transport and Civil Aviation this third day of September 1956

No. IN SEAL REGISTER A4087

An Under Secretary of the
Ministry of Transport and Civil Aviation.

(**a**) 8 & 9 Geo. 6, c. 43. (**b**) 11 & 12 Geo. 6. c. 17. (**c**) 52 & 53 Vict. c. 63.

Figure 101: The Retention of Cables etc (Somersetshire) (No.1) Order 1956 – Page 1 (MT 78/42/1)

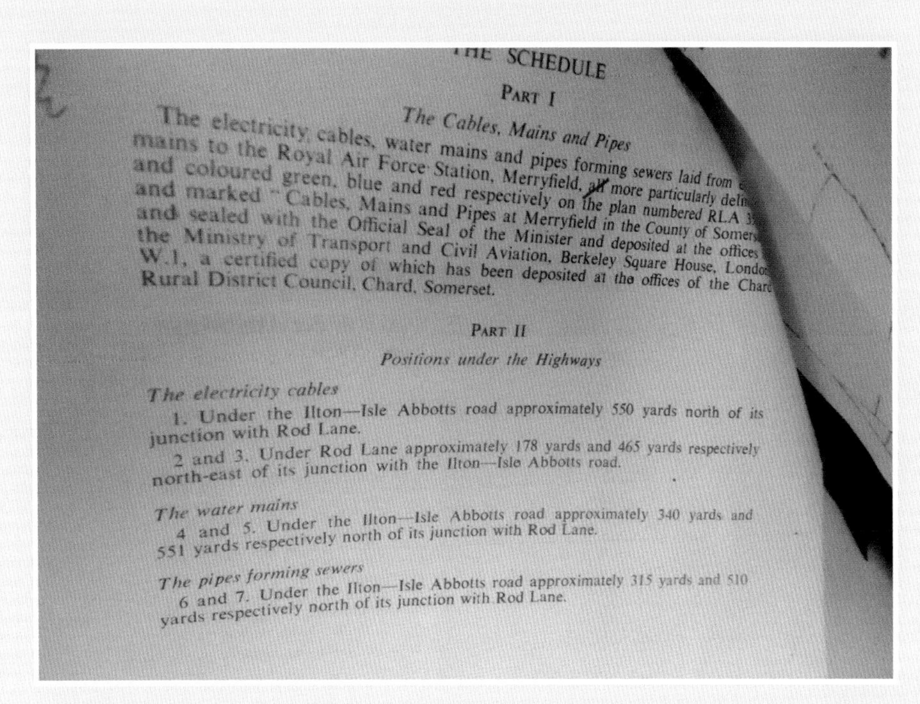

THE SCHEDULE

PART I

The Cables, Mains and Pipes

The electricity cables, water mains and pipes forming sewers laid from [illegible] mains to the Royal Air Force Station, Merryfield, all more particularly deli[illegible] and coloured green, blue and red respectively on the plan numbered RLA [illegible] and marked "Cables, Mains and Pipes at Merryfield in the County of Somers[illegible] and sealed with the Official Seal of the Minister and deposited at the offices [illegible] the Ministry of Transport and Civil Aviation, Berkeley Square House, Londo[illegible] W.1, a certified copy of which has been deposited at the offices of the Char[illegible] Rural District Council, Chard, Somerset.

PART II

Positions under the Highways

The electricity cables

1. Under the Ilton—Isle Abbotts road approximately 550 yards north of its junction with Rod Lane.

2 and 3. Under Rod Lane approximately 178 yards and 465 yards respectively north-east of its junction with the Ilton—Isle Abbotts road.

The water mains

4 and 5. Under the Ilton—Isle Abbotts road approximately 340 yards and 551 yards respectively north of its junction with Rod Lane.

The pipes forming sewers

6 and 7. Under the Ilton—Isle Abbotts road approximately 315 yards and 510 yards respectively north of its junction with Rod Lane.

Figure 102: The Retention of Cables etc (Somersetshire) (No.1) Order 1956 – Page 2 (MT 78/42/1)

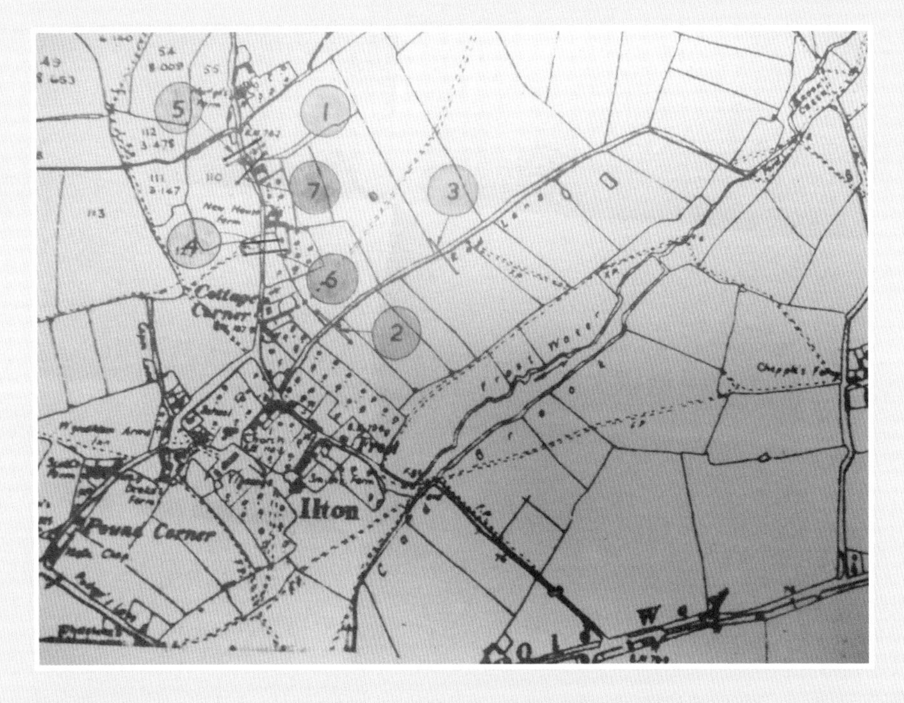

Figure 103: The Retention of Cables etc (Somersetshire) (No.1) Order 1956 – Plan (MT 78/42/1)

The document in the above example is worth five stars (for an application at byway status) because it is referred to as a highway in an order made under statutory powers, but the order did not directly affect the highway; the route is clearly shown in the plan forming part of the order and the text of the order makes its status (as road) clear. Had the route not been a highway, it would not have needed to be mentioned in the order.

3.21 Ministry of Agriculture and Fisheries Farm Survey Records

These records were compiled during the War to collect data on food production. Each farm holding was inspected and a report made. These records include descriptions of the land holding, the crops and livestock, and the people living and working on the land and their standard of farming. The base maps used were the county series Ordnance Survey.

For highways purposes, the MAF 73 records are the most interesting, although other researchers will find a wealth of local history information in MAF 32.

Star Rating	2
Held at	The National Archives, class/series MAF 73 and MAF 32
Coverage	England and Wales
Appearance	MAF 73 are produced in folders containing 4 or 16 individual sheets each (one full sheet, less if there are fewer maps in a grid on the edge of the county); occasionally there are folders for several sets of individual sheets in one box. MAF 32 records are in separate files for each parish and there are three or four forms for each farm.
Shape	MAF 73 are in the Ordnance Survey county grid system, MAF 32 are by parish, and then individual farms within the parish.
Date	1940 to 1944
Use with	The MAF 73 series contains the maps, and the MAF 32 series contains the reports on the individual farms. It is necessary to use the maps first to get the farm numbers for use with MAF 32.
Locating	The MAF 73 series is referenced by county, so each county has a number. This is easily found on the online catalogue (http://www.nationalarchives.gov.uk/catalogue/) by entering the county name in the top box and MAF 73 in the third box on the catalogue search screen. This reveals that Hertfordshire is 18. The required individual sheet number is added to make a reference of MAF 73/18/32 for the MAF record on the Ordnance Survey base map for Hertfordshire XXXII. The example search shows the county first and then starts to list the individual files. This will produce a folder containing either 4 quarter sheets or the 16 smaller sheets in the normal way.

Search the catalogue

Search | Places, prominent people & subjects

Word or phrase (Mandatory)	Hertfordshire
Year range (optional)	to
Department or Series code (optional)	MAF 73

Clear | Search >

Figure 104: TNA search for MAF73 records

Catalogue:

Sort by: Catalogue reference | Former reference | Date range | Relevance ranking

Catalogue Reference	Title/Scope and Content
MAF 73/18	Hertfordshire. Described and orderable at item level

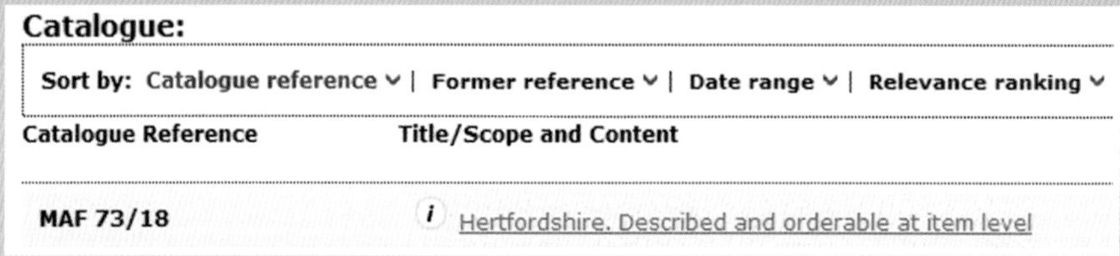

Figure 105: TNA search for MAF73 records – results

The MAF 32 series are referenced by parish. Type the parish name in the top line and MAF 32 in the third line.

So to get the complete record, order the map, and then check the reference number written on the farm holding, which will be a two phase number, the first half is the parish number and the second is the individual farm holding.

Interpretation

MAF 73: The individual farm holdings were identified on the maps by a coloured outline and the farm number. Where the property on either side of a track was in different ownership, the track was usually excluded from either property, which is helpful to show it was not privately owned. Where the track runs between fields which were part of the same farm, the coloured outline includes them.

MAF 32: There are separate records for each farm detailing various data from the standard of farming and crops grown to the type of soil, and the water and road access. Although very interesting and providing information about the people and the farm, the records of the different farms are not usually helpful for highways purposes. Occasionally there will be reference to a road, but it is very unlikely to specify the status of the road.

Example for use in an application[41]

38. Ministry of Food National Farm Survey (1941–2)

a. These records are held at The National Archives in Kew. They are maps prepared in conjunction with the individual farm records of the National Farm Survey conducted by the (then) Ministry of Food (subsequently the Ministry of Agriculture, Fisheries and Food). The maps show the extent of each farm, or other agricultural holding, with its boundaries. The area of each farm is indicated on the map by the use of a colour wash, and its code number is added in black ink. The relevance of these records is that where unproductive land (such as a vehicular highway or river) runs between holdings, it is excluded from the holdings.

b. This application route is on base map Hertfordshire XXXV SW. The relevant document reference at The National Archives is MAF 73/18/35.

c. The application route, Barley Mow Lane, is shown inside the red oval. The continuation of the route to the south is recorded on the definitive map as byway Colney Heath 52, and is shown inside a green rectangle.

d. We can see that the northern part of the application route falls between holdings and is excluded. The southern part of byway Colney Heath 52 also falls between holdings and is excluded. The southern part of the application route and the northern part of byway Colney Heath 52 are inside a land holding and so are not excluded.

e. The applicant draws the conclusion that the northern part of the application route had the same status as the southern part of byway Colney Heath 52, namely that of a vehicular highway.

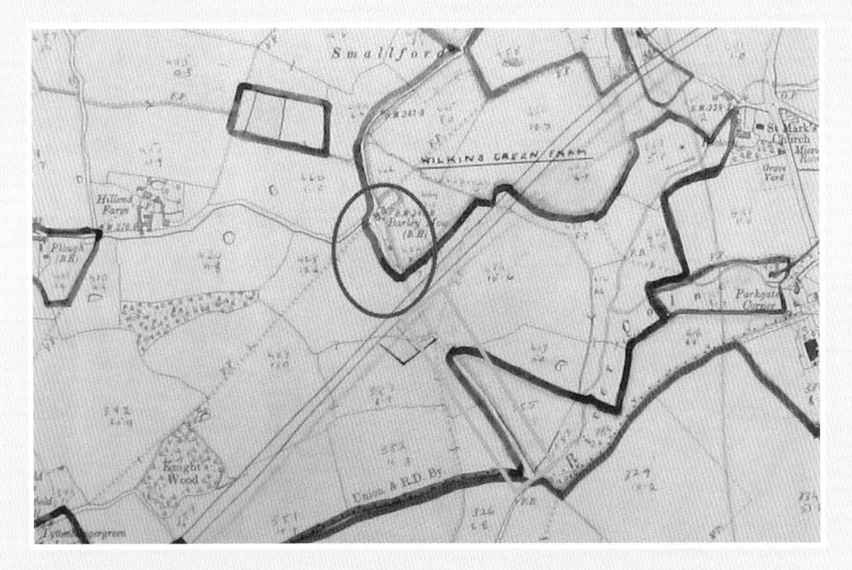

Figure 106: Extract from Ministry of Food Farm Survey Map XXXV SW

41 Application made to Hertfordshire County Council on 25 Jan 2010. Their reference STA/130.

The document in the above example is worth two stars (for an application at byway status) because the valuer considered the routes to be excluded from the agricultural holding. This only occurred when unproductive land fell between holdings. Carriageways are unproductive land. Inspection of the route shows it was not unproductive land of another sort (like a river).

Further Reading

Beech, Geraldine and Mitchell, Rose, (2004) *Maps for Family and Local History*, The National Archives, ISBN 978-1-903365-50-2 (although now out of print, there is at least one copy on the shelves in the Map Room).

3.22 County Council Records

Relevant documents are held by county councils and unitary authorities in their roles as surveying and as highway authorities.

Document	Definitive map original surveys (sometimes erroneously called walking surveys)
Held at	County council and unitary authority offices (variously held by rights of way departments, legal departments or in county record offices)
Value	These are the original surveys, conducted under s.27 National Parks and Access to the Countryside Act 1949 for the purpose of creating the definitive map. Parish councils were required (s.28(3)) to hold a parish meeting for the purpose of considering the information to be provided by the council to the county council. The parish council may have a copy of the information they supplied to the county councils in the 1950s, and the county councils should certainly have the information. It may be held by the rights of way department or legal department rather than the county record office, and enquiries should be made to ascertain this. The records may show whether any status was suggested in the initial surveys, and how it was resolved at the time.

Document	Draft, provisional and definitive maps, and correspondence
Held at	County council and unitary authority offices (variously held by rights of way departments, legal departments or in county record offices)
Value	The process of creating the initial definitive maps was long and provided many opportunities for public involvement. Each stage will have records that may shed light on why a route is or is not recorded today. To allow an understanding of any records uncovered, it is worth explaining the main steps in the process. All section numbers given relate to sections in the National Parks and Access to the Countryside Act 1949. After the initial surveys, surveying authorities were required to produce draft maps of their area, and to make this available for four months for formal public inspection (s.29(1)). Members of the public could make representations or objections to any path shown, or not shown, in the draft map, and the council had to consider these and give the objector a chance to be heard. Any changes the authority decided were needed had to be advertised in the London Gazette and in local newspapers allowing further representations or objections to be made. Where further such objections occurred, the authority again had to give the objector a chance to be

heard before deciding whether a path should be shown or not. Any person still aggrieved after this process could appeal to the Minister (s.29(5)).

When all appeals had been exhausted, the Council prepared a provisional map comprising the particulars in the draft map, as modified by the hearings and appeals that had taken place (s.30). The provisional map was placed on deposit for public inspection but only owners, lessees and occupiers were permitted to object at this stage. Objections were made by way of complaint to Quarter Sessions (s.31).

Once all objections were determined, the authority prepared the first definitive map (s.32).

The notation to be used in the maps was prescribed by Regulations (s.38). The Regulations made provided that maps would show footpaths as solid purple lines, bridleways as solid green lines, and roads used as public paths as green dashes.

Document	Special Review papers
Held at	County council and unitary authority offices (variously held by rights of way departments, legal departments or in county record offices)
Value	Under the Countryside Act 1968, surveying authorities were supposed to reclassify roads used as public paths (RUPPs) on their definitive maps to footpath, bridleway or byway status. Each authority had to conduct either a 'Limited Special Review' of the definitive map in which only the status of RUPPs was considered, or a 'Special Review' in which other changes could also be considered. Many Special Reviews had not been completed by the time the law was changed by the Wildlife and Countryside Act 1981. Where the period for making representations or objections to the draft Special Review map had expired, but the review was abandoned, any change that was proposed in the Special Review that attracted no objections can be made on today's definitive map by an order under s.55(5) of the 1981 Act. Such orders do not require consultation or a further objection period, and come into effect on their being made.[42] If this section applies, no research of documents pre-dating the Special Review map is required.

42 An example is The Hertfordshire County Council (Aldenham 22) Modification Order 1995, which changed a footpath on the definitive map to a bridleway, once it was found that bridleway status on the Special Review map had attracted no objections.

Document	List of streets maintainable at the public expense.
Held at	County council and unitary authority offices (variously held by rights of way departments, roads or highways departments, legal departments or in county record offices)
Value	This is a record that must[43] be maintained by the highway authority. It records those highways that the authority considers are maintainable at the public expense (although does not necessarily mean that they have been spending money on maintenance recently). The showing of a route on the list is good evidence that the route is a highway. In many areas it is possible to advance the argument that because footpaths and bridleways are not shown in the list, carriageway rights are likely to exist on the routes it does include. Unfortunately, there is no public oversight of changes to the list, and some authorities have been found to remove routes in error. Therefore, any copies or extracts of lists can be of great value should such a mistake occur, and it will be evidence that helps add a highway back on the list. Not all removals are mistakes: if a highway is stopped up, or if its maintenance liability is removed by the Magistrates,[44] then it would be a legitimate removal. The list must 'be kept deposited at the offices of the council by whom it was made and may be inspected by any person free of charge at all reasonable hours'. Where a list is created by a county council in an area that also has district councils, 'the county council shall supply to the council of each district in the county an up to date list of the streets within the area of the district that are highways maintainable at the public expense, and the list so supplied shall be kept deposited at the office of the district council and may be inspected by any person free of charge at all reasonable hours'.[45]

43 s.36(6) Highways Act 1980 (previously s.25 Highways Act 1959 and s.1(4) Rights of Way Act 1932).

44 s.47 Highways Act 1980.

45 s.36(7) Highways Act 1980.

Document	Council stopping up and diversion orders
Held at	County council and unitary authority offices (variously held by rights of way departments, legal departments or in county record offices)
Value	It is possible that the route is not recorded today because it has been stopped up or diverted at some time in the past, by an administrative order of a council. This means it won't be found in the Quarter Sessions records (section 3.13) or at TNA (section 3.20). If you are researching just one or two routes, it may be worthwhile asking the highway authority if they have any record of a previous stopping-up or diversion, before investing many hours of research effort. If a diversion is uncovered, don't forget that a diversion of footpath rights where the path historically had higher rights will have left the higher rights in situ. In those circumstances, research will be needed to show the higher rights and so have them recorded.

Document	Landowner Deposits under s.31(6) Highways Act 1980
Held at	County council and unitary authority offices (variously held by rights of way departments or legal departments).
Value	These documents must be made available for public inspection by s.31A Highways Act 1980. They will show any routes admitted to have highway status by a landowner, and are usually accompanied by a statement that no other ways are admitted as highways. Where a route is shown that is not on the present definitive map (or is shown at a higher status than on the present definitive map), this is evidence of landowner dedication, and scores 5 stars under our star scheme.

Document	Side Roads Orders
Held at	Department for Transport, county council and unitary authority offices (variously held by rights of way departments, legal departments or in county record offices)
Value	Side roads orders are the orders made by government departments, usually the Department for Transport, in order to make changes to highways that cross the route of a major road scheme. While copies should reside with the department that made them, they are often hard to locate that way. Most highway authorities will have copies of the side roads orders that affected their area.

They have particular value as they constitute a legal event of the changes they made to highways. If a side roads order is found that placed a footpath or bridleway or road over or under or alongside a new main road, but the path hasn't made it to the current definitive map, the order can be used by the surveying authority to make a legal event order to just add the path to the definitive map without the need for advertisements and potential challenge. This is because the legal change has already happened, and it is only the recording aspect that has yet to take place. The authors have found it helpful to examine the definitive map for changes of status adjacent to major roads, and then to check the side roads orders to confirm all rights are properly recorded.[46]

46 The Hertfordshire County Council (North Mymms 083 and Potters Bar 079) Legal Event Modification Order 2007 was made following one of the authors' finding a copy of The A1(M) Motorway and Connecting Roads (Cecil Road to Roestock Section) Scheme 1975. This enabled a bridge over the motorway to be recorded.

3.23 Other Records

There are various other sources of rights of way evidence. They may provide additional evidence to the sources described above. However, as they have more limited applicability than the foregoing sources we are just listing them here.

Document	Victorian History of England
Held at	The National Archives and some county record offices
Value	Good historical background that usually describes the local road network. It may also direct the researcher to other useful records.

Document	Route cards produced by organisations like the Ancient Order of Packriders.
Held at	Occasionally found in second-hand bookshops
Value	Generally made for travellers, and hence provide evidence of public status.

Document	Parish Minute Books
Held at	Clerk to relevant parish council, sometimes transferred to county record offices
Value	Occasionally entries will be found in parish council minute books making a complaint about a blocked right of way, giving evidence that the parish considered it to be a highway.

Document	Manorial Documents Register
Held at	The official repository of the register is The National Archives. Actual records may be held in a county record office or a private archive. Often these records will be in another part of the country to the land or area concerned.
Value	In general too early to shed much light.

Document	Aerial photographs
Held at	National Monument Record Centre, some county record offices
Value	These will not prove legal rights but may well show where a route went, which will then assist with further research.

Document	Road books such as Paterson's Roads (1808)
Held at	Available as a CD reprint from 'Archive CD books'
Value	Very good evidence of highway rights on various roads across the country. As modern equivalent routes are often along routes that were bypasses to the original roads, these can be more helpful than initially thought.

Document	Quarry Records
Held at	Either CROs or county council offices. Some quarrying companies may also allow access.
Value	Records may relate to planning applications which show diversions or temporary or permanent closures of rights of way. Others may have been created in lieu of those being stopped up.

4. USER EVIDENCE

Historical documents are not the only way of proving current highway status. Highways researchers should be aware that highways still come into being through public use of a route. It is often helpful to surveying authorities to receive any statements of past and current use by members of the public. A full treatment of the subject may be found in Riddall and Trevelyan, page 141.

Further Reading

Riddall, John and Trevelyan, John (2007) *Rights of Way: A Guide to Law and Practice*, 4th edn, Ramblers' Association and Open Spaces Society, ISBN 978-1-901184-99-0.

4.1 Statutory Presumption of Dedication

Section 31 of the Highways Act 1980 provides that where a way, other than a way of such a character that use of it could not give rise at common law to any presumption of dedication, has been actually enjoyed by the public, as of right and without interruption, for a period of 20 years, the way is deemed to have been dedicated as a highway unless there is sufficient evidence that the landowner demonstrated no intention during this period to dedicate the route. The 20 year period applies retrospectively from the date on which the right of the public to use the way was brought into question.

User evidence is needed to show that the route was used for at least 20 years measured back from when use was brought into question (whether by the landowner stopping use or by someone applying for a modification order, or some other means), was use 'as of right', and was by members of 'the public'. Because each requirement is the subject of case law decisions, this method is beyond the scope of this present book.

The statutory presumption of dedication no longer applies to use by mechanically-propelled vehicles.[1]

1 s.66 Natural Environment and Rural Communities Act 2006.

4.2 Dedication of Highway at Common Law

Should the test for statutory dedication fail under section 31 of the 1980 Act then it may be appropriate to consider the dedication of the way at common law. Dedication at common law requires consideration of three issues: whether any current or previous owners of the land in question had the capacity to dedicate a highway, whether there was express or implied dedication by the landowners and whether there is acceptance of the highway by the public. Evidence of the use of a path by the public as of right may support an inference of dedication and may also show acceptance by the public.

Much of the consideration given to dedication at common law relates to whether *implied* dedication can be inferred from the later conduct of the landowner and of the users of the route. There are many legal rules relating to such presumed dedication at common law, and this subject is beyond the scope of this present book. However, where *express* dedication is made, usually in the form of a deed, this can be an extremely quick and powerful method of securing highway status in agreement with a landowner, and without needing any intervention from local authorities. A good treatment of express dedication can be found in Rachel Thompson's guide.

Further Reading

Thompson, R (2011) *Creating Multi-user Public Rights of Way – A Guide for Local Groups*, Ash Tree Publications, ISBN 978-0-9517222-2-0.

4.3 Preventing Dedication through Long User

In simple terms, since 1932,[2] it has been possible for a landowner to deposit declarations and plans with the highway authority stating which highways on his land he admitted existed and that he has no intention of dedicating any further ones. If subsequent declarations were made within six years, this prevented evidence of long user during the period covered by declarations from giving rise to presumed dedication. The present re-enactment of this rule is found in s.31(6) Highways Act 1980, and the maximum time between declarations has been extended[3] to ten years.

2 s.1(4) Rights of Way Act 1932.
3 Countryside and Rights of Way Act 2000 Sch 6 para 3.

Nothing in a deposit made under this section can affect any highway rights that have already come into existence, even if they are not yet recorded.

Some deposits provide positive evidence from the landowner of the existence of rights of way that are not yet on the definitive map. These carry a rating of five stars.

4.4 Effect of Countryside and Rights of Way Act 2000

Some people believe that the cut-off date set by s.53 Countryside and Rights of Way Act 2000 does not apply to user evidence based applications. This is incorrect: s.53 provides that footpaths and bridleways that existed (in law) on 16 December 1949 and are not recorded on 1 January 2026 are extinguished by statute on 1 January 2026, subject to some specific exemptions.

While it will be possible to apply for routes to be recorded as highways after 1 January 2026 on the basis of user or documentary evidence, the surveying authority will then always need to examine when the highway might have come into being. If it was created before 16 December 1949 and is stopped up by s.53, then the fact that it is still in use in 2027 will not give sufficient evidence to meet the 20 year test, as such evidence will only count from 2 January 2026. However, if the route is shown only to have come into existence on or after 17 December 1949, then it will not have been stopped up in 2026, and so user evidence across the cut-off date will still be usable.

At the time of going to press, s.53 has not yet been brought into force by Parliament but it can be brought into force very quickly when the appropriate Minister decides to do so, so this should not be taken as any indication that the power will not be used in due course. The only certain thing is that there is a desire in Parliament to cease recording routes based on historic evidence, so the faster any unrecorded ways are recorded, the better.

5. PREPARING A MODIFICATION ORDER APPLICATION

5.1 Introduction

This chapter explains how to make an application for an order to modify the definitive map and statement. It is concerned with the mechanics of the application rather than the evidence needed to persuade the surveying authority that an order should be made.

Section 53(5) of the Wildlife and Countryside Act 1981 allows any person to apply for an order that modifies the definitive map and statement for the area. The same process applies for applications to add rights to the definitive map and for those to remove rights from the definitive map. Schedule 14 to the Act provides more details about the process.

In May 2012, the government started a consultation[1] on the law relating to changes to the definitive map. We note the main effect of the proposals where it would change the process. However, the authors encourage all who would apply to change the definitive map not to delay pending legislation, as such changes could take several years before they are in force.

5.2 Practice

An application consists of the statutory form, a map showing the route, and copies of the evidence that the applicant believes shows it reasonable to allege that the definitive map and statement require modification. It is usually helpful to submit a statement (as illustrated in the yellow-tinted sections in Chapter 3 and in section 5.8) explaining why the evidence points to the need for an order to be made.

1 DEFRA, *Improvements to the policy and legal framework for public rights of way*, May 2012.

Surveying authorities (county councils and unitary authorities) are required by s.53(2) to modify the definitive map and statement as soon as reasonably practicable after discovering evidence that shows that the map needs to be altered. However, few authorities will do so (except for those modifications following the coming into operation of a legal event like a diversion order) unless they receive an application in the form laid down by the Regulations[2] made under the 1981 Act.

If a formal application is made that is compliant with the 1981 Act and its Regulations, and no action is taken by the surveying authority, a request can be made after 12 months to the Secretary of State asking that he direct the authority to determine the application within a set period of time. However, he will not consider such a complaint unless the formalities have all been complied with. It is therefore advisable always to make applications in the standard form rather than just submitting the evidence under cover of a letter.

In 2008, the Court of Appeal examined[3] what needed to occur for an application to be properly made. It decided that all three requirements of paragraph 1 of Schedule 14 to the Wildlife and Countryside Act 1981 had to be satisfied: (1) the application must be in the form set down by the Regulations; (2) it must be accompanied by a map at the required scale that shows the line of the application route, and (3) it must be accompanied by copies of any (that is, every) document that the applicant wishes to produce in evidence. While the circumstances of the judgment were dependent on when an application had been properly made, as the provisions of another Act depended on this date, the authors believe that it is vitally important always to ensure the paragraph 1 requirements are met in full, since future legislation could also have a test hinging on this point. The authors always ask the surveying authority to confirm compliance with paragraph 1's requirements so that if any defect is found it can be quickly remedied.

2 Wildlife and Countryside (Definitive Maps and Statements) Regulations 1993. SI 1993 No 12.

3 *R (on the application of Winchester College and Humphrey Feeds Ltd) v Hampshire County Council and the Secretary of State for Environment, Food and Rural Affairs* [2008] EWCA Civ 431.

5.3 Before the Application

5.3.1 Collect Evidence

Collect together all the evidence available relating to the path in question. Determine whether the evidence is sufficient, on the balance of probabilities, to show that one of the tests in s.53(3)(b) or (c) is met. For the newcomer to making modification order applications, the authors generally look for at least seven stars worth of evidence (defined in section 3.1) before making an application.

For the addition of a path, the surveying authority has to determine whether the path at the claimed status 'subsists' (on the balance of probabilities) or is 'reasonably alleged to subsist'. Case law[4] makes it clear that these two conditions are distinct. For example, an application based on user evidence showing use of the route and a landowner's evidence saying that it was with permission can still cause the authority to make an order: it is reasonable for the applicant to allege that the route subsists, and only an inquiry will allow sufficient cross-examination for the truth of the landowners' contradiction to be tested.

For changing the status of a path already shown (for example from footpath to bridleway), the surveying authority must be satisfied on the balance of probabilities that the higher rights subsist.

For reducing the rights recorded on the definitive map, the surveying authority must be shown how either an error had been made in the recording process, or that the route has subsequently had its status changed.

5.3.2 Check for Sufficient Evidence

In order to succeed, an application needs both to cause a 'discovery of evidence'[5] and contain enough to show, on the balance of probabilities, that the applied-for highway status exists.

The requirement for the 'discovery of evidence' means that some evidence must be provided with the application which has never been

4 *R v Secretary of State for Wales, ex parte Emery* [1998] 4 All ER 367.

5 *Burrows v Secretary of State for Environment, Food and Rural Affairs* [2004] EWHC 132 (Admin).

considered previously by the surveying authority in connection with a definitive map change. For this reason, it is important not to make half-hearted applications, since then pieces of 'new' evidence may be discovered but not cause a change to the map, so denying someone making a fuller application the ability to have an order made. The need for a discovery of evidence applies equally to applications to add rights as to those seeking to delete rights from the definitive map.

Once new evidence has been found, use the guidance in this book to see how many stars the application scores. (The stars are counted for all available evidence, not just the new evidence.) The authors like to have at least seven stars before making an application, since these are most likely to result in changes to the definitive map, but applications scoring five or more are worthy of consideration.

> The government has proposed that surveying authorities need not process applications that do not meet a 'basic evidential test'. The 'Stepping Forward' report[6] that led to the consultation appears to suggest that applications worth five stars should meet the basic evidential test and so be eligible to be processed by the surveying authority.

5.3.3 Determine the Surveying Authority

This is the council of a London borough, metropolitan district, or unitary authority, or the county council in areas served by both a district and county council. In some of the latter areas, the district council may deal with modification order applications under an agency agreement with the county council (made under the Local Government Act 1972), but the surveying authority remains the county council and any application sent to the county will be valid and will be passed on to the district if necessary. It is recommended that all applications are served on the surveying authority rather than any agents. Where a path is partially in one surveying authority's area and partially in another's, it is recommended that the application be made separately to each of the authorities, and that they are notified that this has been done. It will then be up to the two surveying authorities to decide whether to reach independent decisions on

6 Natural England report NECR035, Stepping Forward, March 2010.

the evidence available or whether one authority should allow the other to process the application on behalf of both authorities. The form and envelope should be addressed to the County Secretary or Chief Executive, unless you already know of a better addressee. Many county councils and unitary authorities produce their own guidance on making modification order applications, and these will usually provide details of where the application should be sent.

5.3.4 Check for an Existing Application

Check with the surveying authority to see if they already have an application for the claimed path, or if there are any nearby. If an application has already been made by someone else, it might be possible to support that application rather than make a separate one. However, the applicant for a path has the power to complain if a decision is not made within a year, and to appeal against a decision not to make an order, while a supporter has neither of these rights. Potential applicants should therefore consider who has made the existing application and whether they wish to make a fresh application in order to have these rights.

5.3.5 Determine Next Steps

Once the pack of evidence has been compiled, consider whether to approach the landowner to ask if, in the light of the evidence, he will agree to the route being recorded. This can be achieved by a simple deed of dedication, or by using the method outlined by Thompson,[7] and can save much time, especially in areas where the surveying authority has a large back log of modification applications to process. Alternatively, proceed to making the application.

7 See further reading in section 4.2.

5.4 Making the Application

5.4.1 Prepare the Application Map

a. The Map. The 1993 Regulations require that the map submitted is of a scale not less than 1:25,000. This is the scale used on Ordnance Survey Explorer maps. Note that the Ordnance Survey Landranger series maps do not meet the requirements. Some authorities may ask for a map on a smaller scale: in such circumstances, it is reasonable to ask the authority to supply the map. The authority cannot refuse to consider an application only on the grounds that they want a smaller scale map, providing that the one supplied is of a scale not less than 1:25,000. Copyright is not infringed by taking a copy of an Ordnance Survey map to submit with the DMMO application.[8] It is suggested that the following label be attached to the map before photocopying.

> Copyright Designs and Patents Act 1988
> Section 46
>
> This copy is made for the purpose of initiating a statutory inquiry and so does not infringe Copyright. Further copies should not be made.

If a map is not easily available, one can be printed free of charge from an online service such as http://www.ordnancesurvey.co.uk, http://www.streetmap.co.uk, http://www.mapmyrun.com or some other reputable mapping service. So long as the scale of the printed version is not less than 1:25,000, it should be acceptable.

b. Showing the Path. The application path should be marked on the map that is to be submitted. The Regulations do not specify any particular notation for the depiction of the path, but the map should be clear and unambiguous. It is advised that a key be added showing the line style used and the status of the path to which it relates. This is especially important where an application is for a number of paths and some are of one status and some of another. Different line styles or colours should be used for different statuses, for clarity.

8 s.46(1) Copyright Designs and Patents Act 1988.

5.4.2 Prepare the Applicant's Statement

Although not required by Regulations, it is considered best practice to prepare an Applicant's Statement for submission with the application. The Applicant's Statement goes through the evidence and suggests what evidential weight can be given to each piece. It should lead the surveying authority to the conclusion that, taking the evidence as a whole, it is reasonable to allege that the requested change to the definitive map should be made. The tellow-tinted examples in Chapter 3 are all suitable for inclusion in the Applicant's Statement. An example of a full Applicant's Statement is given in section 5.8. Note how each entry provides the following information:

- What the record is.
- Where the record is held (and its reference number, if applicable).
- Why it is of use/relevance.
- What the record shows in this instance.
- The conclusion to be drawn.

The Applicant's Statement should summarise the value of each piece of evidence presented. It should then come to a conclusion about the total value. It is worth reiterating that in examining the evidence, it is important to consider the evidence as a whole: over the range of documents and span of time. Each individual map or document may not be conclusive and only suggestive of rights. When this pattern is repeated across many different types of evidence produced by different people for different purposes at different times, though, it suggests that the common theme was that public rights existed.

The production of such a statement, rather than simply attaching photocopies of the raw evidence to the application form, is beneficial for the following reasons.

- It ensures that the applicant has evaluated the evidence sufficiently to believe that an investigation is needed by the surveying authority. This helps avoid poorly argued applications which could cause an application for an order to be turned down. An application must contain at least some new evidence that has not been formally assessed by the surveying authority before in order for there to be the 'discovery' of evidence required by s.53 of the 1981 Act. If new evidence is presented in a poor way, it can deny a future application, since the evidence then will not be new.

- If an applicant wants a second opinion before submitting the application, it enables another person to review quickly all the pertinent information on which to assess the evidence, and give an opinion.
- It discusses the evidence in a form which the surveying authority will understand and quickly assimilate. This cuts down on nugatory effort in resource-limited authorities, and assists them to come to the same conclusion as the applicant.
- It forms a sound basis on which to prepare a statement of case for a public inquiry, should that stage be reached. This ensures that any issues which do not support the recording of a path are addressed well in advance, or at least identified, so allowing the applicant to have a stronger case before inquiry is reached.

5.4.3 Prepare the Application Form

The application must be in the form (or substantially in the form) set out in the Regulations. The form is reproduced (with helpful annotations) in section 5.7.2. The following notes assist in the completion of the application form.

a. Surveying Authority. Enter the name and address of the surveying authority identified above.

b. Applicant. Enter your name as applicant, and either your own address or that of the organisation for which you are an authorised representative. The 1981 Act allows 'any person' to make an application. This means any individual, and any limited company, but not an unincorporated association. So applications made by an unincorporated partnership or an unincorporated bridleways association should be made in the name of one of the members of the partnership or association.

c. Description of Change. For a route that is not currently shown on the definitive map and statement, use the words 'adding the [status of path] from … to …'. If the path is already shown as, for example, a footpath and bridleway rights are alleged, use the form of words, 'upgrading to a bridleway the footpath from … to …'.

The words '[here]' and [there]' in the form relate to the ends of the path, but it is equally permissible to include additional words describing the route of the path. This could be particularly useful for a long and twisty path. If the evidence points to the existence of a limitation or condition on the use of the path by the public, these can be stated using the 'varying/adding to the particulars' section. Here, the applicant is asking for something to be changed in the definitive statement. This is also the place to include a statement about width, if the applicant is not happy for the surveying authority to come to their own conclusion on width. Do take care to ensure that this description of the change sought is accurate. In particular note that many footpaths are in fields alongside but separate from droves, so technically a drove may have no current status and the application will be to add a bridleway or restricted byway, rather than to upgrade the footpath.

d. List of Evidence. Make a concise list of the evidence submitted. An example is given below.

- Dury and Andrews' Map of Hertfordshire, 1766, Hertfordshire Archives.
- Cary's Map of 15 miles around London, 1800.
- Bryant's Map of Hertfordshire, 1822, Hertfordshire Archives.
- Tithe Map of St Stephen's Parish, 1823, Hertfordshire Archives.
- Ordnance Survey 1st edition 25 inch extract from map Hertfordshire 39 – 12, British Library.
- Ordnance Survey Book of Reference for Parish of St Stephen, 1874, British Library.
- OS 26/4976 Ordnance Survey Boundary Book, The National Archives.
- OS 27/2450 Ordnance Survey Boundary Plan, The National Archives.
- OS 35/3393 Ordnance Survey Object Name Book, The National Archives.
- IR 126/8/8 Inland Revenue Valuation plan, 1910, The National Archives.
- MAF 73/18/1 Ministry of Food Valuation plan, The National Archives.
- Hertfordshire County Council Land Charges map, circa 1970.
- Applicant's Statement.

This list is clearly not exhaustive, but is given as a guide to the level of information that should be given on the form. Further information on each piece of evidence will, of course, be given in the Applicant's Statement recorded at the end of the list.

5.4.4 Prepare the Application

Collate the completed application form, the map showing the path, a copy of each of the pieces of evidence listed on the form and the Applicant's Statement on the interpretation of the evidence. Where the Applicant's Statement includes the copies of evidence, they do not need to be attached for a second time. Note that it is essential that copies of all evidence are provided. Failure to send a copy of every piece of evidence listed will mean that the application does not satisfy paragraph 1 of Schedule 14 to the 1981 Act, meaning that the applicant will have no appeal rights, and no right to complain that the application isn't dealt with in a suitable period of time.

It is advisable at this stage to take a photocopy of the evidence bundle. It is important that you retain the originals, especially originals of user evidence, since paperwork can go astray.

Send the original of the application form, and the copy of the evidence bundle to the surveying authority. Although no covering letter is necessary, some applicants find it helpful to include a note asking that receipt of the package be acknowledged. Some applicants send the package by recorded delivery, since this provides a proof of delivery, but this is not usually necessary. The authors recommend that the surveying authority be asked to confirm that the application meets the requirements of paragraph 1 to Schedule 14 of the Wildlife and Countryside Act 1981 before proceeding to the next stage, since if it is not so compliant it will need to be corrected. A suitable covering letter is in section 5.7.1.

Once this step has been completed, a surveying authority is obliged to enter the application in its register of applications within 28 days.[9] It may (in law, should) consider the evidence and, after considering it with other available evidence, make a decision on whether to make an order. However, if the authority takes no action, no complaint will

9 The Public Rights of Way (Register of Applications under section 53(5) of the Wildlife and Countryside Act 1981) (England) Regulations 2005, Regulation 3(6) for England. The Public Rights of Way (Registers) (Wales) Regulations 2006, Regulation 8 for Wales.

be entertained by the Secretary of State unless the authority has been served with a certificate that the owners and occupiers of the land crossed by the path have been notified of the application. It follows that it is in the applicant's interest to notify the owners and occupiers and certify this fact to the authority.

The authors recommend that applicants check that the online register has been updated, to make sure the application is accurately listed. It is possible that correctly recorded applications will be exempted from the cut-off date, and any error in the register could be fatal if the application has not been determined by 2026.

The government has proposed to remove the requirement to submit copies of evidence that are already in the surveying authority's possession. Until any legislation is in place to make this change, take extra care to ensure that copies of every piece of evidence cited in the application paperwork is copied and enclosed.

5.4.5 Notifying the Owners and Occupiers

The first source of the names and addresses of the owners and occupiers of the land crossed by the path is local knowledge. Try to find someone living, working or riding in the area of the path who can advise. Failing this, it might be worth asking parish clerks, parish path liaison officers, local access forums, the local office of the National Farmers Union, or branch of the Country Land and Business Association.

The owner of the land crossed by a path can often be checked at HM Land Registry, although not all land is registered. There is a fee payable for a copy of the register which shows the name and address of the owners. The use of the Land Registry's own search service (http://www.landregistry.gov.uk) tends to be far cheaper than commercially-provided services even though they use essentially the same information.

The occupier of the land crossed by a path can be determined from the electoral register or the register of council tax payers for paths clearly on a farm but these may not help for land which is not clearly attached to any dwelling.

Land that is owned by trustees following a bequest should have the names of the trustees recorded at the Probate Registry.

It is better to notify too widely than not widely enough. If someone has been identified as a likely owner, a notice should be served on him. If any of the evidence suggests that the land is owned by the surveyor of highways, don't forget to serve a notice on the highway authority (even though it should already be aware in its capacity as surveying authority).

The notice that a change to the definitive map and statement has been applied for must be in the form (or substantially in the form) set out in the Regulations. This is reproduced (with helpful annotations) in section 5.7.3. A separate notice is needed for each owner or occupier. The following notes assist in the completion of the notices.

a. Fill in the name and address of the owner or occupier.

b. Fill in the applicant's details, the date the application was made, and the name of the surveying authority. All of this information can be found on the retained copy of the application form.

c. Record the change to the definitive map and statement that has been requested. It is usually easiest to use the same words that were in the application form. It is not necessary to notify an owner of part of a long path about the details of the application at the other end of the path, but can be desirable, especially if the ownership boundary is unclear.

d. People receiving the statutory notice may not have seen one before. The 'Note' at the end of the notice is designed to explain the process in very broad terms, and to give the recipient a point of contact for initial questions. Its use should be tailored to the circumstances, but it is recommended that the name and telephone number of the contact at the surveying authority should always be given.

Take two copies of each of the notices prepared. Send the originals to the owners or occupiers, keep one set for your records and one set will be needed for the surveying authority. There is no need to use a recorded delivery service,[10] although this can be used if desired. Alternatively, the notices can be hand delivered or posted at the counter of a post office, with a request for a certificate of posting.

10 The requirement was removed by s.70A Wildlife and Countryside Act 1981.

The government has proposed to remove the requirement from applicants to notify owners and occupiers and instead to require the surveying authority to do this. Any change to the law is likely to take some time to implement and the authors recommend that applicants do not delay in submitting modification order applications purely in order to take advantage of any potential new regime.

5.4.6 When Some Owners or Occupiers are Untraced

If you believe that there is an owner or occupier that you have been unable to trace, you may ask the surveying authority for permission to post a notice in a prominent position on the land affected. There is no statutory form to request this permission, but a sample letter, which should be adapted for the circumstances, is set out in section 5.7.4. The applicant needs to have made reasonable attempts to have identified the owners and occupiers before asking for permission to post site notices.

The requirement to notify owners and occupiers of land crossed by the path comes from paragraph 2 of Schedule 14 to the Wildlife and Countryside Act 1981. It specifically refers to land crossed by the path, and does not mean all people who own or occupy land that is adjacent to the path.

If permission to post a site notice is given, it should take the form described for personal notices for owners and occupiers, except that instead of the owner or occupier's name and address, you should use the form, 'To the owner [or occupier] of the land known as [address or description of land crossed by the path]'. Take two copies of the site notice: one for your records and one for the surveying authority. It is also worth having a spare copy or two when attending site, in case a user of the route asks for information or clarification.

The notice should be placed in a prominent position on the land, so that an owner or occupier would be able to see it. It should not be positioned so that it is difficult to see, like under a bush. It is good practice to take a photograph of any site notices posted, but this is not a statutory requirement. Contrary to some authorities' requests, there is no obligation to put a notice at each end of the path. It is sufficient to place it in a prominent position on the path such that it is likely to be seen by the owner or occupier when on his land.

5.4.7 Certifying that the Owners and Occupiers have been Notified

Once you believe that all the owners and occupiers of the land crossed by the path have been notified or that you have notified all you can and have received permission to post a site notice and done this, it is necessary to certify this to the surveying authority. The form of words for the certificate is reproduced (with helpful annotations) in section 5.7.6.

The requirement to inform owners and occupiers of the land crossed by the route is exactly that; it does not extend to the owners and occupiers of adjacent landholdings.

The certificate, with a copy of each of the notices served on owners, occupiers, and if applicable placed on site, should be sent to the surveying authority. Although no covering letter is necessary, some applicants find it helpful to include a note asking that receipt of the package be acknowledged. A suitable covering letter is in section 5.7.5. Some applicants send the package by recorded delivery, since this provides a proof of delivery, but this is not usually necessary.

Once this step has been completed, a surveying authority should consider the evidence if it has not yet started to, and, after considering it with other available evidence, make a decision on whether to make an order.

5.4.8 What Happens Next?

In order to determine a modification order application, the surveying authority have to follow a statutory process of consultation and consider not just the evidence from the applicant and consultees but all other relevant evidence available to them,[11] before making a decision on whether the definitive map needs to be altered. The exact process followed varies from authority to authority. The process followed by Hertfordshire County Council is illustrated in the flow charts at Figure 107.

If the authority have failed to make a decision on the application within 12 months of this step, the applicant may ask the Secretary of State to direct the authority to determine the application within a set period of time. See section 5.5 for information on this step.

11 *R. v. Isle of Wight County Council ex parte O'Keefe* (1990) 59 P & CR 283.

If the surveying authority make a decision to make an order, the Schedule 14 procedure is over: the provisions of Schedule 15 to the 1981 Act will apply to any modification order made.

If the surveying authority agree to modify the definitive map and statement, but to a status other than that applied for, there will be an opportunity to consider any other evidence on which they may have relied, and if necessary object and go to the inquiry.

If the surveying authority make a decision that no change to the definitive map and statement is required, there will be an opportunity for the applicant to appeal to the Secretary of State. See section 5.6.

5.5 No Decision After 12 Months

Once the surveying authority have received the certificate that the owners and occupiers have been notified, paragraph 3(1) of Schedule 14 to the Wildlife and Countryside Act 1981 requires the authority to investigate the application, consult with every other local authority in whose area the route falls, and make a decision on whether or not to make an order to change the definitive map as requested. It says that this must be done 'as soon as reasonably practicable'.

To guard against some surveying authorities failing to fulfil their duty to investigate, Parliament provided, at paragraph 3(2) that if the surveying authority have not determined an application within 12 months of getting the certificate that the owners and occupiers have been notified, the applicant can complain to the Secretary of State. After consulting the surveying authority, the Secretary of State can issue a direction that the application be determined within a set period.

The Planning Inspectorate handles complaints that decisions have not been taken within a year on behalf of the Secretary of State. In their guidance[12] they say that the only factors that will be taken into account are:

- the authority's reasons for not reaching a decision and what stage has been reached so far;

12 See http://www.planningportal.gov.uk/planning/countryside/schedule14/schedule14directions.

- the authority's priorities for up-dating its definitive map and statement;
- how the application stands in relation to those priorities;
- the progress it is making in bringing and keeping the definitive map up to date; and
- whether there are reasons why a case should take priority over other cases.

There are no regulations providing forms of complaint, but clearly it will be important to address the factors provided by the Planning Inspectorate. A suggested way forward is provided below, in the form of informal discussion and data collection and then, if necessary, the making of a complaint.

5.5.1 Preliminary Checks

Before complaining to the Secretary of State that the surveying authority have failed to determine the application within the 12 months allowed, check with the authority to see what action has been taken. Find out whether they have started to investigate the application, whether they have consulted the statutory consultees, or whether they are about to make a decision. This step is best performed by telephone, where the applicant will have the opportunity to find out whether there are any particular difficulties that have led to a delay.

Write to the surveying authority setting out the details of the case so far. Tell them the dates of application for a modification order and of the certificate that the owners and occupiers have been notified. Summarise the reasons for their delay, and ask them to confirm that your understanding is correct. Make sure that you ask for a copy of their statement of priorities,[13] and ask when they think they will have made a decision (or even started to investigate the claim for authorities with a back log).

When the statement of priorities is received, look to see that the application is recorded under the appropriate category. Could it

13 In Wales, Department of the Environment Circular 2/93 requires the Secretary of State to take into account any statement of priorities when considering an application for a direction.

be advanced in the list of cases because of grounds of which the surveying authority may not be aware, for example, imminent planning permission or public safety? If there are grounds on which to change its place in any modification order investigation queue, write to the surveying authority and point this out to them and asked for a revised target date for determination of the application.

Once these steps have been taken, it is reasonable to approach the Secretary of State for a direction that the surveying authority determine the application within a set period of time.

Applying for a Secretary of State's direction that the application be determined does not of itself put the applicant at risk of paying costs should the application fail.

5.5.2 Application for a Direction

There is no statutory form, and the layout should be adapted to the circumstances of the case. The following guidance is offered, which should be read in conjunction with the suggested layout for a request to the Secretary of State given at section 5.7.7.

1. History of the Application. It is helpful to summarise the history of the application. Ideally, this will be based on the letter sent to the surveying authority before a direction is sought, modified in the light of information they have provided, so it should represent a common position on the history.

2. Discovery of Evidence. It is useful to show that there is a discovery of evidence, since without this there is no obligation for any investigation. To do this, it is only necessary to point out that some evidence has been provided which has not previously been considered by the authority in connection with its definitive map processes.

3. Statement of the County Council. Set out in a concise form the position of the council for the Secretary of State. Ensure that you quote any of their statements on which you will rely when formulating the special reasons why they should be directed to get on with determining the application.

4. Factors to Consider. This paragraph shows that the applicant understands the framework in which the Secretary of State will make his decision, and then sets out the reasons why the applicant thinks the Secretary of State needs to intervene.

5. Application for Direction. This paragraph asks for the direction. The request that the applicant be allowed to comment on the council's response is important, since otherwise the applicant may not have a chance to refute or comment on some new statement from the surveying authority.

5.5.3 Result of a Direction

If the Secretary of State grants a direction that the application be determined by a set date, make sure that the surveying authority stays on track to reach its decision in time. There are no statutory penalties for an authority that fails, but councillors will usually be unhappy at the prospect of being castigated in the press for failing to act in time and a formal complaint to the leader of the council or the chief executive of the council may assist.

If no direction is made, or if the council fails to meet a date that has been set, it remains open to the applicant to make further requests for directions. This would be particularly useful if the authority has failed to do something it said it would be doing in its submission to the Secretary of State, or if it rewrites its statement of priorities to the disadvantage of an applicant whose application was shortly to be considered under its old rules.

5.6 Appeal Against Refusal to Make an Order

If the surveying authority notify the applicant that no order will be made, paragraph 4(1) of Schedule 14 to the Wildlife and Countryside Act 1981 allows the applicant to appeal to the Secretary of State. Notice of appeal must be served on the Secretary of State and on the authority within 28 days of receipt of the decision not to make an order. It is recommended that the applicant obtains a certificate of posting for his letter of appeal to ensure that he has evidence of compliance with this statutory deadline, should it later be necessary.

A sample appeal letter is provided at section 5.7.8. Once this statutory step has been taken, the Planning Inspectorate will provide forms for completion, and ask for a copy of the application.

Further information about appeals can be found on the Planning Inspectorate's website.[14]

5.7 Precedents: Letters and Forms

The letters and forms used to make an application for a modification order application and its associated activities are contained in this section. Each will need to be modified to address the needs of the actual modification being sought, but they should serve as good starting points. The forms are those prescribed by the 1993 Regulations, as updated, and the letters have been in use by the authors.

14 See http://www.planningportal.gov.uk/planning/countryside/schedule14/schedule14appeal.

INVESTIGATION OF APPLICATION STARTED
HCC researches its "Top 10" historical documents & analyses this and any evidence submitted at the time the application was made e.g. from landowners or people who claim to have used the route. This information is put into an Investigation Report, including interpretation of the evidence. Ownership of the land is also investigated.

CONSULTATION WITH REPORT
Consultation letters are sent, together with the Investigation Report to the landowners, applicant, Parish and District Councils. Consultation letters are sent with list of documents consulted, and the interim finding to the remaining consultees.
Four weeks are allowed for replies

TAKE DECISION
HCC will then decide if an Order (a legal document) is needed to amend the Definitive Map.
This decision is based on the evidence available.
Everyone who is consulted is informed of the decision.

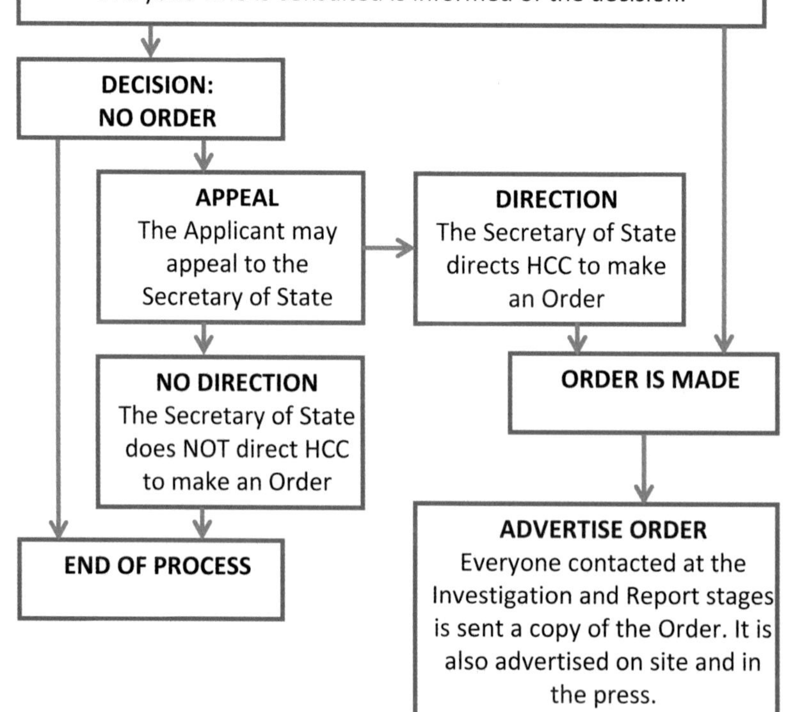

Figure 107 (above and facing page): Flowchart showing the process followed by Hertfordshire County Council when investigating an application

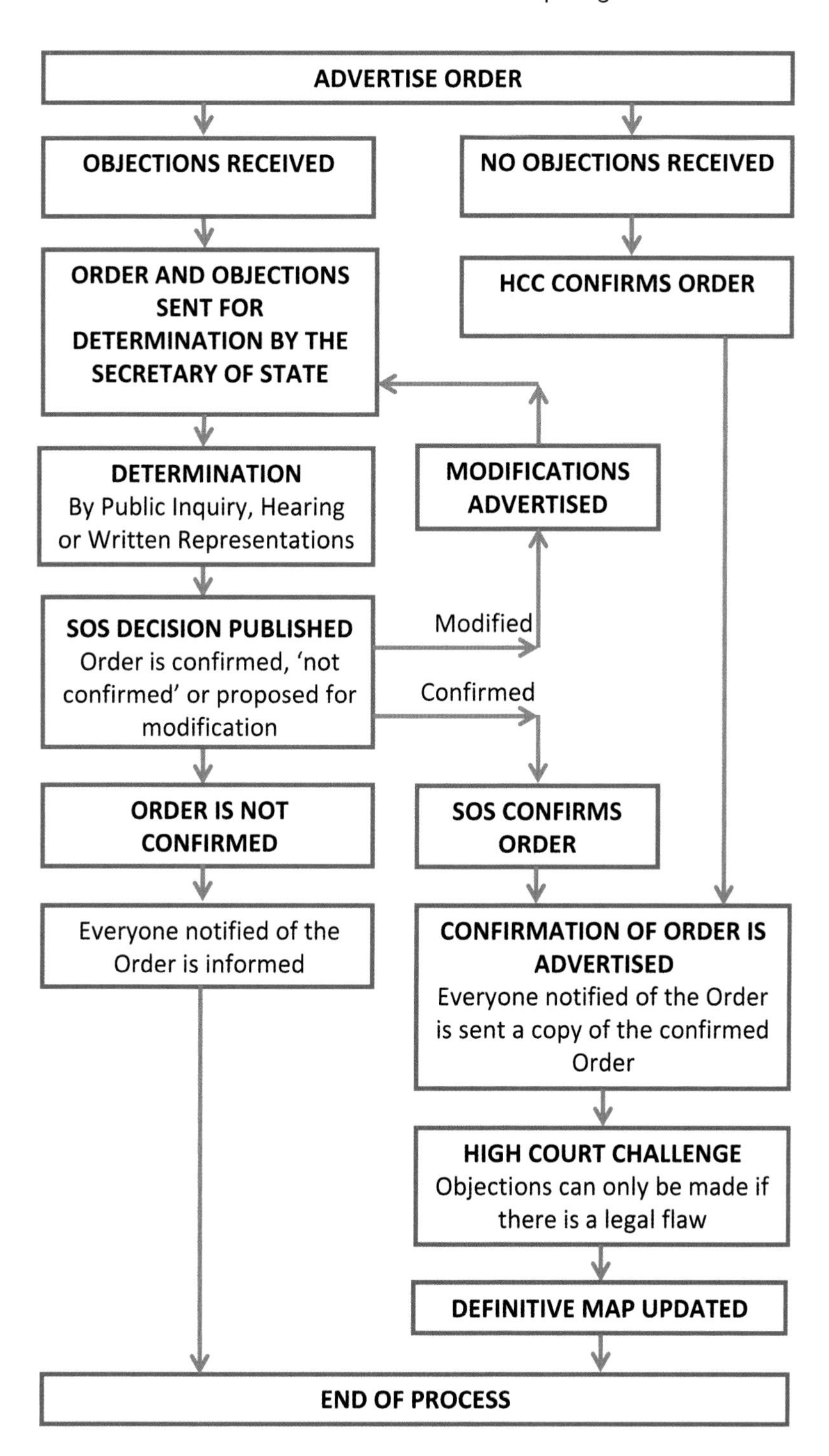
ADVERTISE ORDER
OBJECTIONS RECEIVED
NO OBJECTIONS RECEIVED
ORDER AND OBJECTIONS SENT FOR DETERMINATION BY THE SECRETARY OF STATE
HCC CONFIRMS ORDER
DETERMINATION
By Public Inquiry, Hearing or Written Representations
MODIFICATIONS ADVERTISED
SOS DECISION PUBLISHED
Order is confirmed, 'not confirmed' or proposed for modification
Modified
Confirmed
ORDER IS NOT CONFIRMED
SOS CONFIRMS ORDER
Everyone notified of the Order is informed
CONFIRMATION OF ORDER IS ADVERTISED
Everyone notified of the Order is sent a copy of the confirmed Order
HIGH COURT CHALLENGE
Objections can only be made if there is a legal flaw
DEFINITIVE MAP UPDATED
END OF PROCESS

5.7.1 Covering Letter to the Form of Application for a Modification Order

This is a sample letter that should be adapted to the particular circumstances. The important point is to ask for the application to be acknowledged, and to ask the council to check that the application complies with paragraph 1 of Schedule 14 to the Wildlife and Countryside Act 1981. This point is important, since if the application is not compliant (for example the map supplied is at the wrong scale, or copies of the evidence relied upon are not submitted) then other rights given by the 1981 Act will not apply. It will be better to remake the application before proceeding to notify owners and occupiers.

[Address of applicant]

[Name of surveying authority] [Applicant's reference]

[Address of surveying authority] [Date]

Dear Sirs,

Wildlife and Countryside Act 1981
Application for a definitive map modification order
Route from [here] to [there]

Please find enclosed an application for a definitive map modification order to record a route on the definitive map in [name of parish or locality].

I would be grateful if you would kindly acknowledge receipt of this application, confirm that it is fully compliant with the requirements of paragraph 1 to Schedule 14 of the 1981 Act, and advise which reference number you will be using to track the application.

Yours faithfully,

5.7.2 Form of Application for a Modification Order

The form of application is prescribed by the 1993 Regulations (Regulation 8(1)). The text in square brackets should be replaced as necessary, and the text in italics removed. There is no need to buy specially printed forms or ask for them from a surveying authority: so long as the form of words given is followed, they can be typed or even handwritten. Some surveying authorities are helpful in making their application forms available in electronic copy.

Wildlife and Countryside Act 1981

The Definitive Map and Statement of Public Rights of Way in Blankshire
[The above line is just the title of the Definitive Map and Statement for the Area – check the title with the surveying authority for this and other notices that have to be served]

To: [name of surveying authority]

Of: [address of surveying authority]

I/We, [name of applicant] of [address of applicant][15] hereby apply for an order under section 53(2) of the Wildlife and Countryside Act 1981 modifying the definitive map and statement for the area by:

[adding the footpath/bridleway/restricted byway/byway open to all traffic] from [here] to [there]

[upgrading/downgrading to a footpath/bridleway/restricted byway/byway open to all traffic the footpath/bridleway] from [here] to [there]

[deleting the footpath/bridleway/byway open to all traffic] from [here] to [there]

[[varying] [adding to] the particulars relating to the footpath/bridleway/ byway open to all traffic from [here] to [there] by providing that ...]

and shown on the map accompanying this application.

I attach copies of the following documentary evidence (including statements of witnesses) in support of this application:

[insert list of documents here]

Dated: Signed:

[Applicant's Reference: *this is not a statutory requirement but is useful if you are making a large number of applications*]

15 The address of a headquarters could be used if the applicant is making the application for an organisation.

5.7.3 Notice of an Application for a Modification Order

The form of application is prescribed by the 1993 Regulations (Regulation 8(3)). The text in square brackets should be replaced as necessary.

While it is not a statutory requirement, it is often helpful to provide owners and occupiers with a plan showing the application route, as the textual description often provides only limited information.

Section 53(5) of and Schedule 14 to the

Wildlife and Countryside Act 1981

The Definitive Map and Statement of Public Rights of Way in Blankshire

To: [name of owner or occupier]

Of: [address of owner or occupier]

I/We, [name of applicant] of [address of applicant] hereby give notice that on [date] I/we made application to the [name and address of surveying authority] that the definitive map and statement for the area be modified by:

[description of change – use the same form of words as in this part of the application for the order, or for a long path, use similar words but just relating to the portion on this owner or occupier's land]

Dated: Signed:

[Applicant's Reference: *this is not a statutory requirement but is useful if you are making a large number of applications*]

[The following text does not form part of the statutory notice, but often helps explain what the notice is about, especially when used on a site notice or where a path is generally accepted as a highway of the status applied for.]

Note not forming part of the Statutory Notice

This is an application for the map and statement that record details about public paths to be changed because it appears that a route is missing or that the statement does not fully legally define the path.

No new rights are created by a definitive map and statement modification order. An order only records those rights that already legally exist.

[continued]

This application is made in order to assist the county council in its statutory duty to correct the incomplete record of public rights of way.

The council will be able to answer any questions on the procedure that is to be followed.

5.7.4 Request for Permission to Post Site Notices

This is a sample letter that should be adapted to the particular circumstances. There is no statutory form. The letter should normally be sent to whoever acknowledged the initial application.

[Address of applicant]

[Name of surveying authority] [Applicant's reference]

[Address of surveying authority] [Surveying authority's reference]

[Date]

Dear Sir,

Wildlife and Countryside Act 1981 Schedule 14 Paragraph 2(2)

Application for a definitive map modification order

Route from [here] to [there]

On [date] I applied for an order modifying the definitive map and statement by [insert brief details of the application]. I now wish to serve a notice of my application on the owners and occupiers of the land crossed by the path in my application.

I have [asked local people][performed a search at HM Land Registry][consulted the electoral register] *[Describe here the efforts made to determine who the owners and occupiers are. The words given are examples only, but it is good practice to show that the applicant has made reasonable attempts. If this information is not given, the surveying authority may just write back and suggest these things be tried rather than give permission.]*

I have been unable to determine any of the owners or occupiers of the land crossed by the path in my application. *[Use this line if no owners or occupiers have been found.]*

I have served notices on the owners and occupiers listed at Annex A, but believe that there may be others. *[Use this line if one or more owners and occupiers have been found, and add an Annex to the letter.]*

[continued]

I request permission to post a site notice in accordance with Paragraph 2(2) of Schedule 14 to the Wildlife and Countryside Act 1981. I look forward to hearing from you.

Yours faithfully,

[Annex A
List of names and addresses of those owners and occupiers that have been identified and on whom notices have been served. The authority may use this list to help them determine other owners and occupiers.]

5.7.5 Letter Covering the Certificate that Notices have been Served

This is a sample letter that should be adapted to the particular circumstances. It covers both the situation where the landowners and occupiers have been identified, and that where permission to post site notices has been obtained because the owners or occupiers are untraceable. The important point is to ask for the certificate to be acknowledged, and to ask the council to confirm that the statutory requirements have all been satisfied.

[Address of applicant]

[Name of surveying authority] [Applicant's reference]

[Address of surveying authority] [Surveying authority's reference]

[Date]

Dear Sirs,

Wildlife and Countryside Act 1981

Application for a definitive map modification order

Route from [here] to [there]

Please find enclosed the certificate that I have complied with the requirements of paragraph 2 of Schedule 14 to the Act in respect of my modification order application, and copies of the notices served.

I would be grateful if you would confirm by letter that the application is fully compliant with paragraphs 1 and 2 of Schedule 14 to the Wildlife and Countryside Act 1981.

I look forward to hearing from you.

Yours faithfully,

5.7.6 Certificate that Notices have been Served

The form of application is prescribed by the 1993 Regulations (Regulation 8(4)). The text in square brackets should be replaced as necessary.

This certificate should be sent, with copies of the notices served on owners and occupiers or posted on site, to the surveying authority.

Wildlife and Countryside Act 1981

The Definitive Map and Statement of Public Rights of Way in Blankshire

Certificate of Service of Notice of Application for Modification Order

To: [name of surveying authority]

Of: [address of surveying authority]

I/We, [name of applicant] of [address of applicant] hereby certify that the requirements of paragraph 2 of Schedule 14 to the Wildlife and Countryside Act 1981 have been complied with.

Dated: Signed:

[Applicant's Reference: *this is not a statutory requirement but is useful if you are making a large number of applications, especially as nowhere on the Certificate is the application path described.*

5.7.7 Letter to Secretary of State if No Decision has been Made After a Year

This is a sample letter that should be adapted to the particular circumstances. There is no statutory form. Fill in the items in square brackets with the appropriate information.

[Address of applicant]

The Secretary of State
Rights of Way Section
The Planning Inspectorate
Room 4/05 Kite Wing
2 The Square
Temple Quay
Bristol
BS1 6PN

[Applicant's reference]
[Surveying authority's reference]

[Date]

Dear Sir,

Wildlife and Countryside Act 1981 Section 53(5)

Application for a Direction under Paragraph 3(2) of Schedule 14

[The Definitive Map and Statement of Public Rights of Way in Blankshire]

Route from [here] to [there]

1. History of the Application. On [date] I applied for a definitive map modification order modifying the definitive map and statement by [insert brief details of the claim]. I served the Certificate that I had notified all the owners and occupiers of the land crossed by the route on [insert date]. The application was acknowledged by the surveying authority, [insert name of council], on [date].

2. Discovery of Evidence. As part of my application, I submitted [insert reference to some of the new evidence sent in]. This amounts to a discovery of evidence under S.53(3)(c) so enabling the surveying authority to consider making an order.

3. Statement of the County Council. On [date], I wrote to the Council, outlining the history of the application (as in paragraph 1 above) and asking when they thought they might be able to make a decision on the application.

[continued]

On [date] they responded, saying [insert salient points of their reply, ensuring that any dates and any reasons for the delay are quoted].

4. Factors to Consider. The Secretary of State normally considers the Council's published statement of priorities for bringing and keeping its definitive map and statement up to date, how the application stands in relation to those priorities, the progress the authority is making in bringing its definitive map up to date and whether there are reasons why a case should take priority over other cases I put forward the following special reasons:

[List and number the special reasons here]

5. Application for Direction. For the [insert number] special reasons given above, I ask the Secretary of State to direct the Council to determine the present application within a set period of time. I also make the special request that I be allowed to have sight of and comment on the Council's response to the Secretary of State before a decision is reached.

Yours faithfully,

5.7.8 Letter to Initiate an Appeal Against Refusal to Make an Order

This is a very simple letter to initiate an appeal against the refusal of an authority to make an order. It must be sent within 28 days of receipt of the authority's decision, and it must be copied to the surveying authority within the same 28 day period. Once this statutory timescale has been met, the Planning Inspectorate will provide forms and a timetable for the appeal.

[Address of applicant]

The Secretary of State
Rights of Way Section
The Planning Inspectorate
Room 4/05 Kite Wing
2 The Square
Temple Quay
Bristol
BS1 6PN

[Applicant's reference]
[Surveying authority's reference]

[Date]

Dear Sir,

Wildlife and Countryside Act 1981 Section 53(5)

Appeal against the decision of [Blankshire] Council to Modify the Definitive Map

Route from [here] to [there]

On [date] I applied for a definitive map modification order modifying the definitive map and statement by [insert brief details of the claim].The application was determined by the surveying authority, [insert name of council], on [date], and notified to me on [date of receipt of letter].

I appeal against this decision.

I have sent a copy of this letter to the surveying authority.

Please advise me what information is now required, for the Secretary of State to reach a decision.

Yours faithfully,

5.8 Example Applicant's Statement

As an example of how to put together an applicant's statement, an example in Hertfordshire follows. This route reached 21 stars without checking the inclosure or tithe evidence (which were held in a different record office from the other evidence presented). Even if the route had been stopped up in the inclosure process, the route still has 16 stars from after that time.

While only the relevant extracts of documents are included in the applicant's statement, case law[16] says that documents must be read in context. So if only a portion of a longer document is included, attach a copy of the full document to the modification order application.

THE APPLICATION ROUTE

1. The application route runs from Burymead Lane (Cottered 17 BOAT) to a junction of Cottered 14 FP and the county road at Cottered Warren. It is shown from A (junction with Cottered 17) to B (Flanders Green) to C (junction with Cottered 20) to D (Cottered Warren) below. The part from A to B is currently recorded on sheet 23 of the definitive map of rights of way for Hertfordshire as a bridleway, while the part from B to D is not recorded.

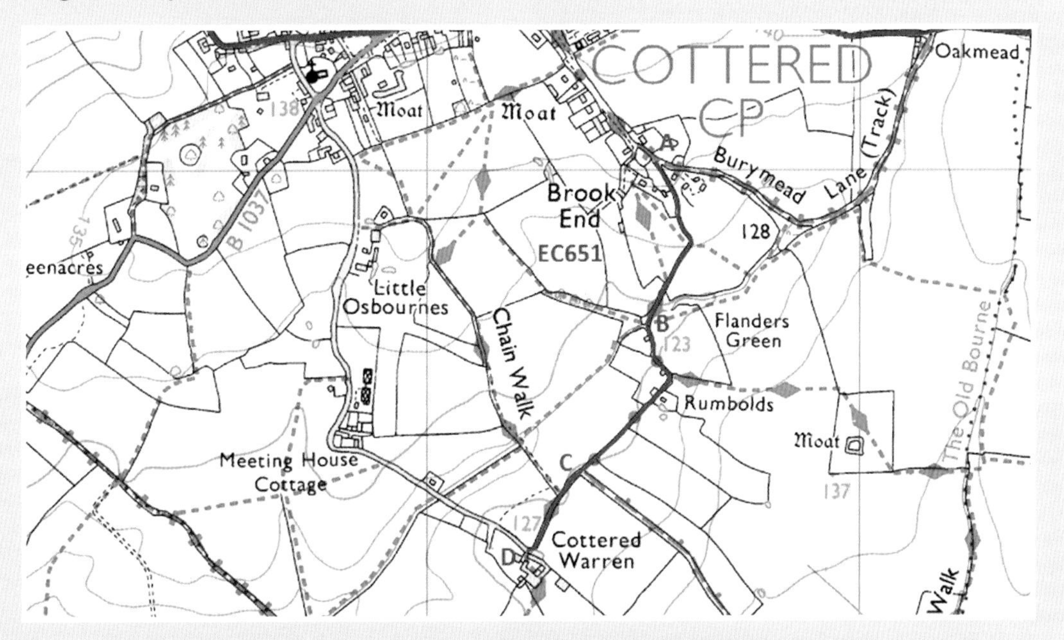

Figure 108: Ordnance Survey 1:25000 scale map extract showing application route

16 *O'Keefe v Secretary of State for the Environment and Isle of Wight County Council* (1997) *The Times*, 5 Aug 1997.

DOCUMENTARY EVIDENCE OF HIGHWAY STATUS

2. In order to be able to modify the definitive map and statement, the Surveying Authority needs to have a discovery of evidence which shows, on the balance of probabilities, that highway rights exist. The use of the 'balance of probabilities' test rather than 'beyond reasonable doubt' was confirmed by the High Court in *Todd, Bradley v SOS for EFRA* [2004] 4 All ER 497.

3. While no single piece of evidence is conclusive, the applicant believes that taken as a whole the pieces of evidence demonstrate highway reputation over many years, indicating that the route does indeed have highway status, and that prior to the Natural Environment and Rural Communities Act 2006, there were full vehicular rights.

4. <u>Dury and Andrews' Map of Hertfordshire (1766)</u>

a. An original is held by the Hertfordshire Archives and Local Studies (HALS), under reference CM26.

b. This was made for sale to the public, and so is unlikely to show routes that the public could not use. It has a key in which different types of route are distinguished.

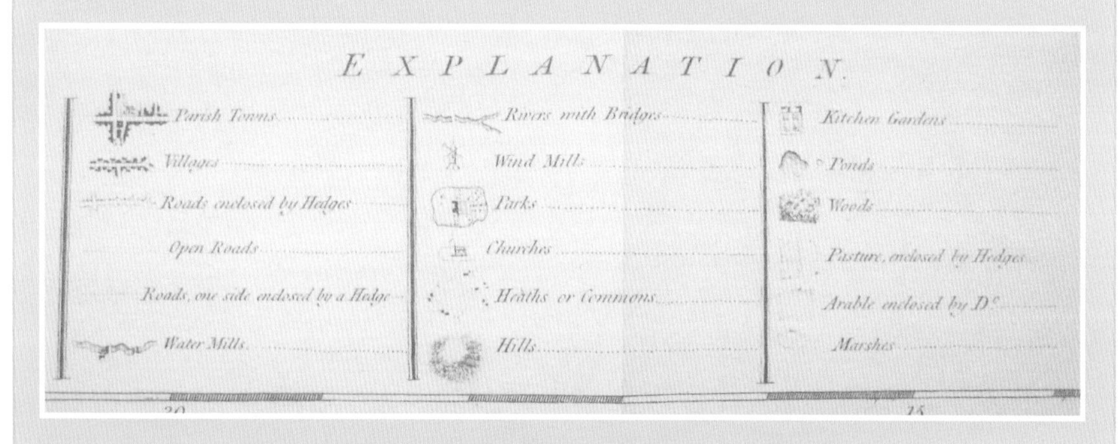

Figure 109: Extract from Dury and Andrews' Map (1766) showing the Key

c. The route is shown in the manner of an 'Open Road'. This suggests that the route was considered to have vehicular rights in 1766.

d. In *Rights of Way: Restoring the Record*, this evidence is rated as two stars.

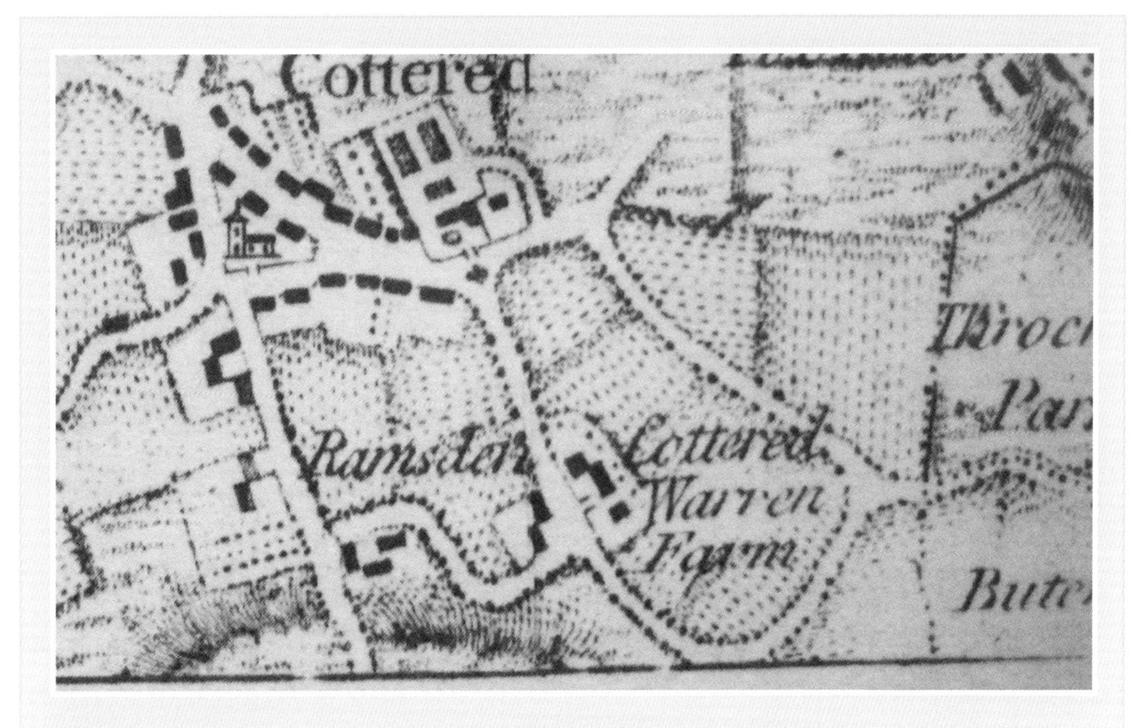

Figure 110: Extract 1 from Dury and Andrews' Map (1766) showing the application route

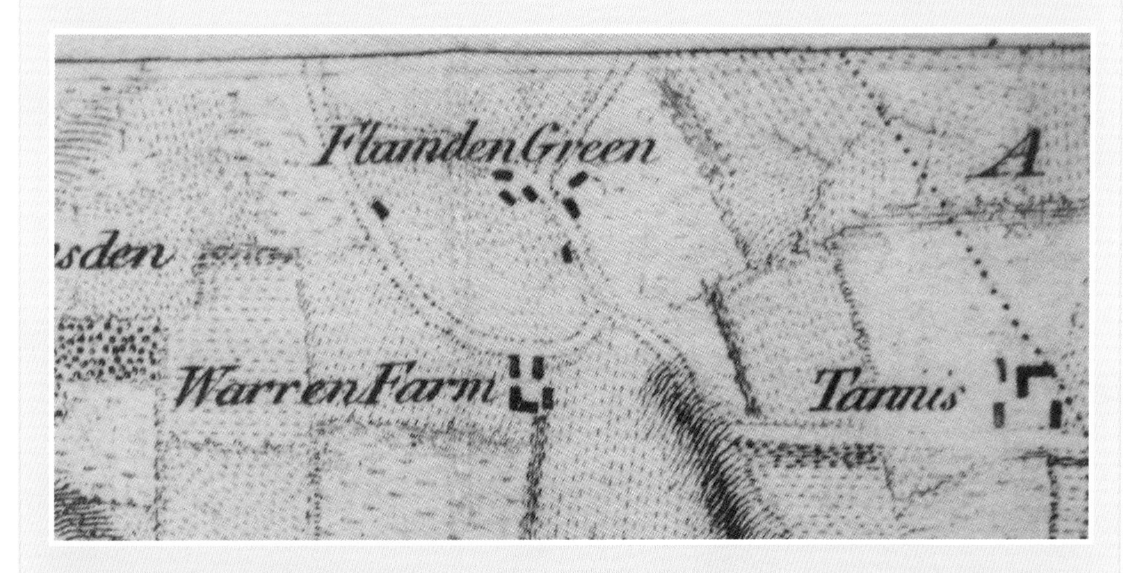

Figure 111: Extract 2 from Dury and Andrews' Map (1766) showing the application route

5. Bryant's Map of Hertfordshire (1822)

a. An original is held by the Hertfordshire Archives and Local Studies (HALS), under reference CM88.

b. This was made for sale to the public, and so is unlikely to show routes that the public could not use. It has a key in which different types of route are distinguished.

c. The route is shown in the manner of a 'Lanes or bridleways'. This suggests that the route was considered to have at least equestrian, but more likely vehicular rights in 1822.

d. In *Rights of Way: Restoring the Record*, this evidence is rated as two stars.

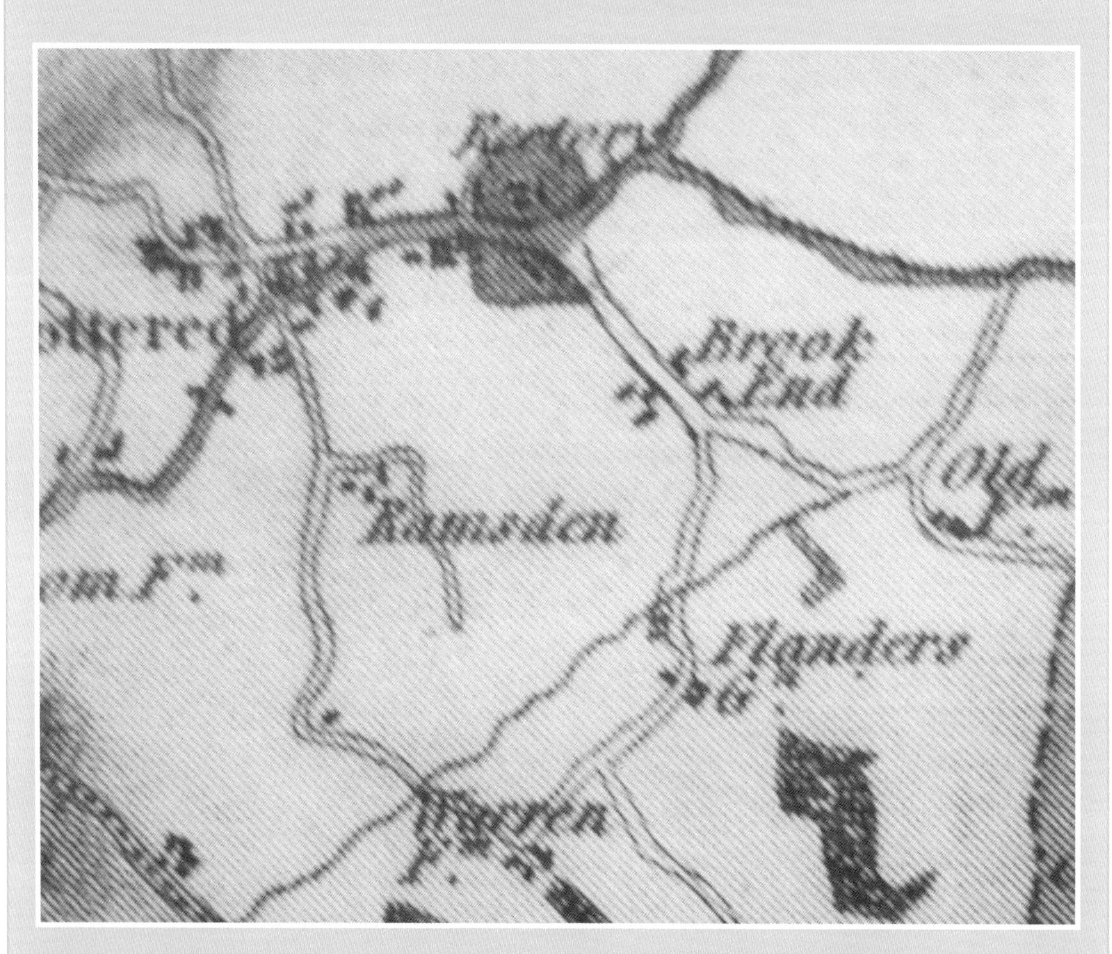

Figure 112: Extract from Bryant (1822) showing the application route

The Turnpike & Mail Roads
Good Grofs or Driving Roads
Lanes & Bridle Ways

Figure 113: Extract from Bryant (1822) showing the Key

6. Ordnance Survey First Edition 25 inch

a. Copies of the first edition Ordnance Survey 25 inch maps are held by the British Library. As well as originals, they have created microfiche copies, which can be inspected by the public. The extracts here are taken from the microfiche The Ordnance Survey (OS) maps are not usually of use for rights of way purposes as they usually purport only to show physical features and not legal rights. However, the early maps in the first edition series contain valuable extra information when cross referenced to the books of reference, often called simply the 'area books', that were published to go with them. The British Library holds these books of reference. These are indexed by parish.

b. The application route is shown on the OS map as land parcel number 297 in Cottered. These extracts of OS sheets Hertfordshire 13 – 3 and 13 – 7 were obtained from the British Library.

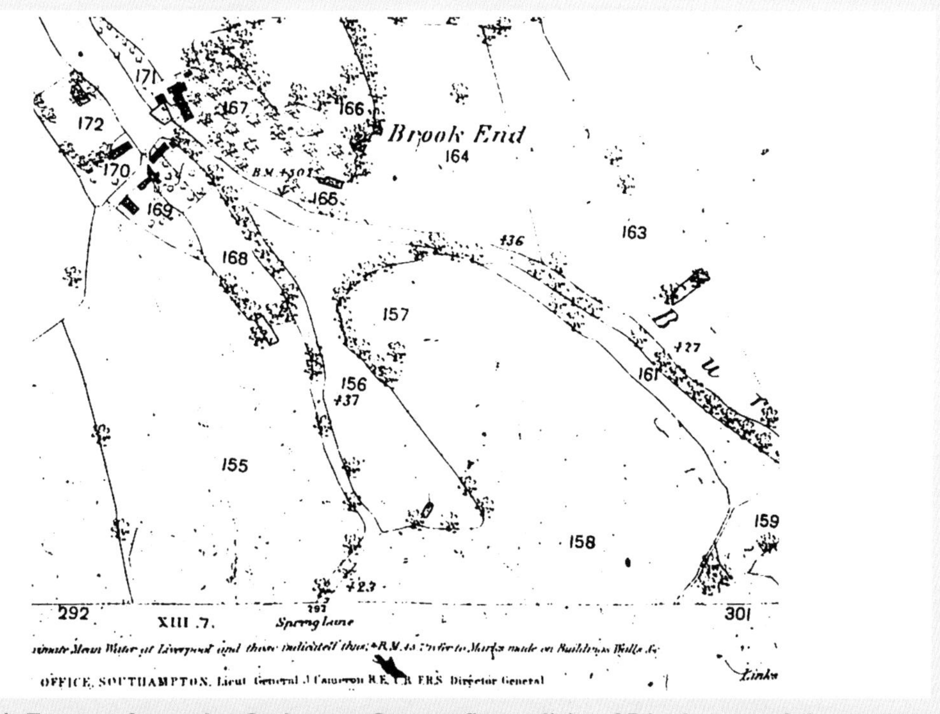

Figure 114: Extract from the Ordnance Survey first edition 25 inch map of the area, sheet Hertfordshire 13 – 3 showing the application route

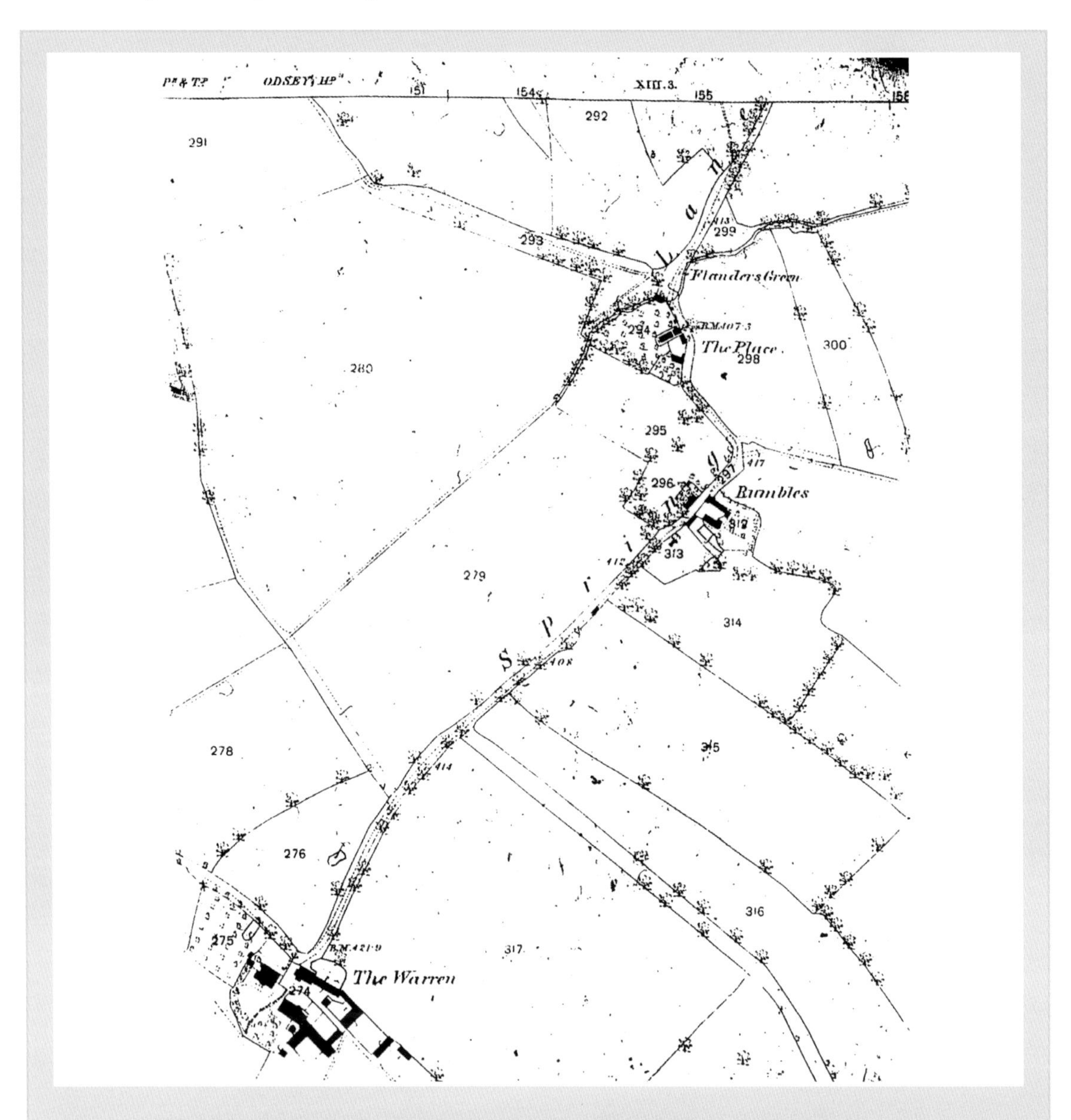

Figure 115: Extract from the Ordnance Survey first edition 25 inch map of the area, sheet Hertfordshire 13 – 7 showing the application route

c. In the entry for the Area Book for Cottered, there is a description for land parcel 297. The description reads, 'Road'.

d. In *Rights of Way: Restoring the Record*, the map on its own would be worth one star for physical evidence, but coupled with the 'road' description in the area book, it is worth three stars.

4 PARISH OF COTTERED.

No. on Plan.	Area in Acres.	Remarks.
278	5·053	Arable.
279	9·719	Arable, &c.
280	17·067	Arable, &c.
281	7·609	Arable.
282	·412	House, gardens, &c.
283	3·117	Road.
284	4·339	Arable.
285	3·051	Arable.
286	10·255	Arable.
287	1·557	Pasture, &c.
288	3·392	Arable, &c.
289	·203	Wood.
290	3·495	Arable.
291	5·682	Arable.
292	5·031	Arable.
293	1·355	Pasture.
294	·713	Houses, gardens, &c.
295	2·154	Pasture.
296	·054	House, garden, &c.
297	2·243	Road.
298	3·309	Arable, &c.
299	·368	Pasture, &c.
300	2·239	Pasture, &c.
301	15·560	Arable, &c.
302	19·496	Arable, &c.
303	1·304	Road.
304	·165	Wood.
305	3·641	Arable.
306	4·049	Arable.
307	9·825	Arable.
308	7·180	Pasture, &c.
309	·257	Water (moat).
310	·138	Wood.
311	3·427	Pasture.
312	·451	Houses, garden, &c.
313	·350	Stackyard, &c.
314	3·093	Pasture.
315	7·104	Arable.
316	7·000	Arable.
317	14·286	Arable.
318	22·191	Pasture, &c.
319	2·092	Wood.
320	69·323	Arable.
321	·472	Arable.
322	7·348	Arable.
323	3·700	Road.
324	3·613	Arable.
325	·715	Pasture.
326	2·987	Arable, &c.
327	·168	Road.
328	·544	Pasture.
329	64·553	Arable, &c.
	1832·659	

RECAPITULATION.

Area in Acres.	Remarks.
1787·870	Land.
1·027	Water.
43·762	Roads.
1832·659	Area of the Township of Cottered.

TOWNSHIP OF BROADFIELD.

No. on Plan.	Area in Acres.	Remarks.
1	30·962	Arable.
2	12·079	Pasture, &c.
3	2·353	Arable.
4	2·813	Ornamental ground, &c.
5	16·306	Arable.
6	15·912	Arable, &c.
7	6·406	Pasture, &c.
8	3·846	Arable.
9	·415	Wood.
10	·613	Pasture.
11	19·219	Arable, &c.
12	10·458	Arable, &c.
13	1·337	Arable, &c.
14	·439	Pasture.
15	1·217	Arable.
16	16·169	Arable.
17	7·140	Ornamental ground, &c.
18	5·660	Ornamental ground, &c.
19	7·045	Arable, &c.
20	14·673	Arable.
21	6·532	Ornamental ground, &c.
22	7·258	Ornamental ground, &c.
23	·406	Stackyard, &c.
24	·286	Houses, gardens, &c.
25	9·166	Ornamental ground, &c.

Figure 116: Extract from the Book of Reference to the Plan of the Parish of Cottered, published by the Ordnance Survey of England in 1878

7. Ordnance Survey Boundary Sketch Map

a. The Ordnance Survey was given the duty of ascertaining and recording all public boundaries by the Ordnance Survey Act 1841. Of particular value for determining highway status are the sketch maps (OS 27) and boundary books (OS 26). These were produced under parliamentary authority (the 1841 Act), with the power to summon the Clerk of the Peace and any books, maps, papers or other documents he held (s.5 of the 1841 Act) and under provisions that an offence be committed for obstructing or hindering the surveyor appointed under the 1841 Act (s.8 of the 1841 Act). The Boundary Sketch Map was advertised for public inspection. The records have been held in official custody, firstly by the Ordnance Survey, and latterly by The National Archives.

b. The OS Boundary Sketch Maps in TNA class OS 27 show the whole of a parish, and indicate which of the Boundary Books is needed to look at a specific section of the parish boundary.

c. This route does not cross a parish boundary and so these records can provide no inference.

8. Ordnance Survey Boundary Remark Books

a. The Ordnance Survey was given the duty of ascertaining and recording all public boundaries by the Ordnance Survey Act 1841. The OS Boundary Remark Books, held at The National Archives ('TNA') in class OS 26, are the results of the Ordnance Survey's checking of the boundaries with the meresmen from the parish each side.

b. This route does not cross a parish boundary and so these records can provide no inference.

9. Ordnance Survey Object Name Book

a. The Ordnance Survey needed a reliable way of determining the names put on their maps. They recorded the authority for the names and the modes of spelling. Their record books give other information.

b. The Object Name Book for map Hertfordshire XIII NE, held as TNA document OS 35/3264 records the name of the application route as Spring Lane. The description given is 'A public lane extending NE from The Warren to Brook End'.

c. In *Rights of Way: Restoring the Record*, this evidence is worth four stars.

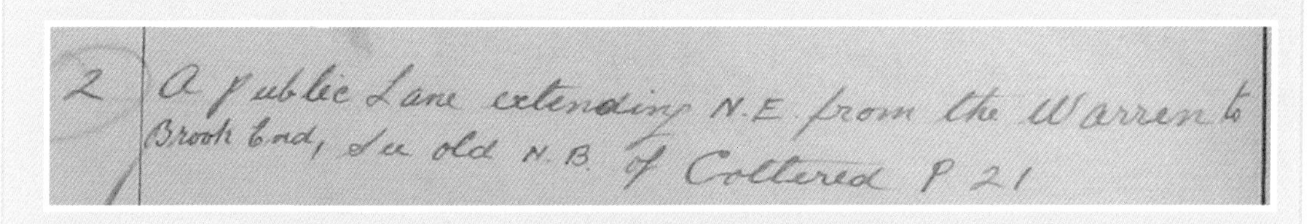

2 A public Lane extending N.E from the Warren to Brook End, See old N.B. of Cottered P 21

Figure 117: Enlarged extract from the OS Object Name Book OS35/3264

Figure 118: Whole page extract from the OS Object Name Book OS35/3264

10. <u>Inland Revenue Valuation</u>

a. The Finance (1909–10) Act 1910 provided for land valuations to take place across the country so that the increase in its value could be taxed. Deductions from the assessable value could be claimed by landowners where the land was crossed by a footpath or bridleway. Where a vehicular highway crossed land, it was usually omitted from the valuation, and shown on the Inland Revenue's plans as a 'white road'.

b. The extracts below are from the records that were passed from the IR Valuation Offices to The National Archives at Kew. Reference IR126/4/121 Part 1 covers base map Hertfordshire XIII 7. Reference IR126/4/117 covers Hertfordshire XIII 3.

c. In both maps, the application route is shown as a white road. The applicant draws the conclusion that it was a vehicular highway.

d. In *Rights of Way: Restoring the Record*, this evidence is rated as five stars.

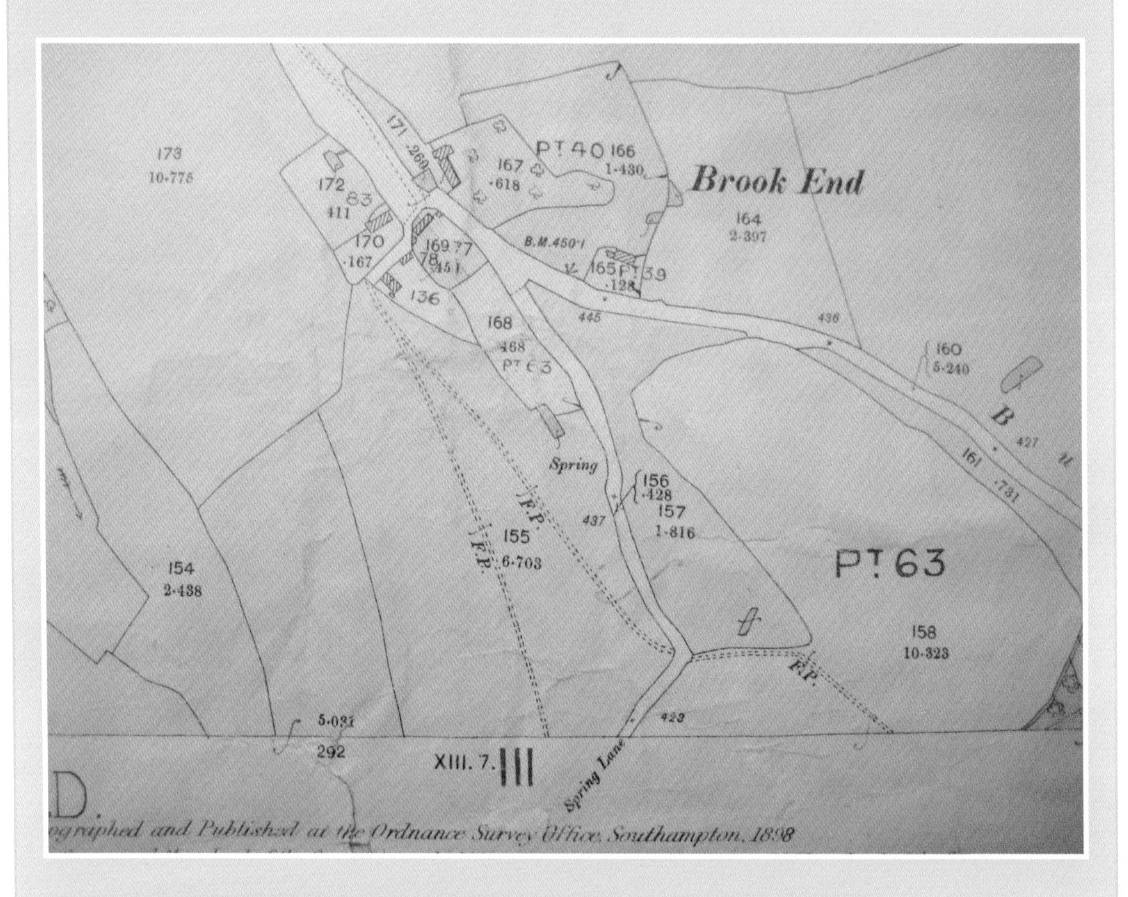

Figure 119: Extract from Inland Revenue Valuation Map IR126/4/117

Figure 120: Extract from Inland Revenue Valuation Map IR126/4/121 Part 1

11. Map of Main and County Roads (1927)

a. This document is held by Hertfordshire Archives and Local Studies (HALS) under reference 'Off Acc 732 (unboxed)'.

b. Under s.15 Highways and Locomotives (Amendment) Act 1898, it was enacted that where it appears to any Highway Authority that any Highway within their District ought to become a Main Road by reason of its being a medium of communication between great towns, or a thoroughfare to a railway station, or otherwise, such Highway Authority may apply to the County Authority for an Order declaring such road as to such parts as aforesaid to be a Main Road and the County Authority, if of opinion that there is probable cause for the application, shall cause the road to be inspected, and if satisfied that it ought to be a Main Road shall make an Order accordingly.

c. The map below is an extract from a map created by the county council to index which routes had been taken over as Main Roads. Part of the application route appears to have been included as Main Road number 780.

d. This indicates to the applicant that it was considered to carry vehicular rights at the time the map was drawn up.

e. In *Rights of Way: Restoring the Record*, this evidence is rated as five stars.

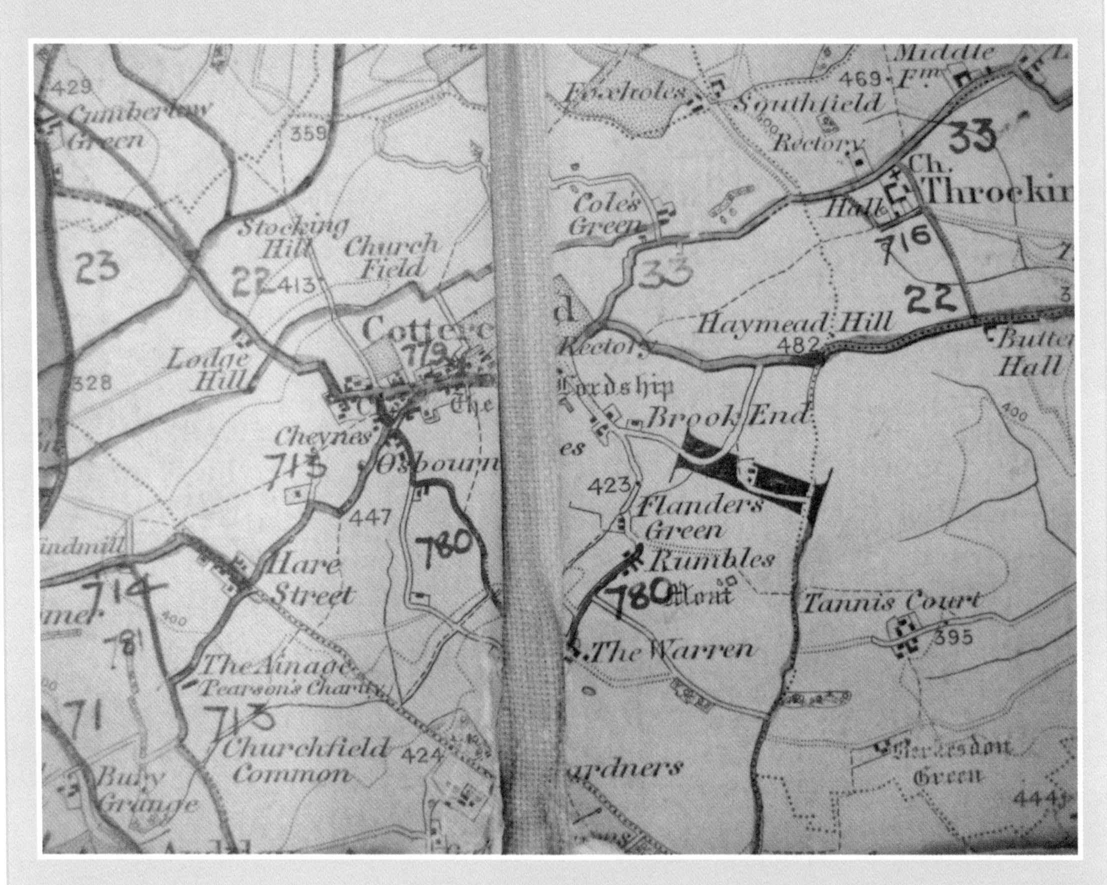

Figure 121: Extract from the Hertfordshire Main and County Roads Map (1927)

CONCLUSIONS

12. In short, all the evidence produced for the application route suggests that vehicular rights existed at the times the various pieces of evidence were created. While no single piece is conclusive of highway status, the fact that every standard piece of evidence leans towards vehicular rights means that, on the balance of probabilities, such rights existed prior to the commencement of the Natural Environment and Rural Communities Act 2006.

13. In the scoring scheme suggested by *Rights of Way: Restoring the Record*, the evidence presented appears to be worth 21 (= 2 + 2 + 3 + 4 +5 + 5) stars. This is more than the suggested value for the basic evidential test (5).

REQUEST

14. The Applicant requests the surveying authority to add the route to the definitive map as a byway. (The type of byway – restricted or open to all traffic – will depend on the application of the Natural Environment and Rural Communities Act 2006).

6. HELPFUL HINTS AND PRACTICAL SUGGESTIONS

6.1 Research Materials

Mark up and maintain a 'research index map' and develop a list of potential application routes within a parish. Keep a summary sheet for each route investigation (see section 2.2).

Build up an electronic library of photographs of documents. The authors have found it best to collect the photographs of each document in a file, and all those of a similar document type (sales particulars, tithe records, inclosure awards etc) within a folder. It is important to use this as a reference library, and only 'cut and paste' when using any photograph for an application. So stored, the photographs can be shared with other researchers, and so reduce the number of times the original documents are handled. It is important, on a regular basis, to back this information up to safeguard against the repercussions of the failure of one computer.

6.2 Preparations Before Visiting a Record Office

While almost every visit to a record office can be helpful and provide new evidence, in order to get the most out of limited visiting time, researchers may find the following pointers helpful.

- Check the website for details of opening times, temporary closures, travel possibilities, reader's ticket requirement, and restrictions, if any, on camera use.
- Check their online catalogue and make a list of references of all relevant documents.
- Pre-order if possible. Some record offices cannot accept pre-orders without a current reader's ticket. Most limit the number of documents that can be pre-ordered, so order your next batch as soon as you arrive.
- Some documents are stored offsite and may require prior notice (this should be apparent when pre-ordering online).

- Photographs and negatives are usually stored chilled and will therefore require ordering in advance.
- Some record offices (The National Archives for example) allow bulk orders (possibly up to 30 pieces) to be pre-ordered, but this may be restricted and will need more notice.
- Some records are stored in boxes of ten or more consecutive documents, therefore, when requiring a large block of these, order 1 from each box rather than consecutively numbered documents.
- Some record offices have very limited space but will allow a map table to be booked. Check whether you need to do this.
- If the record office requires gloves to be worn, consider buying a pair of inexpensive cotton gloves rather than having to use the plastic ones provided.
- Consider buying a second battery for your camera, so you can change them over when at a record office and so always have one charging up.
- If there are practical alternatives, decide which record office to use for particular documents, some charge for camera use and some do not allow it; some have records on microfiche and others produce the originals.
- If photography and photocopying are not allowed, check whether tracing paper is permitted, and if so take some with you.

6.3 Visiting Record Offices

6.3.1 Things to Take When Visiting

- The reader's card for the record office, or appropriate forms of identification if you need to get a new or replacement reader's card.
- A copy of this book.
- A pencil (without an eraser) and a note pad.
- Take in your own research index map (described in section 2.2). Put your name on it and inform the record office staff that you have it with you so they do not think you are writing on or taking one of theirs out with you. If carrying out research on an area or parish, take a note of the list/index of routes within each parish which you already believe are worthy of further investigation.

- A list of the documents you have pre-ordered and further documents to order.
- A camera with a fully charged battery, and, if intending to take a large number of photographs, the computer and cord to download the photographs and the camera battery charger.
- Your laptop computer, if you need to check your records or download photos.

6.3.2 At the Record Office

- Order documents as soon as you arrive so they will be ready when the pre-ordered ones have been scrutinised.
- When applying for a reader's card at a record office or archive library, say that you are working on a long term project and would like the card to run for two or three years.
- Ask if they have any advisory leaflets. The National Archives has a good collection.
- Note any local requirements for handling documents. Archive offices have a duty to preserve the documents and on occasion will say that a document is too fragile for production. In such cases, a researcher may be allowed to view the document under supervision.
- Archiving of records is an ever-changing and improving system and more and more document references are being added to electronic catalogues. Ask at a record or archive office if they are cataloguing any documents which might be of interest for rights of way research.
- Some record offices have ring binders or card indexes listing maps by parish, which can be useful, although references for sales documents, 1910 Domesday books and other documents will have to be found using the online catalogue.
- Ask if records such as the Quarter Sessions or Highway Board minutes have been catalogued (either by staff or volunteers).
- Know what you want to look at or research before you go, or you will get side-tracked.
- If considering researching more routes and in several parishes, take photographs of the whole county's listings in Kain and Oliver's book on tithe maps, then you will always have the information, particularly the date and TNA reference number, of every tithe map.

- Some private collections deposited at a record office may have restrictions on their availability and permission to photograph these particular documents may be required.
- Many maps of the counties on the eastern seaboard and London were marked up to show bomb damage and air raid routes during both world wars. These are often on Ordnance Survey maps. Many can be found in the Metropolitan Archives and County Record Offices.
- In large archive offices, type in the county name and 'map' and see if any other references are shown.

6.3.3 Collecting the Documentary Evidence

6.3.3.1 General points

- Keep a record of what documents you have looked at so that you do not re-order documents which you have already photographed or which have no useful information.
- If you see a particular track or feature which is important to you, photograph that section of your research index map (possibly with your finger pointing to it) and then the same feature/track on the document, it will make it easier to find the relevant photo when you need it.
- Take a blank shot (e.g. the floor) in between individual documents which makes it easier to see where each set of photographs starts and ends when filing them later.
- Be careful when photographing not to turn over two pages at once – check the page numbers if there are any.
- Always check that you have taken all the relevant photos. Some documents, for example the Boundary Remark Books in The National Archives, have several blank pages in the middle after the maps and then descriptions and verifications near the back of the book.
- When considering a route near a parish boundary, the adjacent parish's documents may also provide supporting evidence.

6.3.3.2 For each document

- Always look on the back of a document (occasionally it has notes or endorsements and some have the reference number).

- When photographing, always photograph the outside of the document if it has the name and/or reference number on it, and possibly also the reference slip.
- Always photograph the whole of the document (unless completely impracticable).
- Always take a photograph of the key to any map or plan. This will be important in the evaluation of the evidence.
- If possible, take a photo of a whole map and then photograph smaller sections in more detail. (Some record offices have a step stool to aid this.)
- Always include any compass mark showing 'N' (for north) on at least one of the photographs, to aid in orienting the map later. This is especially important if north is not obviously at the top of the map, for example, in railway plans.
- Check, and possibly photograph, a note of the scale and units: e.g. some lengths are given in perches (1 perch = 5.5 yards = 5.08 metres), chains (22 yards = 20.4 metres) or furlongs (220 yards = 203.8 metres).
- In general, it is worthwhile to note as much as is available of the following information when taking information from or photographing any document:
    - The archive office.
    - The reference number of the document.
    - The date of the document.
    - Parish(s).
    - The coordinates.
    - Status of the track on the definitive map (and this may change along the length of the track).
    - Lengths (where appropriate, and units e.g. furlongs, perches etc).
    - Distances (where appropriate, e.g. from the start of a railway line).
    - Owners (where given).
    - Responsibility for maintenance (where given).
    - Easements (where given).
    - Adjoining routes ('meets another district road' etc).
    - If appropriate, draw the line of the document route on the research index map with the reference number, this is helpful for railway records and river authority records.

6.3.3.3 When a reference is not easy to find

- If a tithe map is proving difficult to find, look at the map in Kain and Oliver's book and see if you can identify the parish or a parish nearby, then use the number of the identified parish and see what name it relates to; quite often it is the right parish, but the spelling has changed (e.g. the Rimpton tithe map number is 'under' 'Rympton'), or the name has changed slightly (for example, King Weston to Kingweston) and this is enough of a change to make finding the reference more difficult. In place names 'y' can change to 'i' and 'a' to 'o' and vice versa over the years.
- Sometimes 'l's and 'e's get added or left off.
- Some names can be catalogued in different ways, e.g. East Chinnock might be under Chinnock East. Also, some names have joined and/or changed such as 'Whitestaunton' is catalogued under 'White Staunton'. This can even apply to sister series, e.g. at The National Archives, the Boundary Remark Books (OS26) entry is under 'Combe Saint Nicholas' and the Boundary Sketch Map (OS27) is found under 'Combe St. Nicholas'.
- In the tithe apportionment the numbers may be in any order, sometimes in alphabetical order of the owner's name. Tracks and Roads often do not have an apportionment number, and many tracks and roads which were allotted an apportionment number do not have an entry of any amount in the 'amount of rent charge apportioned upon the several lands' column, which would be the case for titheable land, so a quick check in the rent charge column may 'indicate' such untithed apportionments. It should be remembered that some routes, such as wide droves, were titheable, if a crop could be taken from them. In some apportionments the roads were grouped together at the end.
- Sometimes the parishes have since been combined (or split), and the area of the one that was subsumed has the tithe map covering the missing area. If you suspect this to be the case, either check the map in 'Kain and Oliver's' listing, or the edge of the tithe map near the required area and look for the name of the adjoining parish which has been subsumed.
- Yorkshire is catalogued as one county for some documents and as three or four separate sections (North Riding, West Riding, East Riding and Ainsty) in other series.
- Hampshire sometimes appears under Southhampshire.

- Railway documents are sometimes catalogued by their termini.
- Where a book of reference (for railway and river/drainage records) has been stored in the roll with the map, it might be very curled up. It is worth photographing the whole of the book of reference, possibly printing off a copy of the photographs so the original document can be spared excessive handling. Find the crossings on the map, and then check them on the book of reference.
- If a book of reference is missing from one archive office, check if another archive office which holds the same document has a copy of the missing book of reference.
- If it is difficult to identify the correct field book for the 1910 Finance Act records, see the locating advice in section 3.17.
- Canals usually had reservoirs, and before construction the rights of way which would be covered by the new reservoir would have had to be diverted, so check the information on the area for the reservoirs as well as the ribbon of land used by the actual canal.
- Even if a proposed canal or railway line was not built, the deposited plans will be useful because they show the situation at every place where the line crosses a right of way.
- Occasionally some counties will have two parishes with the same name, for example Appledore in Devon. Take care to check the correct records if this happens in your county.
- Most record offices have the volumes of Kelly's for their county. These directories came out regularly and contain information on parishes, including, sometimes, which rural or urban district they were in, which can be useful for locating relevant highway board records.
- If documents have information with field numbers but no map, the number will probably refer to either apportionment numbers on the tithe map, or the OS field numbers printed on the County series maps, or possibly lot numbers in an auction catalogue. The date of the document should give a clue as the people compiling the document will probably have used the best map available at the time – often the tithe map.

6.4 Private Archives

- Some large estates have private collections and may employ an archivist. It may be possible to gain information or view documents from such collections if the owner and archivist are willing.
- Records may be held by university libraries, local history societies, museums, or local libraries. Information about such locations is beyond the scope of this book.
- Some private collections are held by public record offices and the owner's permission may be required, or charged for, if the document is to be used at a public inquiry.

6.5 Away from the Record Offices

- Buy, beg or borrow any old maps (including touring – cycling or motoring) or road atlases whenever available. Photocopy or photograph them.
- Sometimes historical documents and old maps may come up as lots at local auction houses. Look out for these, where possible.
- Visit second-hand bookshops to buy old maps and guides.

6.6 Looking at Landscape and Physical Features

- The presence of milestones is usually regarded as evidence of a turnpike road, these were indicated by MS or MP on the Ordnance Survey 1:50,000 Landranger maps.
- Consider the gradient of a route. Bridleways could be steeper than carriageways.
- What might now appear to be a cul-de-sac route may have (or have had) as its destination a place of public interest and so could have public rights. Check whether there were any markets, important houses, ferry/ quay, church or such places near the application route, particularly near the end or as a continuation, as this could have been why the route was in use, and, possibly why it became less important because the place of interest lost its status (for example, a priory, or a market that ceased to be held).

- A track called 'Hangman's Lane' even if a dead end, most likely went to a place of public resort and therefore probably had public rights.
- A mill suggests there was public access to it, and this would have been with carts since sacks of grain are heavy.
- When there has been a prolonged period without rain, go and check where there may have been fords. Occasionally old cobbles or stoned ramps may be found. A ford would be for the use of ridden or driven horses and other animals, whereas a footbridge would only accommodate walkers.
- Measure the width of railway bridges, the width is significant in determining what level of highway passed under it – see section 3.9 on Railway and Canal Records.
- Bridges, check their construction:
    - a simple lightweight plank bridge is indicative of a footpath, but it may be shown alongside a ford which would indicate there was route with higher rights alongside the bridge.
    - a stone or arched packhorse bridge would also probably be alongside a ford which would have been used by ridden horses and possibly coaches.
    - a stone arched bridge wide enough for carriages would probably have been constructed over rivers that were not easily fordable.
- Hawthorn hedges were often planted to mark out the line of inclosure roads where walls were not built.
- Where there is a place name with 'gate' in it, consider if it might have been a turnpike gate, and check for turnpike records.
- If a name has 'common' in it or the route runs up to a common, check the commons register (at the county council or unitary authority), or check the records to see if the land was rejected as a common at the time they were originally registered. Commons often carried public rights, so preventing a route leading to a common from being a dead-end.
- The General Turnpike Act of 1773 extended the privilege of erecting gates on side roads to foil toll evasion by travellers using circuitous routes.
- Where there is a lay-by opposite a track, it might have been for the carriages to swing round out of what was a carriage road coming in across the road, and which now may only be recorded as a footpath.

- Old stoned tracks have probably never been ploughed, and can still be distinguished between cultivated lands; prodding with a stave/stake will indicate that there is still a stoned/hard surface underneath. These tracks may also, occasionally, be raised from the surrounding land.

6.7 Checking a Particular Route on the Ground

This may only be possible if the route already has recorded public rights (for example a footpath when the historical evidence suggests higher rights), or is in regular use by the public.

- When going out to check a route, take a photocopy of the relevant section of your research index map rather than the original as it may get wet or damaged. Also take a pen to make notes on where there are landmarks, gates etc.
- Take a camera with a fully charged battery.
- Make a note of the date the route was checked, and again if checked at on another date.
- Note if there are hoof prints on the ground, and if there are horses in fields adjoining the route.
- As well as the ends of the route where it joins other routes, photograph distinctive features such as where the track is higher or lower than the surrounding ground, goes through gates or gaps. Mark the place and number of the photograph on the copy of the research index map.
- Make a note of any gates into fields off the route, which obviously use the track as access to the field.
- Note if there is a stile alongside but not on the line of what you believe to be the legal line of a route with higher rights. The stile might have been installed alongside a gate which has now been locked or replaced with fencing.
- If there is a manhole cover set into the track, check which utility company has responsibility for it and whose land they think it is on.
- Consider where a route may have been headed. Old public routes would have led to places that the public wanted to reach.
- If there is a property reached from the application route which is not served by any other public highway, remember to check the records for any easement mentioned in earlier

sales documents. If none, then it would appear that the property was accessed by a public road, unless the drive appears on the deeds.

- If there are horse signs on the road near the junction of an application route with the road, check, if possible, when and why they were sanctioned or erected. It might have been put up when the application route was acknowledged as a bridleway by the highway authority.
- Have a look at the track and check whether it is double-hedged – or might have been had one or both hedges not been taken out. This often indicates bridleway or carriageway status (although sometimes can just be a farm track).
- If the route is at the edge of an agricultural field, check whether the ground is the same as the rest of the field or if it has a hard surface under the top few inches of soil. A different surface or subsoil could indicate that that strip of land was treated differently from the rest of the field, which would be consistent with highway rights.

6.8 Traditional Beliefs That May Assist in Identifying Routes

These may assist in guiding research, but should not be quoted in an applicant's statement without corroboration!

- Holly trees were often planted at junctions of coaching roads because they were easier to see at night.
- A holly tree or groups of Scots Pines were often used as landmarks on long distance routes to indicate the route and where accommodation could be found.
- Where there are stinging nettles, there was human habitation.

6.9 Modification Orders

There are some points which should be bought to the surveying authority's attention, if they apply:

- It is not unusual for two footpaths to join a track a few hundred yards apart, and it could be assumed that the public would have used the section of the connecting track to travel between one footpath and the next, rather than have two cul-de-sac footpaths. So where two footpaths join a route (which is not a public road or a route on the definitive map) at different places, it suggests that the route connecting the ends of the two footpaths should also have public rights, and of a higher status – or it would have been recorded at the time as a footpath too. Therefore, if an application route is joined at different places by footpaths which would otherwise be cul-de-sacs, it is almost certain that the application route was perceived by the surveyor at the time to have public status, and of higher rights than the footpaths and bridleways they were recording. Likewise for any route which is joined by a footpath which would, if the route had no public status, be a cul-de-sac. Similarly for bridleways; if one ends at a track which is not recorded, and would have been the obvious connection between that bridleway and another definitive bridleway or road, it can be inferred that the unrecorded route was considered to be a road at the time of the 1950s surveys.
- There are cases where a definitive footpath runs in a field alongside a drove. This often came about because a drove could become excessively muddy or impassable when full of moving animals and the public preferred to walk in the field alongside. As a result, when the definitive map was prepared, the footpath was recorded. However, the drove was missed off as it was thought to be a road and that information was not required at that time. When making a modification order application, take care to distinguish between adding a route (on the line of the drove), and upgrading the footpath which is in the field. It is important that the evidence relates exactly to the line of the application route, and it is doubtful that the footpath in the field carried any higher rights. The application should be to add the rights on the drove, probably of restricted byway status. This also offers the opportunity to discuss whether the footpath rights in the field could be diverted onto the drove road.

- Parish and county boundaries may have changed, so if a route/parish is anywhere near a boundary, be prepared to check the records for the adjoining county, for example Belton on Norfolk/Suffolk boundary. This may also lead to making a definitive map modification order for the continuation of the route in the adjoining county.

6.10 Miscellaneous Notes

- It can be helpful to consult contemporary dictionaries for the meaning of words at that period in time.
- Check if the landowner has deposited a section 31(6) Highways Act 1980 statement saying that he has not dedicated and has no intention of dedicating any routes other than shown on his deposited plan. This would affect any user-evidence based applications but could not be used to undo historical evidence already in existence. It may, however, provide further evidence of status if the route were admitted in the deposit as a highway.
- If the route used to be recorded as a footpath and was diverted, this will not have diverted any higher rights which will remain on the original line. A definitive map modification order will be required to record these higher rights.
- Ask the county council's right of way office if they have any information on the route or whether any previous investigation of the route's status has taken place.
- Maintenance carried out at public expense would not have been legal if it was for routes not available to the public, therefore maintenance records are important to rights of way researchers. Even if maintenance was requested by a parish but refused by the highway authority, it indicates that the parish asking for it believed the route to be available to the public at large.
- If, on the balance of probability, a route does not appear to have historical rights, question why you believed it might – such as an express dedication or evidence that it should have been created in lieu of a route being legally stopped up – and then decide whether to pursue further evidence.
- A highway needs to go from one highway to another, or to a place of public interest (such as a church, monument, ford, watering place or perhaps a nice view). If your route does not

link two highways, consider why it might have stopped at a cul-de-sac point.

- Avoid confusion between 'handover maps' around 1929/30 and maps from the 'Highway and Locomotive Act maps' up to 1927.
- 'ford' on old maps is helpful, especially where there is a footbridge alongside. This would have been put on the map for the benefit of travellers. Note packhorse bridges were for pack animals, they would have had low parapets, and generally be for animals crossing in single file. The ridden horses and carriages would have used the ford.

7. NATIONAL ARCHIVE AND RECORD OFFICES

7.1 Introduction

The internet is the best source of up to date information on the various record and archive offices, so we only provide essential information here. Of particular interest to the researcher will be whether cameras and laptops can be used, or whether tracings and notes have to be taken longhand; whether a membership scheme operates (and hence whether identity documents need to be taken on a first visit); whether parking facilities are available; and whether there is somewhere to eat nearby.

While the list of offices is initially accurate, from time to time archive offices will be closed for refurbishment, or will change location. Most will close for a week or two each year for stock taking. The authors strongly recommend that the office's website be consulted or a telephone call made to check that a journey will not be wasted.

Under s.2(3) of the Public Records Act 1958, it is the duty of the Keeper of Public Records to take all practicable steps for the preservation of records under his charge. This means that where a document is particularly fragile, it may not be produced, or may be produced with special handling instructions.

7.2 The National Archives

<table>
<tr><td>Bessant Drive
Kew
Richmond
London
TW9 4DU

020 8876 3444

Nearest tube: Kew Gardens</td><td>TNA Reader's Ticket

Photography allowed

Parking available

Café on site

Currently closed on Mondays</td></tr>
<tr><td colspan="2">http://www.nationalarchives.gov.uk. Up to 6 documents can be pre-ordered (or up to 20 if they are consecutively numbered). When pre-ordering, ask for a seat in the map room or select the option for large or bulky documents.</td></tr>
</table>

7.3 The British Library

<table>
<tr><td>96 Euston Road
London
NW1 2DB

Nearest tube: King's Cross, St Pancras, Euston</td><td>BL Reader's Ticket

No photography

No parking available

Café on site

It takes about 70 minutes from ordering a document to its production, so pre-ordering is valuable.</td></tr>
<tr><td colspan="2">http://www.bl.uk</td></tr>
</table>

7.4 Parliamentary Archives

<table>
<tr><td>The Parliamentary Archives
Houses of Parliament
(Black Rod's Garden Entrance)
London
SW1A OPW

Nearest tube: Westminster</td><td>Photographic identification required

Appointment required

Photography allowed

No parking available

Refreshments available nearby</td></tr>
<tr><td colspan="2">http://www.parliament.uk/archives
The Parliamentary Archives hold a copy of every Act of Parliament and many supporting documents, such as deposited plans in support of a private railway Act.</td></tr>
</table>

7.5 English Heritage National Monuments Record Centre

Great West Village Kemble Drive Swindon SN2 2GZ 01793 414600	Pre-ordering of documents is required Photography allowed Parking available Refreshments available on site
http://www.englishheritagearchives.org.uk http://www.english-heritage.org.uk/daysout/properties/national-monuments-record-centre/ National Monuments Record Centre. This office holds millions of aerial photos from when the RAF first started taking them. The requirement for advance notice is so that the photos which are stored chilled can be bought up to ambient temperature slowly. They also hold hard copies of sales documents of major land holders such as the Universities, the Church Commissioners and other large estates.	

7.6 Newspaper Library

This is now part of the British Library.

7.7 National Library of Wales – Llyfrgell Genedlaethol Cymru

The National Library of Wales Aberystwyth Ceredigion Wales SY23 3BU	NLW Reader's Ticket Photography allowed Parking available Café on site
http://www.llgc.org.uk	

7.8 Church of England Archives

15 Galleywall Road South Bermondsey London SE16 3PB 020 7897 1030	Reader's Ticket Introductory letter needed – see website Pre-ordering of documents is required No photography Secure parking available Refreshments available nearby
http://www.lambethpalacelibrary.org/content/cerc	

7.9 Royal Mail Archive

Freeling House Phoenix Place London WC1 0DL (This is part of the Mount Pleasant Sorting Office) 020 7239 2570 Nearest tube: Farringdon (10 min walk)	Photographic identification required An appointment is advised Photography allowed Parking available Café nearby
http://www.postalheritage.org.uk	

8. 'COUNTY' ARCHIVE AND RECORD OFFICES

8.1 Introduction and Key

The archiving of records is an ever-changing and improving system and more and more document references are being put on the electronic catalogues. Many record offices receive additional records rendering any book showing the office's holdings out of date. Accordingly, we provide information about county and local record offices here, and advise researchers to check online or by telephone should specific documents be required.

Some archive offices offer a research service which is usually charged out at an hourly rate. Details of such services can be obtained from the appropriate office.

Local government changes over the years have made finding local historic records difficult in places. The researcher may need to consider more than one record office as 'local'. We list here record offices in England by region, followed by record offices in Wales, with notes on coverage areas where needed.

Rules on the need for reader's tickets vary. The authors recommend that you take two forms of identification when visiting an office for the first time, to save a wasted journey should requirements have been tightened since this guide was published. CARN stands for County Archive Research Network.

Many record offices have excellent guidance leaflets, and a new researcher should check what is available. In particular, always ask if there is any guidance on what is available on estates and collections particular to the county or locality.

While the list of offices is initially accurate, from time to time archive offices will be closed for refurbishment, or will change location. Most will close for a week or two each year for stock taking. Some offices need a few days' notice to retrieve documents held off site. Others have days or half-days when they are not open to the public. **The authors strongly recommend that the office's website be consulted or a telephone call made to check that a journey will not be wasted**.

8.2 County and Local Record Offices in England

8.2.1 North East

8.2.1.1 Northumberland Record Offices

Woodhorn QEII Country Park Ashington Northumberland NE63 9YF 01670 528080	Local Reader's Ticket Photography allowed for some documents Parking available Refreshments available on site or nearby
http://www.northumberland.gov.uk/collections Covers the whole of the county except the area around Berwick and south to Ellingham and across to the Cheviots.	

Berwick-upon-Tweed Council Offices, Wallace Green, Berwick-upon-Tweed, TD15 1ED 01289 301865	No Reader's Ticket required No photography Parking available Refreshments available on site or nearby
http://www.northumberland.gov.uk/collections Former Berwick Borough, south to Ellingham, west to Ingram, north to Carham.	

8.2.1.2 Durham County Record Office

County Hall Durham DH1 5UQ 0191 383 3253	No Reader's Ticket; Appointment required. Photography allowed 'sometimes' Parking available Refreshments available on site or nearby
http://www.durham.gov.uk/recordoffice Counties of Durham and Darlington plus some ecclesiastical research information include Sunderland.	

8.2.1.3 Tyne and Wear Records Office

Newcastle Discovery, Blandford Square, Newcastle Upon Tyne, Tyne And Wear NE1 4JA 0191 232 6789	CARN Reader's Ticket Photography allowed Parking available nearby Café in building or seating area for own food
http://www.tyneandweararchives.org.uk Newcastle, Gateshead, Sunderland, South Tyneside, North Tyneside.	

8.2.1.4 Teesside Archives

Exchange House 6 Marton Road Middlesborough TS1 1DB 01642 248391	Admission Free Photography allowed Parking available Refreshments available on site or nearby
http://www.middlesbrough.gov.uk/ccm/navigation/leisure-and-sulture/archives/ Former county of Cleveland. Note: Cleveland was formed from areas previously in County Durham, North Riding of Yorkshire and Teesside County Borough (which included some of County Durham, North Riding & Middlesbrough County Borough). Many records remain with the Durham and North Riding archives.	

8.2.2 North West

8.2.2.1 Cumbria Records Offices

Cumbria Records Office – Barrow 140 Duke Street Barrow-in-Furness LA14 1XW 01229 407377	Local Reader's Ticket Photography allowed Parking available Refreshments available on site or nearby
http://www.cumbria.gov.uk/archives/recordoffices Barrow, and estate papers of Duke of Buccleuch.	

Cumbria Records Office – Carlisle The Castle Carlisle CA3 8UR 01228 227285/227284	Local Reader's Ticket Photography allowed Parking available Refreshments available on site or nearby
http://www.cumbria.gov.uk/archives/recordoffices The historic county of Cumberland north of the Derwent.	

Kendal County Offices Kendal LA9 4RQ 01539 713540/713539	Local Reader's Ticket Photography allowed Limited parking available Refreshments available on site or nearby
http://www.cumbria.gov.uk/archives/recordoffices Records relating to the historic county of Westmorland, and also some for the Sedbergh-Dent district (formerly in the West Riding of Yorkshire) and for the Cartmel district (formerly in Lancashire North of the Sands).	

Cumbria Record Office – Whitehaven 1 Scotch Street Whitehaven CA28 7NL 01946 506420	Local Reader's Ticket Photography allowed Limited parking available Drinks machine available on site
http://www.cumbria.gov.uk/archives/recordoffices West Cumbria bounded by the River Derwent in the north and River Duddon in the south.	

8.2.2.2 Lancashire Record Office

Bow Lane Preston PR1 2RE 01772 533039	Local Reader's Ticket Photography allowed Parking available Drinks machine and rest area
http://www.lancashire.gov.uk/education/record.office Lancashire	

8.2.3 Greater Manchester Record Office

56 Marshall Street New Cross Manchester M4 5FU 0161 832 5284	CARN Reader's Ticket Pre-booking essential Photography allowed Parking available nearby Refreshments available nearby
http://www.manchester.gov.uk/info/448/archives_and_local_studies Covers all of Greater Manchester and Manchester City plus Bolton, Bury, Rochdale, Salford, Stockport, Oldham, Tameside (Ashton) and Trafford.	

<table>
<tr><td>The Manchester Room @ City
Library
Elliot House
151 Deansgate
Manchester
M3 2HN

0161 832 5284</td><td>CARN Reader's Ticket

Pre-booking recommended

Photography allowed

Parking available nearby

Refreshments available nearby</td></tr>
<tr><td colspan="2">http://www.manchester.gov.uk/info/448/archives_and_local_studies
The Greater Manchester County Record Office's key non-original sources are now available in the Manchester Room@City Library, rather than at Greater Manchester County Record Office.</td></tr>
</table>

8.2.3.1 Liverpool Records Office

<table>
<tr><td>Central Library
William Brown Street
Liverpool
L3 8EW

0151 233 5817</td><td>CARN accepted

Photography allowed

Parking available

No café, but seating area</td></tr>
<tr><td colspan="2">http://www.liverpool.gov.uk/archives
Covers Merseyside and Liverpool.</td></tr>
</table>

8.2.3.2 Cheshire Record Office

<table>
<tr><td>Duke Street
Chester
CH1 1RL

01244 972574</td><td>CARN Reader's Ticket

Photography allowed by agreement only

Parking available for disabled only

Drinks machine and rest area</td></tr>
<tr><td colspan="2">http://archives.cheshire.gov.uk/
This archive office acts on behalf of both Cheshire West and Chester, and Cheshire East Councils.</td></tr>
</table>

8.2.3.3 Cheshire (Wirral) Record Office

<table>
<tr><td>Lower Ground Floor
Cheshire Lines Building
Canning Street
Birkenhead
Wirral
CH41 1ND

0151 606 2929</td><td>No admission card is needed

Photography allowed

Parking available (pay and display)

Refreshments available nearby</td></tr>
<tr><td colspan="2">http://www.wirral.gov.uk/my-services/leisure-and-culture/wirral-archives-service
Wirral Archives Service was founded in 1974 upon the creation of the Metropolitan Borough of Wirral, a borough of Merseyside. Previously, the Wirral peninsula had been a part of the County of Cheshire.</td></tr>
</table>

8.2.4 Yorkshire

8.2.4.1 York City

<table>
<tr><td>Archives and Local History
York Explore Centre
Museum Street
York
YO1 7DS

01904 552800</td><td>Identification required

Photography allowed

No parking on site, available at Maygate

Café on site

Documents must be pre-ordered by at least 48 hours</td></tr>
<tr><td colspan="2">http://www.york.gov.uk/archives
Mainly the city of York.</td></tr>
</table>

<table>
<tr><td>Borthwick Institute for Archives
University Library & Archives
University of York
Heslington
York
YO10 5DD

01904 321166</td><td>Photography allowed – only with prior notice

Booking advised

Parking nearby

Cafés nearby</td></tr>
<tr><td colspan="2">http://www.york.ac.uk/library/borthwick/
Includes papers from the Diocese of York.</td></tr>
</table>

8.2.4.2 West Yorkshire Archive Service

Central Library Northgate Hose Northgate Halifax HI IUN 01422 392636	CARN Reader's Ticket Photography allowed Parking available Refreshments available nearby Appointment advisable
http://www.archives.wyjs.org.uk/ Mostly Calderdale.	

Bradford Central Library Princes Way Bradford BDI INN 01274 435099	CARN Reader's Ticket or other identification Photography allowed Parking available Vending machines available on site
http://www.archives.wyjs.org.uk/ Bradford, Ilkley, Skipton, Leeds.	

Central Library Princess Alexandra Walk, Huddersfield HDI 2SU 01484 221966	CARN Reader's Ticket Photography allowed Parking available nearby Refreshments available nearby
http://www.archives.wyjs.org.uk/ Dewsbury, Huddersfield, Denby Dale, Holmforth, Kirkburton, Honley, Batley, and surrounding areas.	

Registry of Deeds – Wakefield Newstead Road Wakefield WFI 2DE 01924 305980	CARN Reader's Ticket or other identification Photography allowed Parking available Picnic area available
http://www.archives.wyjs.org.uk/ Old county of the West Riding plus other records.	

Leeds Record Office Chapeltown Road Sheepscan Leeds LS7 3AP 0113 214 5814	CARN Reader's Ticket or other identification Photography allowed Parking available (on street) Rest area available
http://www.archives.wyjs.org.uk/ Old West Riding	

8.2.4.3 North Yorkshire Archive Service

County Record Office Malpas Road Northallerton DL7 8TB 01609 777585	Make appointment to visit No photography Parking available (limited) Refreshments 10 min walk away
http://www.northyorks.gov.uk/archives North Yorkshire (Old West Riding documents are in Leeds, Old East Riding documents are in Beverley). Some records are held in Teesside (see 8.2.1.4) or York or Borthwick (see 8.2.4.1).	

8.2.4.4 Barnsley Archives and Local Studies

Barnsley Central Library Shambles Street Barnsley South Yorkshire S70 2JF 01226 773950	Free admission Photography permitted – £1 per document Parking available at nearby retail sites Café nearby
http://www.barnsley.gov.uk/barnsley-archives-and-local-studies Barnsley Metropolitan Borough	

8.2.4.5 Rotherham Archives and Local Studies Service

Rotherham Central Library Walker Place Rotherham S65 1JH 01709 823616	Sign in, no identification or ticket required Photography not allowed – but possibly at the discretion of the staff Parking available in library car park or multi-storey car park Safe in library
http://www.rotherham.gov.uk/info/448/records_and_archives-information_and_advice Rotherham	

8.2.4.6 Sheffield Archives and Local Studies

52 Shoreham Street Sheffield S1 4SP 0114 203 9395	Sheffield Archives Reader's Ticket Photography allowed Parking available nearby Café nearby
http://www.sheffield.gov.uk/libraries/archives-and-local-studies This office used to have the records for South Yorkshire, now they mainly have records for the Sheffield area and the records of the Dioceses of Sheffield. They also have the estate papers of the Wentworth estates, even though this estate is nearer to Rotherham.	

8.2.4.7 Doncaster Archives

Doncaster Archives King Edward Road Balby Doncaster DN4 0NA 01302 859811	Doncaster Library Card Photography allowed Parking available Sandwich shops, café and pubs nearby
http://www.doncaster.gov.uk/doncasterarchives/ Archdeaconry of Doncaster and Doncaster Metropolitan Borough.	

8.2.4.8 East Riding Archives and Local Studies Service

East Riding Archives and Local Studies The Treasure House Champney Road Beverly HU17 9BA 01482 392790	CARN Reader's Ticket Booking essential Photography allowed Parking available at nearby supermarket or railway station Café on site
http://www2.eastriding.gov.uk/leisure/archives-family-and-local-history/ East Riding of Yorkshire and some archives for Hull.	

8.2.4.9 Hull City Archives

Hull History Centre Worship Street Hull HU2 8BG 01482 317500	CARN Reader's Ticket Booking available Photography allowed Parking available nearby Café on site
http://www.hullhistorycentre.org.uk/ Hull History Centre is the new home for Hull City Archives, Hull Local Studies Library and Hull University Archives.	

8.2.5 East Midlands

8.2.5.1 Nottinghamshire Record Office

<table>
<tr><td>Nottinghamshire Archives and
Southwell & Nottingham Diocesan
Record Office
County House
Castle Meadow Road
Nottingham
NG2 1AG

0115 958 1634</td><td>CARN Reader's Ticket
Photography allowed
Limited parking available
Refreshments available nearby</td></tr>
<tr><td colspan="2">http://www.nottinghamshire.gov.uk/home/leisure/archives.htm
Nottinghamshire (and some Peterborough records).</td></tr>
</table>

8.2.5.2 Derbyshire Record Office

<table>
<tr><td>County Hall
Matlock
Derbyshire
DE4 3AG

01629 539207

(Note planned office move in 2013)</td><td>CARN Reader's Ticket
Pre-booking (5 days) essential
No photography
Parking available nearby
No refreshments on site</td></tr>
<tr><td colspan="2">http://www.derbyshire.gov.uk/recordoffice
Derbyshire, Derby City and the Diocese of Derby.</td></tr>
</table>

8.2.5.3 Leicestershire and Rutland County Record Office

<table>
<tr><td>Long Street
Wigston
Leicester
LE18 2AH

0116 257 1080</td><td>Local Reader's Ticket
Photography allowed
Parking available
Refreshments available on site or nearby</td></tr>
<tr><td colspan="2">http://www.leics.gov.uk/recordoffice
This office covers both Leicestershire and Rutland records.</td></tr>
</table>

8.2.5.4 Northamptonshire Record office

Wootton Hall Park Northampton NN4 8BQ 01604 767562 or 01604 762129	CARN Reader's Ticket Photography allowed Parking available Area for eating
http://www.northamptonshire.gov.uk. Follow the 'Community and Living' option on the left of the page, and then 'Record Office'. Holds records for Northamptonshire. It is also the Peterborough Diocesan Record Office and holds some records for Peterborough.	

8.2.5.5 Lincolnshire Archives

St Rumbold Street Lincoln LN2 5AB 01522 782040	CARN Reader's Ticket plus other identification Photography allowed Parking available Refreshments available nearby
http://www.lincolnshire.gov.uk/residents/archives/ Lincolnshire	

8.2.6 West Midlands

8.2.6.1 Herefordshire Record Office

Harold Street Hereford HR1 2QX 01432 260750	CARN Reader's Ticket Photography allowed Parking available Eating area available, no food sold on site
http://www.herefordshire.gov.uk/archives	

8.2.6.2 Worcestershire Record Office

County Hall Spetchley Road Worcester WR5 2NP 01905 766351	CARN Reader's Ticket Photography allowed Parking available Refreshments available on site or nearby
http://www.worcestershire.gov.uk/records	

8.2.6.3 Shropshire Archives

Castle Gates Shrewsbury SY1 2AQ 01743 255350	Local Reader's Ticket Photography allowed Parking available Eating area available
http://www.shropshirearchives.org.uk	

8.2.6.4 Staffordshire and Stoke on Trent Archive Service

Staffordshire Record Office Eastgate Street Stafford ST16 2LZ 01785 278379	Local Reader's Ticket Photography allowed No parking available Drinks machine on site, cafés nearby
http://www.staffordshire.gov.uk/leisure/archives/contact/sro/home.aspx Records for Staffordshire are also held at Litchfield. This is the Bishop's collection which has a more complete set of tithe maps.	

<table>
<tr><td>Lichfield Record Office
The Friary
Lichfield
WS13 6QG

01543 510720</td><td>Local Reader's Ticket
Appointment essential
Photography allowed
Parking available nearby
Cafés nearby</td></tr>
<tr><td colspan="2">http://www.staffordshire.gov.uk/leisure/archives/contact/LichfieldRecordOffice/home.aspx
Holds the Bishop of Litchfield's collection and the Diocesan records, plus some tithe maps for Staffordshire and Shropshire and some estate and inclosure maps.</td></tr>
</table>

<table>
<tr><td>Stoke on Trent City Archives
City Central Library
Bethesda Street
Hanley, Stoke on Trent
Staffordshire
ST1 3RS

Tel: 01782 238420</td><td>Local Reader's Ticket
Photography allowed
Parking available nearby
Cafés nearby</td></tr>
<tr><td colspan="2">http://www.staffordshire.gov.uk/leisure/archives/contact/stoke/home.aspx
Holds records for the north of the county and the Potteries.</td></tr>
</table>

8.2.6.5 Warwickshire County Record Office

<table>
<tr><td>Priory Park
Cape Road
Warwick
CV34 4JS

01926 738959</td><td>CARN Reader's Ticket
Photography allowed
Limited parking available
Tearoom available on site</td></tr>
<tr><td colspan="2">http://www.warwickshire.gov.uk/archivesunlocked</td></tr>
</table>

8.2.7 East of England

8.2.7.1 Bedfordshire and Luton Record Office

Borough Hall Cauldwell Street Bedford MK42 9AP 01234 228833	No Reader's Ticket required Photography allowed Limited parking available Refreshments available on site
http://www.bedford.gov.uk/archive The historic county of Bedfordshire including Luton.	

8.2.7.2 Cambridgeshire Archives and Local Studies

Box RES 1009 Shire Hall Castle Hill Cambridge CB3 0AP	CARN Reader's Ticket Photography allowed Parking available Refreshments available on site or nearby
http://www.cambridgeshire.gov.uk/leisure/archives/ Holds records relating to the former counties of Cambridgeshire and the Isle of Ely, all archived records of Cambridgeshire County Council from 1974 onwards and records dating from before 1974 which cover both the old Cambridgeshire and Huntingdonshire areas. Historical records relating to Thorney, previously in the former county of the Isle of Ely and now in the Peterborough City Council area, are still held in Cambridgeshire Archives.	

8.2.7.3 Huntingdonshire Record Office

<table>
<tr><td>Huntingdon Archives and Local Studies
Huntingdon Library and Archives
Princes Street
Huntingdon
PE29 2PA

01480 372738</td><td>CARN Reader's Ticket
Photography allowed
Limited parking available
Refreshments available nearby</td></tr>
<tr><td colspan="2">http://www.cambridgeshire.goc.uk/leisure/archives
Holds records relating to the former county of Huntingdonshire, an area largely coinciding with today's Huntingdonshire District Council, and the Archdeaconry of Huntingdon. This includes Alwalton, Stanground, the Ortons, and Fletton, which were historically part of Huntingdonshire but which today form part of Peterborough City Council.</td></tr>
</table>

8.2.7.4 Peterborough Record Office

<table>
<tr><td>The Central Library
Broadway
Peterborough
PE1 1RX

01733 864160</td><td>No Reader's Ticket
Photography allowed
Parking available nearby
Refreshments available nearby</td></tr>
<tr><td colspan="2">http://www.vivacity-peterborough.com/libraries-and-archives/archives/
The Northamptonshire Record Office is also the Peterborough Diocesan Record Office.
Records relating to Peterborough can be found in a variety of places: Cambridgeshire Archives, Huntingdonshire Archives, Northamptonshire RO, or Peterborough Archives Service.
Quarter Sessions records and so on for the Peterborough area north of the River Nene (the former Soke of Peterborough) are held at Northamptonshire Record Office, while those for the area south of the River Nene are held at Huntingdonshire Archives.</td></tr>
</table>

8.2.7.5 Essex Record Office

<table>
<tr><td>Wharf Road
Chelmsford
CM2 6YT

01245 244644</td><td>CARN Reader's Ticket
Photography allowed
Parking available
Refreshments available on site</td></tr>
<tr><td colspan="2">http://www.essexcc.gov.uk/ero
Essex</td></tr>
</table>

8.2.7.6 Hertfordshire Archives and Local Studies

<table>
<tr><td>Register Office Block
County Hall
Pegs Lane
Hertford
SG13 8EJ

0300 123 4049</td><td>CARN Reader's Ticket
Photography allowed
Parking available
Refreshments available on site or nearby</td></tr>
<tr><td colspan="2">http://www.hertsdirect.org/services/leisculture/heritage1/hals/
Note that some parts of Hertfordshire that used to be Middlesex have records at the London Metropolitan Archives.</td></tr>
</table>

8.2.7.7 Norfolk Record Office, at The Archive Centre

<table>
<tr><td>The Archive Centre
Martineau Lane
Norwich
NR1 2DQ

01603 222599</td><td>CARN Reader's Ticket
Photography allowed
Parking available
Refreshments available on site or nearby</td></tr>
<tr><td colspan="2">http://www.archives.norfolk.gov.uk/</td></tr>
</table>

8.2.7.8 Suffolk Record Offices

Lowestoft Record Office Clapton Road Lowestoft NR32 1DR 01502 405357	CARN Reader's Ticket Photography allowed Parking available nearby Café on site
http://www.suffolk.gov.uk/LeisureAndCulture/LocalHistoryAndHeritage/SuffolkRecordOffice/HowToUseTheSuffolkRecordOffice/OnlineCatalogues.htm This office collects material relating to North East Suffolk. Major collections include the records of the Boroughs of Lowestoft, Beccles and Southwold.	

Ipswich Record Office Gatacre Road Ipswich IP1 2LQ 01473 584560	CARN Reader's Ticket Photography allowed Parking available nearby Area for eating available
http://www.suffolk.gov.uk/LeisureAndCulture/LocalHistoryAndHeritage/SuffolkRecordOffice/HowToUseTheSuffolkRecordOffice/OnlineCatalogues.htm Holdings mostly cover East Suffolk.	

Bury St Edmunds Record Office 77 Raingate Street Bury St. Edmunds IP33 2AR 01284 741212	CARN Reader's Ticket Photography allowed Parking available nearby Area for eating available
http://www.suffolk.gov.uk/LeisureAndCulture/LocalHistoryAndHeritage/SuffolkRecordOffice/HowToUseTheSuffolkRecordOffice/OnlineCatalogues.htm Holdings mostly cover West Suffolk.	

8.2.8 London

8.2.8.1 London Metropolitan Archives

London Metropolitan Archives 40 Northampton Road Clerkenwell London EC1R 0HB 020 7332 3820	City of London Reader's Ticket Photography allowed Parking available Refreshments available on site or nearby
http://www.cityoflondon.gov.uk/lma Covers the City of London from 1067, London and Middlesex County Councils from 1889, and Greater London from 1965.	

8.2.9 South East

8.2.9.1 Berkshire Record Office

9 Coley Avenue Reading RG1 6AF 0118 9375132	CARN Reader's Ticket Photography allowed Parking available Refreshments available on site or nearby
http://www.berkshirerecordoffice.org.uk Former county of Berkshire, including Reading.	

8.2.9.2 Buckinghamshire County Archives and Local Studies Library

County Hall Walton Street Aylesbury Bucks 01296 382587, map room 01296 382250	CARN Reader's Ticket Photography allowed Parking available in town centre Refreshments available nearby
http://www.buckscc.gov.uk/bcc/archives/Centre_for_Buckinghamshire_Studies.page? Buckinghamshire	

8.2.9.3 Oxfordshire Record Office

<table>
<tr><td>St. Luke's Church
Cowley
Oxford
OX4 2HD

01865 398200</td><td>CARN Reader's Ticket
Photography allowed
Parking available
Refreshments available on site or nearby</td></tr>
<tr><td colspan="2">http://www.oxfordshire.gov.uk/wpa/portal/publicsite/councilservices</td></tr>
</table>

8.2.9.4 East Sussex Record Office

<table>
<tr><td>The Maltings
Castle Precints
Lewes
BN7 1YT

01273 482349</td><td>CARN Reader's Ticket
No photography
Parking available nearby
Café available nearby</td></tr>
<tr><td colspan="2">http://www.eastsussex.gov.uk/leisureandtourism/localandfamilyhistory/esro/collections/
East Sussex, Brighton and Hove</td></tr>
</table>

8.2.9.5 West Sussex Record Office

<table>
<tr><td>West Sussex Record Centre
3 Orchard Street
Chichester
West Sussex
PO19 1DD

01243 753602</td><td>CARN Reader's Ticket
Photography allowed
Parking available
Refreshments available on site or nearby</td></tr>
<tr><td colspan="2">http://www.westsussex.gov.uk/ro
West Sussex</td></tr>
</table>

8.2.9.6 Hampshire Record Office

Sussex Street Winchester Hampshire SO23 8TH 01962 846154	Local Reader's Ticket Photography allowed Parking available (telephone to reserve space) Drinks machine and rest area available
http://www3.hants.gov.uk/archives.htm Hampshire	

8.2.9.7 Isle of Wight Records Office

Isle of Wight Record Office 26 Hillside Newport PO30 2EB 01983 823820/1	CARN Reader's Ticket Photography allowed Parking available Cafes nearby, not on site
http://www.iwight.com/recordoffice Isle of Wight	

8.2.9.8 Kent History and Library Centre

James Whatman Way Maidstone Kent ME14 1 XQ 08458 247200	CARN Reader's Ticket Photography allowed No parking on site (unless disabled). Short term parking on surrounding streets or pay and display at the 'White Rabbit' Small café nearby
http://www.kent.gov.uk/archives Kent excluding Medway.	

8.2.9.9 Medway Archives and Local Studies Centre

Clocktower Building Strood Rochester Kent ME2 4AU 01634 332714	CARN Reader's Ticket – by appointment only Photography allowed Parking available No eating area on site
http://www.medway.gov.uk/leisureandculture/libraries/archivesandlocalstudies.aspx Medway area, from Dartford and Gravesend to Rainham.	

8.2.9.10 Surrey History Centre

Surrey History Centre 130 Goldsworth Road Woking GU21 6ND 01483 518737	Reader's Ticket Photography allowed Limited parking available Refreshments available nearby
http://www.surreycc.gov.uk/surreyhistoryservice Surrey and parts of Middlesex.	

8.2.10 South West

8.2.10.1 Bristol Record Office

'B' Bond Warehouse Smeaton Road Bristol BS1 6XN 0117 922 4224	No Reader's Ticket needed Photography allowed Parking available Refreshments available on site or nearby
http://www.bristol.gov.uk/recordoffice Holds records for Bristol, some records for North Somerset, and some for South Gloucestershire.	

8.2.10.2 Cornwall Record Office

Old County Hall Truro Cornwall TR1 3AY 01872 323127	CARN Reader's Ticket Photography allowed Parking available Refreshments available nearby
http://www.cornwall.gov.uk/default.aspx?page=24656 There are other libraries in Cornwall which may have historical documents.	

8.2.10.3 Devon Record Office

Great Moor House Bittern Road Sowton Industrial Estate Exeter Devon EX2 7NL 01392 384253	CARN Reader's Ticket Photography allowed Parking available Refreshments available on site or nearby
http://www.devon.gov.uk/record_office.htm This office houses all types of historical records relating to the County of Devon, the City of Exeter, and east, mid and south Devon, including Torbay. It also holds the ecclesiastical records of the Diocese of Exeter.	

North Devon Record Office Tuly Street Barnstable EX31 1EL 01271 388607/8	Take proof of identity and address Photography allowed Parking available Refreshments available on site or nearby
http://www.devon.gov.uk/record_office.htm North Devon and Torridge District Councils, Barnstable, Bideford, South Molton and Great Torrington.	

Plymouth and West Devon Record Office 3 Clare Place Plymouth PL4 0JW 01752 305940	CARN Reader's Ticket Photography allowed Parking available Refreshments available nearby
http://www.plymouth.gov.uk/archives North Devon and Torridge District Councils, Barnstable, Bideford, South Molton and Great Torrington.	

8.2.10.4 Dorset Record Office

Bridport Road Dorchester DT1 1RP 01305 250550	CARN Reader's Ticket Photography allowed Parking available Common room with tea/coffee
http://www.dorsetforyou.com/archive Dorset including Poole and Bournemouth.	

8.2.10.5 Somerset Heritage Centre

Somerset Heritage Centre Brunel Way Norton Fitzwarren Taunton TA2 6SF 01823 337600	Local Reader's Ticket Photography allowed Parking available No refreshments
http://www.somerset.gov.uk/archives Covers Somerset.	

8.2.10.6 Gloucestershire Record Office

Clarence Row Alvin Street Gloucester GL1 3DW 01452 425295	Local Reader's Ticket Photography allowed Parking available Coffee lounge available on site
http://www.gloucestershire.gov.uk/archives/107703 Gloucestershire and South Gloucestershire.	

8.2.10.7 Wiltshire and Swindon History Centre

Cocklebury Road Chippenham Wiltshire SN15 3QN 01249 705500	Local Reader's Ticket Photography allowed Parking available Eating area available
http://www.wiltshire.gov.uk/leisureandculture/museumhistoryheritage.htm Wiltshire, including Swindon.	

8.3 County and Local Record Offices in Wales

Useful information about archive offices in Wales can be found at: http://www.archiveswales.org.uk. Be prepared for a mixture of Welsh and English versions of place names.

8.3.1.1 Anglesey County Record Office

Anglesey Archives Industrial Estate Road Bryn Cefni Industrial Estate Llangefni Anglesey LL77 7JA 01248 751930	CARN Reader's Ticket Booking required Photography allowed Parking available Eating area available
http://www.anglesey.gov.uk/leisure/records-and-archives/	

8.3.1.2 Brecon – see Powys

8.3.1.3 Caernarvon – see Gwynedd or Conwy

8.3.1.4 Carmarthenshire Archive Service

Parc Myrddin Richmond Terrace Carmarthen SA31 1HQ 01267 228232	Archives Wales Reader's Ticket No photography Parking available No eating area available
http://archives.carmarthenshire.gov.uk Carmarthenshire	

8.3.1.5 Ceredigion Archives

<table>
<tr><td>Ceredigion Archives
County Offices
Marine Terrace
Aberystwyth
Ceredigion
SY23 2DE

01970 633697</td><td>CARN Reader's Ticket
Photography allowed
Parking available (on street)
Cafés available nearby</td></tr>
<tr><td colspan="2">http://archifdy-ceredigion.org.uk</td></tr>
</table>

8.3.1.6 Conwy Archive Service

<table>
<tr><td>The Old Board School
Lloyd Street
Llandudno
LL30 2YG

01492 577550</td><td>CARN Reader's Ticket
No photography
Parking available
Cafés nearby</td></tr>
<tr><td colspan="2">http://www.conwy.gov.uk/archives
Conwy County</td></tr>
</table>

8.3.1.7 Denbighshire Record Office

<table>
<tr><td>Ruthin Gaol
46 Clwyd Street
Ruthin
Denbighshire
LL15 1HP

01824 708250</td><td>CARN Reader's Ticket
Photography allowed
Parking available
Café nearby and eating area available</td></tr>
<tr><td colspan="2">http://www.denbighshire.gov.uk/en-gb/DNAP-6ZQKTQ</td></tr>
</table>

8.3.1.8 Flintshire County Records Office

The Old Rectory Rectory Lane Hawarden Flintshire CH5 3NI 01244 532364	CARN Reader's Ticket Booking required Photography allowed Parking available Eating area available with drinks machine
http://www.flintshire.gov.uk and search for 'record office'. Historic and modern Flintshire.	

8.3.1.9 Glamorgan Archives – Archifdy Morgannwg

Clos Parc Morgannwg Lekwith Cardiff CF11 8AW 029 2087 2200	Local Reader's Ticket Photography allowed Parking available Eating area and drinks machine available
http://www.glamro.gov.uk/ Glamorgan Archives serves the County Borough Councils of Bridgend, Caerphilly, Merthyr Tydfil, Rhondda Cynon Taf, Vale of Glamorgan and the City and County of Cardiff.	

8.3.1.10 Gwynedd Archives Service

Caernarfon Record Office Swyddfa'r Cyngor Caernarfon Gwynedd LL55 1SH 01286 679095	CARN Reader's Ticket No photography Parking available nearby Café nearby
http://www.gwynedd.gov.uk/archives/	

Meirionnydd Archives Ffordd y Bala Dolgellau Gwynedd LL40 2YF 01341 424682	CARN Reader's Ticket No photography Parking available nearby Cafés nearby
http://www.gwynedd.gov.uk/archives/ Includes information for Corwen area (which is now in Denbighshire).	

8.3.1.11 Merioneth – see Gwynedd

8.3.1.12 Monmouth – see Gwent

8.3.1.13 Montgomery – see Powys

8.3.1.14 Pembrokeshire Record Office

The Castle Haverford West SA61 2EF 01437 763707	Reader's Ticket Photography allowed Parking available Café 5 min walk away
http://www.pembrokeshire.gov.uk and look for record office under 'R'. County of Pembrokeshire but other records may be kept in Cardiganshire Record Office or Carmarthenshire Record Office or the National Library of Wales at Aberystwyth.	

8.3.1.15 Powys County Archives Office

Powys Archives County Hall Llandrindod Wells Powys LD1 5LG Tel 01597 826088	Archives Wales Reader's Ticket Booking essential Photography allowed Parking available Eating area available
http://archives.powys.gov.uk/ Includes the area of the former counties of Breconshire, Radnorshire and Montgomeryshire.	

8.4 Gwent Archives

Steelworks Road Ebbw Vale Blaenau Gwent NP23 6DN 01495 353363	CARN Reader's Ticket Photography allowed Parking available Eating area available
http://www.gwentarchives.gov.uk/ Serves the areas covered by these authorities: Blaenau Gwent County Borough Council, Caerphilly County Borough Council (former Islwyn Borough area), Monmouthshire County Council, Newport City Council and Torfaen County Borough Council.	

8.4.1.1 Radnor – see Powys

8.4.1.2 Wrexham Archives and Local Studies Service

Wrexham County Borough Museum and Archives Regent Street Wrexham LL11 1RB 01978 297480	CARN Reader's Ticket Booking advisable (there are only 6 seats) No Photography Parking available in NCP next door Café in the same building
http://www.wrexham.gov.uk/english/heritage/archives/index.htm	

9. GLOSSARY AND ABBREVIATIONS

Accommodation Road. For our purposes, this is a route constructed to allow an owner or occupier access to land when a railway or motorway is built. It may or may not carry public rights.

Application Route. The name given to a route that is the subject of a definitive map modification order application.

Apportionment. The act of distributing or allotting in proper shares and the results of such action. Part of the tithe record.

Award. The final document produced in the Inclosure process (see section 3.5). It records the decisions made by the Inclosure Commissioners, describes the new allocations of land, and is legally binding.

Basic Evidential Test. This is proposed in the May 2012 government consultation as being a minimum amount of evidence to enable a modification order application to be accepted by the surveying authority. It appears to be broadly equivalent to 5 stars worth of evidence under this book's scheme.

Bridleway. A highway over which the public have a right of way on foot and horseback or leading a horse, with or without a right to drive animals of any description along the highway (s.329 Highways Act 1980). The showing of a public footpath on the definitive map, however, only means that the public had a right on foot there without prejudice as to whether any other rights existed (s.56 Wildlife and Countryside Act 1981).

BL. The British Library.

'Blue Book'. Short-hand reference to *Rights of Way: A Guide to Law and Practice* by Riddal and Trevelyan.

BOAT. Byway Open to All Traffic. A highway over which the public have a right of way for vehicular and all other kinds of traffic, but which [at the time a route is considered for addition to the definitive map] is used by the public mainly for the purpose for which footpaths and bridleways are so used (s.66 Wildlife and Countryside Act 1981).

Book of Reference. (1) A book created under statutory authority listing the owners and occupiers of land affected by proposed canal, navigation, railway and other works, and often detailing land use. It will be accompanied by a map or plan showing which information goes with which land plot, and the pair will have been deposited with the Clerk of the Peace. (2) A book produced and sold by the Ordnance Survey to provide acreage of individual parcels of land shown on the first edition county series 25 inch to the mile maps. Also known as an 'area book'. See section 3.10. Those before about 1879 also contain land use information.

Byway. We use this term as a collective for both 'Restricted Byway' and 'Byway Open to All Traffic'.

CARN. County Archive Research Network. A reader's ticket issued by a county record office that is a member of the CARN network will be accepted by other members.

Carriageway. A highway over which the public have a right of way for the passage of vehicles (s.329 Highways Act 1980). This term includes restricted byways and byways open to all traffic, as well as ordinary roads.

Case Law. Reported decisions from courts of record (High Court, Court of Appeal, House of Lords and the Supreme Court) which can be cited as precedents in future legal proceedings. Case law supplements statute law by providing decisions on how Acts and Regulations are to be interpreted, understood and applied.

Clerk of the Peace. The principal officer who kept the records of the quarter sessions and lieutenancy. In recent times, functions relating to highways and land take over have become those of the local authority for the area.

County Road. A road for which the county council is the Highway Authority (s.29 Local Government Act 1929). Strictly, this is an obsolete term, but it is still frequently encountered.

County Record Office (CRO). The usual name for archive offices maintained by local authorities under powers given by the Local Government (Records) Act 1962.

CRB. Public Carriage [or cart] Road mainly used as a Bridleway. This was a term suggested by the Open Spaces Society in its guide to surveys and maps of rights of way, published in 1950, and adopted by many surveying authorities. In legal terms, a CRB is a RUPP.

CRF. Public Carriage [or cart] Road mainly used as a Footpath. This was a term suggested by the Open Spaces Society in its guide to surveys and maps of rights of way, published in 1950, and adopted by many surveying authorities. In legal terms, a CRF is a RUPP.

Cross Roads. Ogilvy described 'cross roads' as roads that connected or linked the 'direct roads' or 'post roads' which radiated out of London and were used by the mail coaches. Originally these were thought of as public roads other than post roads, and later as public roads other than turnpike roads.

Customary Ways. An old term for ways that belonged to the parish which the parish was liable to maintain as it was to maintain highways, but only parishioners could complain if the way was out of repair. Most have been absorbed into the highway network (Sugden, 1995).

Definitive Map and Statement. These are documents maintained by the surveying authority under s.53 Wildlife and Countryside Act 1981 that provide conclusive proof in law of the existence of the rights shown on them.

Deposited Plan. A map or plan compiled under statutory authority and deposited with the Clerk of the Peace, usually in connection with canal, navigation or railway works. It will be accompanied by a book of reference.

Drift. The collective noun for packhorses.

Driftway. (1) Alternative name for Drove Road. (2) A highway which affords a right of passage for cattle, as well as for riding animals and pedestrians. In this definition, 'Cattle' includes all animals capable of being driven. Driftways are now of less importance for their original purpose than formerly, although for walkers and riders they may be of considerable value, being usually unmetalled and not legally open to motor cars (Hobhouse Report, p. 3).

Drove Road. This is a highway (usually of ancient origin) mainly used for the long distance driving or herding of cattle, sheep, pigs or poultry to market towns. It also carried public rights of way on foot and horseback. Also known as Driftway.

Enclosure. The process of physically enclosing land, for example by fencing. See also 'inclosure'.

Footpath. A highway (other than a footway by the side of the road) on which the public have a right on foot (s.329 Highways Act 1980). The showing of a public footpath on the definitive map, however, only means that the public had a right on foot there without prejudice as to whether any other rights existed (s.56 Wildlife and Countryside Act 1981).

Green Lanes. Non-statutory term for unmetalled track.

Hereditament. Formally, any property that can be inherited. For our purposes the term hereditament is encountered when looking at valuations from the Inland Revenue survey of c.1910 where each parcel of land (with or without buildings) that was valued is included in a hereditament and given a hereditament number.

Highway. Where the public have the right to pass and re-pass along a linear route, that linear route is a highway. Examples of highways are footpaths, bridleways and carriageways.

Highways Agency. This is an Executive Agency of the Department for Transport (DfT), and is responsible for operating, maintaining and improving the strategic road network in England on behalf of the Secretary of State for Transport. It is also responsible for crossings of these roads. Do not confuse this term with Highway Authority.

Highway Authority. The public body (a county council, unitary authority or government department) responsible for the highways in an area, as defined in s.1 Highways Act 1980.

Horse. In highways definitions, this term includes pony, ass and mule, and 'horseback' is to be construed accordingly (s.329 Highways Act 1980).

Inclosure. The process of combining, reallocating and fencing land, and reducing common land, authorised by Act of Parliament. See section 3.5.

Inland Revenue Valuation. This is the valuation conducted under the Finance (1909–10) Act 1910. Some rights of way researchers tend to refer to 'Inland Revenue valuation maps' while others refer to 'Finance Act maps'. Either term is acceptable in general use, providing it is clear in any application that the maps are actually those prepared by the Inland Revenue pursuant to the requirements of the Finance (1909–10) Act 1910.

List of Streets. Every county council and unitary authority must maintain a list of streets maintainable at the public expense (s.36 Highways Act 1980). This list should include all highways that are maintainable, whether or not they are currently maintained. Some authorities have failed to include minor highways in their List of Streets, but the law is clear that all those that are maintainable at public expense should be listed.

Lost Ways. Routes used by the public in the past that are not recorded as being public today.

Made-up Carriageway. A carriageway which has been metalled or in any other way provided with a surface suitable for the passage of vehicles

Meresman. A man appointed to find out the exact boundary of a parish.

Minor Highway. Any highway other than clearly identifiable public roads. In broad terms, this means all public footpaths and bridleways, and any carriageways that are either more used as footpaths and bridleways, or have had their motor vehicular rights stopped up, or are in danger of being forgotten about because they're not made up specifically for motor vehicles' use.

Occupation Road. This term was used in the Inclosure Act 1845 in the phrase 'private or occupation roads' and has been used in railway records to describe some pre-existing road crossings. The Ordnance Survey appear to have used it in the object names books to describe what had been awarded as private carriage roads at enclosure. Such routes will carry private rights and may or may not carry public rights of the same or lower status.

ORPA. Other Routes with Public Access. Symbols denoting this status are used on OS Explorer and Landranger maps for some routes, not on the definitive map. The relevant highway authority should be consulted for details of the rights it believes exist. Consideration should be given to having the route recorded on the definitive map, if the evidence and circumstances suggest this is appropriate.

OS. Ordnance Survey.

Overseer. A paid official with highway responsibilities.

Parochial Road. A road whose maintenance liability fell to the parish.

Private Carriage Road. Term used in Inclosure Acts. See section 3.5.

Proof of Evidence. The Planning Inspectorate defines this as 'a document containing the written evidence which a person at a public inquiry will speak about. It should not rehearse all of the available evidence but should focus on the matters in dispute. It should not contain supporting documents.'

Public Carriage Road. Term used in Inclosure Acts. See section 3.5.

Public Path. A highway being either a footpath or a bridleway (s.69 Wildlife and Countryside Act 1981).

RDC. Rural District Council.

Restricted Byway. A highway over which the public have a right of way on foot, on horseback or leading a horse, and in vehicles other than mechanically propelled vehicles, with or without a right to drive animals of any description along the highway (s.48 Countryside and Rights of Way Act 2000).

Riders. We use the word riders to indicate horse riders. Those who use bicycles are cyclists.

Road Used as a Public Path (RUPP). The original definition was a highway, other than a public path, used by the public mainly for the purposes for which footpaths or bridleways are so used (National Parks and Access to the Countryside Act 1949). The showing of a highway on the definitive map as a RUPP is conclusive proof that the public had a right on foot, horseback or leading a horse there without prejudice as to whether any other rights existed (s.56 Wildlife and Countryside Act 1981). RUPPs were converted into Restricted Byways by s.47 Countryside and Rights of Way Act 2000 if they had not already been reclassified.

RWLR. Rights of Way Law Review. A specialist publication for those interested in highway law as it applies to minor highways.

Statement of Case. The Planning Inspectorate defines this as 'a written statement containing full particulars of the case which a person proposes to put forward at a hearing or Inquiry. It includes copies of any supporting documents which that person intends to refer to or put in evidence, and a list of those documents.'

Statement of Priorities. A statement made by a surveying authority setting out their priorities for bringing and keeping the definitive map up to date. Department of the Environment Circular 2/93 (also known as Welsh Office Circular 5/93) recommends that surveying authorities maintain such a statement. Since 2009, this Circular is only valid in Wales, but the concept remains good, and many authorities in England continue to publish this statement of priorities.

Surveying Authority. This is the county council, county borough council, metropolitan district or London borough council responsible for maintaining the Definitive Map and Statement for the area (s.66 Wildlife and Countryside Act 1981).

Surveyor of Highways. An appointed official for the parish who was charged with a duty to keep under review the condition of the roads within the parish (s.2 Statute for the Mending of Highways 1554). Subsequently surveyors of highways have been appointed for districts or counties. Alternative names have included Overseers, Supervisors of Highways, Waymen, Waywardens, Boonmasters, Stonewardens and Stonemen.

Terrier. Land ownership records of local authorities and the Church.

TNA. The National Archives.

Trunk Road. A principal road for through traffic for which a Minister is the highway authority (instead of the relevant local authority) (s.1 Trunk Roads Act 1936). Any route that used to be a trunk road will have carried vehicular rights, and if no longer in use as a road, should be investigated to see whether it was stopped up by a process of law, or just fell into disuse.

UDC. Urban District Council.

Unclassified County Road (UCR). Originally, a county road which had not been given a letter classification. The term was repealed in 1972 but has been retained in use by many county councils as shorthand for any such route on the list of streets maintainable at public expense.

Unsealed Unclassified County Road (UUCR). Non-statutory term. An unclassified county road which has not been tarmacked.

White Roads. The showing of a route as a 'white road' on Inland Revenue valuation maps, that is, excluded from the adjoining coloured hereditaments, is a primary indicator of carriageway rights at that time, and hence that there is an investigation to complete, as described in section 3.17.

10. FURTHER READING

10.1 Orders and Applications

Many organisations will provide help and advice to their members through the publication of leaflets or in some cases, personalised advice. Those listed here are just a small selection. Their contact details may be found via any good internet search engine.

The British Horse Society (BHS). The BHS is a registered charity representing the interests of the 4.3 million people in the UK who ride or who drive horse-drawn vehicles. It has a network of volunteer access and bridleways officers who can advise on modification order applications.

http://www.bhs.org.uk/

Byways and Bridleways Trust (BBT). The Byways & Bridleways Trust is a registered charity, created to protect the public rights that exist over the many ancient lanes that form part of the British landscape and traditional means of travel.

http://www.bbtrust.org.uk/

Country Land and Business Association (CLA). A membership organisation for owners of land, property and businesses in rural England and Wales.

http://www.cla.org.uk/Policy_Work/Public_Rights_of_Way

Institute of Public Rights of Way Management (IPROW). This is the professional body representing public rights of way practitioners. Advice can be found on their website.

http://www.iprow.co.uk/

National Farmers Union (NFU). The NFU publish business guides for members.

http://www.nfuonline.com

NFU business guide 400, *Rights of Way: Public Inquiries and Hearings.*

NFU business guide 402, *Unrecorded Historic Rights of Way and Definitive Map Modification Orders based on Historic Documentary Evidence.*

The Open Spaces Society (OSS). The OSS is a charity founded in 1865. It has a network of local correspondents working on rights of way matters. It provides information on its website.

http://www.oss.org.uk/

The Planning Inspectorate (PINS). PINS provides the secretariat for the processing of definitive map modification order inquiries and hearings. The Inspectorate produces consistency guidelines for Inspectors and the public which can be found on their website. These are the primary reference material for Inspectors in determining orders. PINS also provides advice notes on a range of topics.

http://www.planningportal.gov.uk/uploads/pins/row/consistency_guide.pdf

http://www.planningportal.gov.uk/planning/countryside/rightsofway/advicenotes

The Ramblers. The Ramblers is Britain's walking charity, working to safeguard the footpaths, the countryside and other places people go walking in England, Scotland and Wales. Information on modification orders can be found under 'definitive maps' on the knowledge portal part of its website.

http://www.ramblers.org.uk/

10.2 Proposed Changes to Definitive Map Legislation

DEFRA, *Improvements to the policy and legal framework for public rights of way A public consultation*, May 2012 (available at http://www.defra.gov.uk/consult/open).

Natural England NECR035, *Stepping Forward – The Stakeholder Working Group on Unrecorded Public Rights of Way: Report to Natural England*, March 2012 (available at http://www.naturalengland.org.uk).

10.3 Useful Resources

For checking local government changes, try: http://www.visionofbritain.org.uk.

For checking the content of legislation, visit http://www.legislation.gov.uk. Since being managed by The National Archives, the legislation website has started to republish old Acts in their original form, as well as providing the currently in force versions.

10.4 Background Reading

Barker, Katherine and Kain, Roger JP (eds) (1991) *Maps and History in South-west England*, University of Exeter Press, ISBN 978-0-85989-373-2.

Beech, G & Mitchell, R (2004) *Maps for Family and Local History*, The National Archives [2nd edn], ISBN 978-1-903365-50-2.

Carter, P & Thompson, K (2005) *Sources for Local Historians*, Phillimore & Co Ltd, ISBN 978-1-86077-358-7.

Clifford, S & King, A (2006) *England in Particular*, Hodder & Stoughton, ISBN 978-0-340-82616-4.

Coombs, Douglas (1990) *Highway use and control up to 1895*, Rights of Way Law Review, section 1.1 pp 1–7.

Davies, Hugh (2008) *Roman Roads in Britain*, Shire Publications Ltd, ISBN 978-0-7478-0690-5.

Friar, Stephen (2001) *The Sutton Companion to Local History*, Sutton Publishing Ltd, ISBN 978-0-7509-2723-9.

Gelling, Margaret (1978) *Signposts to the Past*, Phillimore & Co Limited, ISBN 978-1-86077-376-1.

Hey, David (1996) *The Oxford Companion to Local and Family History*, Oxford University Press, ISBN 978-0-19-211688-8.

Higley, Chris (2011) *Old Series to Explorer, A field Guide to the Ordnance Map*, The Charles Close Society, ISBN 978-1-870598-30-9.

Hindle, Paul (2001) *Roads and Tracks for Historians*, Phillimore & Co Ltd, ISBN 978-1-86077-182-8.

Hindle, Paul (2009) *Medieval Roads and Tracks*, Shire Publications Ltd, ISBN 978-0-7478-0390-4.

Hippisley Cox, R (1923) *The Green Roads of England*, Methuen & Co Ltd.

Hollowell, Steven (2000) *Enclosure Records for Historians*, Phillimore & Co Ltd, ISBN 978-1-86077-128-6.

Kain RJP & Oliver, RR (1995) *The Tithe Maps of England and Wales – A Cartographic Analysis and County-by-County Catalogue,* Cambridge University Press, ISBN 978-0-521-44191-9.

Lively, Penelope (1976) *The Presence of the Past, an introduction to landscape history*, William Collins & Sons Limited, ISBN 978-0-00-195462-5.

Masters, Charles (2009) *Essential Maps for Family Historians*, Countryside Books ISBN 978-1-84674-098-5.

Ministry of Town and Country Planning (1947), *Footpaths and Access to the Countryside*, Cmd 7207. This is commonly known as the *Hobhouse Report* as Sir James Hobhouse chaired the committee that prepared it.

Oliver, R (2005) *Ordnance Survey Maps, a concise guide for historians*, The Charles Close Society [2nd edn] ISBN 978-1-870598-24-8.

Richardson, John (2003) *The Local Historian's Encyclopedia*, Historical Publications Ltd [3rd edn], ISBN 978-0-948667-83-1.

Scott-Giles, CW (1946) *The Road Goes On*, The Epworth Press.

Seymour, WA (ed.) (1980) *A History of the Ordnance Survey*, Wm Dawson & Sons Ltd, ISBN 978-0-7129-0979-2.

Sugden, J (1995) 'Highway Authorities since 1800', Rights of Way Law Review, section 1.1 pp 31–48.

Sugden, J (2000) *On the Right Track*, The British Horse Society, ISBN 978-1-899016-25-9.

Tate, WE (1983) *The Parish Chest*, Phillimore & Co Limited, [3rd edn], ISBN 978-1-86077-611-3.

Taylor, Susan (1997) *What is a Cross Road?*, South Pennine Packhorse Trails Trust, ISBN 978-0-9530573-0-6.

West, John (1997) *Village Records*, Phillimore & Co Ltd, ISBN 978-1-86077-040-1.

Winterbotham, HSL (1936) *A Key to Maps*, Blackie and Son, London.

Wright, Geoffrey N (2008) *Turnpike Roads*, Shire Publications Ltd, ISBN 978-0-7478-0155-9.

11. REFERENCE MATERIAL

11.1 Highway Authorities by Date

The Highway Act 1555 made parishes responsible for repairing the King's Highway. This was achieved using statute labour organised by the parish way wardens and enforced through the Quarter Sessions (see section 3.13).

As the volume of traffic, in particular wheeled carts, increased, the wear and tear on the roads increased to the point where the parishes through which heavily used roads passed were unable and unwilling to carry out the works. The turnpikes then took over some of these roads (see section 3.4). At a similar period the inclosure acts awarded maintenance responsibility for the awarded roads to landowners (see section 3.5). Railway companies became responsible for the tunnels, bridges and their approaches where they had been created to allow the railway to be built (section 3.9).

The Public Health Acts of 1848 and 1875 and the Local Government Acts of 1888 and 1894 forced the parishes to combine their highway responsibilities. Various Highway(s) Acts also made changes, as described in section 11.2. By 1913 there were nearly 1,900 different councils responsible for highways in their area (section 3.11).

The dates for which different bodies were responsible for the maintenance of highways are given in Figure 122.

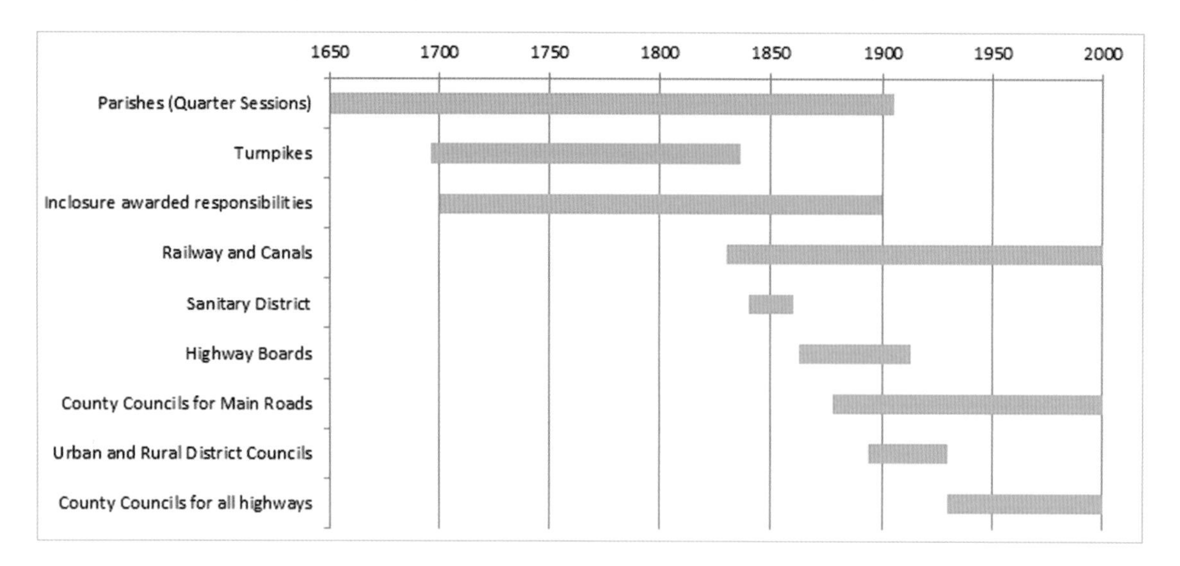

Figure 122: Suggested document sources for maintenance records and the years to which they typically apply

11.2 Selected Legislation by Date

The regnal year is also given in the first column, until its use ceased in 1962, as an aid to cross referencing the text in old Acts of Parliament.

1189	This marks the start of legal memory. Evidence from before this date will not usually be helpful.
1554 2 & 3 Phil & Mar c.8	The Statute for the Amending of Highways requires two persons to be appointed as surveyors of highways and gives them the power to direct the parishioners in the mending of highways on four days to be announced in church (s.1).
1773 13 Geo. 3 c.78	The Highway Act 1773 allowed diversions of highways, which previously had required the King's licence or special legislation.
1801 41 Geo. 3 c.109	The Inclosure (Consolidation) Act 1801 provided that public carriage roads had to be set out before allocating lands, and that they had to be at least 30 foot wide (s.8). Commissioners were empowered (but not obliged) to stop up an existing road (s.8). The forming and repair of awarded public carriage roads and highways had to be at the expense of the Surveyor, or the Surveyor would be fined (s.9) Private roads, bridleways and footways were also to be set out and the forming and maintenance of these was to be at the expense of the owners of the land being enclosed (s.10). Grass and herbage on public and private roads and ways would belong to the abutting landowner to the crown of the road (s.11). The Commissioners did not have the power to change or divert any Turnpike road without the consent of the

	majority of the turnpike trustees (s.11). The award was to deposited with the courts at Westminster or with the Clerk of the Peace (s.35). Rights of the Lord of the Manor were not altered (s.40).
1815 55 Geo. 3 c.68	The Highway Act 1815 required the Surveyor of Highways to maintain every public cartway leading to a market town to a width of 20 ft at least, every public horseway to at least 8 ft, and every public footway by the side of any carriageway or cartway to at least 3 ft.
1835 5 & 6 Will. 4, c. 50	The Highway Act 1835 abolished statute labour for the repair of highways (s.1), caused elections for the position of Surveyor of Highways (s.6) and gave parishes the right to combine to form highway districts (s.13). New vehicular highways (and routes awarded as *private* driftways or horsepaths in Inclosure Awards) would not be maintainable at the public expense unless statutory procedures were followed (s.23). Guide posts were to be erected where two or more ways meet (s.24) giving the name of the next market town, village or other place. There may be copies of the records of maintenance take over in local authority records or in local record offices; they are not held at TNA.
1836 6 & 7 Will. 4 c.71	The Tithe Act 1836 set out the process to be followed in order to commute the tithes payable in a parish. A full description is given in section 3.6.
1836 6 & 7 Will. 4 c.115	The General Inclosure Act 1836 updated the Acts of 1801 and 1820 relating to inclosures. A full description is given in section 3.5.
1842 5 & 6 Vict. c.94	The Defence Act 1842 consolidated and repealed previous Acts relating to defence (s.2). It gave an express power to Officers of Her Majesty's Ordnance (now the Ministry of Defence) to stop up and divert any public or private footpaths or bridle roads (s.16), but required the provision of a replacement footpath or bridle road at the expense of the Ordnance Department in lieu of the route stopped up (s.17).
1845 8 & 9 Vict. c.118	The General Inclosure Act 1845 gave the Commissioners the power to set out parish boundaries (s.39), to set out and make, stop up, and divert public roads and ways (s.62) with objections going to Quarter Sessions (ss.63–4) and to set out public roads and ways with widths stated in the Highway Act 1835.
1845 8 Vict. c.20	The Railway Clauses Consolidation Act 1845 provides (s.49) for minimum widths, heights and spans for bridges carrying the railway over specified highways, unless a different value is authorised under a special Act for a particular railway. The minimum width is given as 35 feet, 25 feet and 12 feet for a Turnpike Road, public Carriage Road and private Road respectively. Further requirements are noted in section 3.9.

1847 10 & 11 Vict. c.104	The Tithes Act 1847 provides (s.2) that every Instrument purporting to be an Instrument of Apportionment, confirmed under the Hands and Seal of the Tithe Commissioners, is absolutely confirmed and made valid in all respects (subject to provisions of the Tithe Commutation Act of 1836).
1862 25 & 26 Vict. c.61	The Highway Act 1862 allowed Justices in Quarter Sessions to compel parishes to combine into highway boards (although some parishes became urban sanitary districts).
1864 27 & 28 Vict. c.101	The Highway Act 1864 is a supplement to, and is to be read as one with, the Highway Act 1862 (s.2). It defined a highway parish as a place that could maintain its own highways (separately from the highway district) and have its own waywarden (s.3). A highway board could apply for maintenance responsibility to be removed (s.21). Waywardens could levy a highway rate (s.31).
1872 35 & 36 Vict. c.79	The Public Health Act 1872 transferred the jurisdiction held by the Secretary of State for highways and turnpike roads to the Local Government Board (s.36). It established rural and urban sanitary districts for all areas of England (s.3). Expenses of the urban and rural sanitary authorities were able to be charged to the rates (ss.16, 17).
1875 38 & 39 Vict. c.55	The Public Health Act 1875 is a consolidation Act. England remains divided into urban and rural sanitary districts, under the jurisdiction of urban and rural sanitary authorities (s.5). Every urban sanitary authority is the highway authority for its area (s.144). Provision for parishes maintaining their own highways was maintained outside urban areas (s.216).
1878 41 & 42 Vict. c.77	The Highways and Locomotives (Amendment) Act 1878 allowed a rural sanitary authority to take over the powers and duties of a highway board, where their respective areas were coincident (s.4). It permitted any two or more highway boards to unite in appointing and paying a district surveyor of highways (s.6). It provided that roads which were dis-turnpiked after 31 December 1870 shall be deemed to be main roads, and half of their future maintenance was to come from the county rate (s.13). S.14 provided that the highways areas shall be those of urban sanitary districts, highway districts and highway parishes not falling in the other categories. S.15 set out the procedure for routes other than the dis-turnpiked ones to become main roads. S.21 provided for bridges to be declared as maintainable by the county inhabitants (that is, from the county rate).
1888 51 & 52 Vict. c.41	The Local Government Act 1888 created elected councils for each county. These took over the administrative functions of the Quarter Sessions, and county boroughs came into existence. Main roads were to be subsidised by the county rates.

1891 54 & 55 Vict c.63	The Highways and Bridges Act 1891 allowed county councils and highway authorities to make agreements regarding the costs of bridges wholly or partially within their areas (s.3). It modified s.16 Highways and Locomotives Amendment Act 1878 to make it easier to reduce the status of a main road to that of an ordinary road (s.4). This did not affect the type of traffic entitled to use the route, so records of main road status remain useful for modification order applications.
1894 56 & 57 Vict. c.73	The Local Government Act 1894 changed urban sanitary districts into urban districts. Parish councils, the civil successors to parish vestries, were established. They were obligatory for (civil) parishes with 300 or more inhabitants, and were discretionary for smaller parishes. Rural district councils took over from the highway boards and became the highway authorities for all but the main roads. District councils were given the statutory duty to protect public rights of way and to prevent obstruction (s.26). Parishes no longer had responsibility for their roads.
1910 10 Edw. 7 c.8	The Finance (1909–10) Act 1910 created 'increment value duty' of 20 per cent for the increase in value of real property, payable when the property changed hands on sale or death, or periodically in the case of land held by a corporation (s.1). The Commissioners were tasked with valuing all land in the United Kingdom, to form a starting point for future increment value duty calculations (s.26). There were exemptions for land held by rating authorities (s.35). See section 3.17 for a fuller treatment of this Act and its relevance.
1929 19 Geo. 5 c.17	The Local Government Act 1929 made the county council the highway authority for all main roads in its area and renamed 'main roads' and any other roads for which the county council became highway authority as 'county roads' (s.29). The county councils became the highway authorities for all roads in rural district council areas (s.30). All classified roads within urban districts were transferred to the county council (s.31). Urban districts having sufficient population were empowered to claim the right to maintain county roads within their areas (s.32) and all districts were able to agree with the county council to take over maintenance (s.35).
1932 22 & 23 Geo. 5 c.45	The Rights of Way Act 1932 introduced the rule (s.1) that 20 years user as of right could lead to a presumption of prior dedication, and created the possibility of a landowner depositing a map and statement with the district and county councils and making periodic declarations to prevent further dedications. [This is now part of s.31 Highways Act 1980.] It specified (s.3) the matters a court or tribunal needs to consider when assessing evidence of highway status. [This is now s.32 Highways Act 1980.]

1947	The report of the Hobhouse Committee, *Footpaths and Access to the Countryside*, was presented to Parliament. This led to the 1949 Act.
1949 12, 13 & 14 Geo. 6 c.97	The National Parks and Access to the Countryside Act 1949 started the process of compiling information for the definitive map and statement.
1959 7 & 8 Eliz. 2 c.25	The Highways Act 1959 consolidated earlier highways legislation, including the 1932 Act. Any duty of 'the inhabitants at large of any area' for maintenance of highways was removed (s.38(1)). It was replaced with the concept of 'highways maintainable at public expense'. Councils of every county and every urban district were required to maintain a list of highways maintainable at the public expense and to keep it available to be inspected by any person free of charge at all reasonable hours (s.38(6)).
1968	The Countryside Act 1968 created (s.27) the power for a highway authority to waymark minor highways and the duty for signs to be erected where a minor highway leaves a metalled road. Over bridleways, it created a right of way on bicycle (s.30) subject to giving way to walkers and riders.
1980	The Highways Act 1980 consolidated the Highways Act 1959 and various amendments that had been made subsequently. It is the main statute for highways law at the time this book went to press.
1981	The Wildlife and Countryside Act 1981 is the current Act containing the definitive map related powers and duties. Section 53 sets out the definition of 'definitive map and statement' and requires the surveying authority (county council or unitary authority) to keep it up to date. It allows any person to apply for a definitive map modification order, following the provisions of Schedule 14. The making, validity and date of coming into force of modification orders is governed by Schedule 15. Section 56 sets out the effect of a route being shown on the definitive map and statement, and provides that it is legally conclusive. Section 66 contains definitions, including that for 'byway open to all traffic'.

2000	Part II of the Countryside and Rights of Way Act 2000 contains the rights of way matters. Section 48 provides that all routes shown as 'Roads Used as Public Paths' (RUPPs) on definitive maps shall carry restricted byway rights, subject to specified exemptions. Restricted byway rights are defined as being a right of way on foot, on horseback or leading a horse, and for vehicles other than mechanically-propelled vehicles. Section 49 provides that all restricted byways coming into being by operation of s.48 shall be maintainable at the public expense. Section 53 extinguishes unrecorded footpaths and bridleways that existed on 1 January 1949 and which are neither recorded nor exempted on the cut-off day. Section 54 contains the (limited) exemptions. Section 56 sets the cut-off date as 1 January 2026 but gives (limited) powers to the Secretary of State (for England) or National Assembly (for Wales) to set a later date, but for most of England and Wales this can be no later than 1 January 2031.
2006	Part 6 of the Natural Environment and Rural Communities Act 2006 (at s.66) abolished the presumed dedication of public rights of way by mechanically propelled vehicles. Section 67 extinguished existing public rights of way for mechanically propelled vehicles that were not shown as byways open to all traffic (BOATs) unless one of the five exemptions applied, or an application to have the route recorded as a BOAT had been made before 20 January 2005 (where the highway is in England) or 19 May 2005 (where the highway is in Wales).
2010	The *Stepping Forward* report published by Natural England made recommendations to changes in how definitive maps are to be updated.

11.3 Measurements and Scales

In the tables that follow, the equivalence of different imperial units is exact, and the conversion to metric is approximate.

11.3.1 Linear Measurements

1 mile = 8 furlongs = 1760 yards = 1609 metres

1 furlong = 10 chains = 40 poles = 220 yards = 201 metres

1 chain = 4 poles = 22 yards = 20.1 metres

1 pole = 5.5 yards = 5.03 metres

1 pole = 1 rod = 1 perch (different names for the same length)

See also the term 'perch' as an area measurement

1 yard = 3 feet = 91.4 cm

1 foot = 12 inches = 30.48 cm

1 inch = 2.54 cm (statutory definition)

11.3.2 Area Measurements

1 square mile = 640 acres = 2.6 km^2

1 acre = 4840 sq yards = 1 furlong x 1 chain = 10 square chains = 4 roods = 0.4047 ha

1 rood = 1210 sq yards = 1 furlong x 1 pole = 40 perches (area) = 0.25 acre

1 perch (area) = 1 perch (length) x 1 perch (length)

1 sq yard = 9 sq feet = 0.836 m^2

The OS Area Books (see section 3.10) helpfully include the conversion from decimal fractions of an acre to roods and perches. To convert 633.357 acres, take the decimal part (0.357) and multiply by 4 (1.428).

The whole number is the number of roods (1). Then take the decimal part (0.428) and multiply by 40 (17.120). The whole number is the number of perches. So, 633.357 acres is equivalent to 633 acres, 1 rood and 17 perches.

11.3.3 Map Scales

Researchers will encounter many maps with many different scales. Some of the most frequently found scales are given below.

1:2,500	25.344 inches to the mile (commonly referred to as 25 inch to the mile). This is used for the County Series of maps.
1:10,560	Six inches to the mile.
1:25,000	This scale is used by the Ordnance Survey for the current Explorer maps, which replaced the Pathfinder series. These are coloured maps and ideal for working research maps and show parish boundaries and contours. A plan forming part of a definitive map modification order application must be on a scale of not less than 1:25,000.[1]
1:50,000	This scale is used by the Ordnance Survey for the current Landranger maps. Note that this scale must not be used for the plan attached to the application form for a definitive map modification order.
1:63,360	One inch to the mile. These are excellent for an overview. The combination of the Old Series, Revised New Series, and Popular Series, now rescaled to 1:50,000 and reprinted by Cassini, can be used easily with the current OS Landranger series (1:50,000).
1:126,720	Half inch to the mile; two miles to one inch.
1:253,440	Quarter inch to the mile; four miles to one inch.
1:633,600	Ten miles to one inch.

Other maps can be of varying scales. In general, tithe maps are scaled at anything from 3 to 6 chains to the inch.

1 The Wildlife and Countryside (Definitive Maps and Statements) Regulations 1993, reg 2 and 8.

11.4 National Grid References

The OS maps are produced to a National Grid system. The country is divided into 100 km by 100 km squares each of which has a unique 2 letter identification code, shown in blue on the Explorer maps, such as ST or TQ. These letters form the first part of any National Grid Reference. The remaining digits identify where in the 100 km by 100 km any particular point is.

Rather than have a lengthy explanation here, the reader who wishes to understand and use grid references is referred to the excellent Ordnance Survey tutorial at:

http://www.ordnancesurvey.co.uk/oswebsite/gi/nationalgrid/nghelp1.html

Although the reader will find grid references that do not show the prefix letters, the authors recommend that they are always given, since otherwise the reference repeats every 100 km across the country.